MORE CHESS FOR CHILDREN

R. BOTT and S. MORRISON

MORE CHESS FOR CHILDREN

With a foreword by
H. GOLOMBEK

Illustrations by
PATRICIA LINDSAY

COLLINS
LONDON AND GLASGOW

ACKNOWLEDGMENTS

The authors acknowledge their indebtedness to R. G. Wade for his helpful criticism of the manuscript and to A. S. Russell for checking the proofs.

First published as the *Chess Apprentice*
This new edition first published 1968
This impression 1973
Published by William Collins Sons and Company Limited, Glasgow and London

Printed in Great Britain
ISBN 0 00 10611 9

CONTENTS

THERE SHALL BE MORE JOY

The little angels of Heaven
Each wear a long white dress,
And in the tall arcadings
Play ball and play at chess;

FORD MADOX FORD
from *The Golden Staircase*

FOREWORD

Chess is such a delightful game that it would be a great pity not to play it as well as you can. Yet quite often you see players who know the moves and perhaps a little more, but who are content to play a standard of chess that is really well below their powers. Either they do not know they can improve or else they do not care. This would not matter very much if chess were the sort of game which could be enjoyed equally whether it were played well or badly. But the truth is that apart from the considerable pleasure you can gain from winning, there is also a deeper enjoyment to be obtained from chess if you understand the game properly so that you know exactly what you are doing.

The game has never been so popular amongst boys and girls as it is to-day. Here, in this book, is a chance for them to improve their play, to acquire that deeper understanding and consequently to enjoy chess all the more. The authors, Messrs. Bott and Morrison, have taught countless children how to play, more particularly in their elementary book, *Chess for Children,* and we older inhabitants of the chess world owe a great debt of gratitude to them for widening this world and making it more populous. Now they have followed it up with another work designed to take the young player a stage further. The pictorial method has been wisely employed: wisely because it is a comparatively painless method of absorbing instruction and also because it is likely to be effective in view of the average chess-player's tendency to have, or to develop, a visual memory.

Turning to the actual contents, I note with great satisfaction that the authors begin with the end-game and devote considerable space to that all-important phase of the game. I would appeal to any boy or girl who may chance to read these words not to neglect the endings but to devote even greater attention to them than they do to the openings. Their elders too might profit much from this advice. In going up and down the country, as I do frequently, either to give a simultaneous display or a lecture or else to report a chess event, I have noticed time and again how weak the average player is in the end-game. And yet, the endings show you chess in its purest form; there is just as much beauty in the ending as there is in the opening or the middle-game, and after all, you cannot hope to win many games unless your knowledge of the endings is at least on a par with that of your opponent.

Casting back in my mind for the way in which I improved my chess when I was a boy, I find another piece of practical advice. Play over the games of master players whenever you can find them. Puzzle out for yourselves why they play the moves they do, and you will find that, in addition to getting a great deal of enjoyment, you will have improved your own play considerably.

Having written this, let me step aside and allow you to get on with the book. You will find it well worth your while to study it carefully and I know that you will enjoy reading it and looking at the various examples the authors have chosen to illustrate their ideas.

H. Golombek

INTRODUCTION

In selecting and preparing the material for this book, we have assumed that the reader will already understand the simple elements of the game. This we attempted in *Chess for Children,* in response to the needs of the army of young chess players who are asking for instruction in the first principles of the game. In that book we explain the more elementary aspects of chess including how the pieces move, simple attack and defence, and so on. Having mastered these first principles, young players are now ready to use this knowledge to develop chess ideas in an imaginative and adventurous way.

Probably no other game has been the subject of so many books. One reason for this is that new ideas about chess are written in new books. One difficulty in attempting to understand these changing ideas has been the fact that many books were written by master players out of touch with the average player. These books often covered too much ground, and were frequently too deep. Notable exceptions there were of course and in recent years many brilliant chess players have combined this knowledge with a very readable style for club players. We have been anxious to select ideas from such modern chess writers which would be suitable for the younger player to use. In this connection we have found the various works of Capablanca, Nimzowitsch and Znosko-Borovsky invaluable for the purpose.

Accompanying some of the usual chess diagrams are others of a military type, which show at a glance areas dominated by either side, and points of attack and defence. The extensive use of chess diagrams that we have adopted in this book is, we believe, the clearest way of presenting our chess ideas. It is our view that the reading of large quantities of text and game quotes, unrelieved by diagrams, is a wearisome affair. But we want to go further, and by making the chess diagram the main focus of attention we seek to give the reader visual pictures of the structural patterns to which we refer in the text, making absorption more certain and more rapid.

Having read the first two chapters of *More Chess for Children,* readers will find that we then deal with the development of the game, starting with the end game and concluding with the opening. This reversal of the order in which a game is played should be helpful, for after mastering some of the principles of the end game, a player is better fitted to understand the needs of the middle game. Only then can he continue his apprenticeship with a proper understanding of the motives of opening play.

We believe that games played by juniors are rarely published in books. Although the quality of such games cannot compare with master chess, nevertheless their publication serves a useful purpose. It gives valuable information to other young players of the kind of standards they can achieve or improve upon. If the practice is continued in future junior chess books, and we feel it should be, it will provide a permanent record of the development of young chess players. Certainly with the growing popularity of the game among the younger generation, we are going to see qualitative advances in their standards. We hope this book is one contribution towards this advance, and proves to be of help to many of our young friends in the world of junior chess.

R. Bott
S. Morrison

Patterns of Checkmate

In Africa several years ago an entomologist (scientist who studies insects) was digging over a piece of ground in search of the remains of a certain kind of insect he was studying. Quite by accident his attention was directed to a fossilised specimen of a beetle he had unearthed. Upon examining it he discovered it was a kind which was not thought to have existed in that particular area. On further investigation of the place he had dug over he rapidly found dozens of other remains of this beetle. The extraordinary fact was that although he had been diligently searching at that spot for many weeks, he had never noticed this beetle before, which was nevertheless there in large numbers under his very nose!

The important point about this true story is that almost always we only see or recognise things that we expect to see. The scientist was not looking for the beetle and so did not notice it but once his attention was drawn to it he had no difficulty in recognising others.

It is for this reason—rapid recognition—that we are giving you many examples of common mating patterns. By retaining a memory picture of them you will readily see when they may be used to bring games to a satisfactory conclusion.

A REMINDER

The minimum material necessary to *force* checkmate is:

(*a*) King and Queen.
(*b*) King and Rook.
(*c*) King and two Bishops.
(*d*) King, Knight and Bishop.
(*e*) King and three Knights. (This unlikely situation only arises when a Pawn has been promoted to a Knight.)

You *cannot* force checkmate with:

(*a*) King and Bishop against King.
(*b*) King and Knight against King.
(*c*) King and two Knights against King unless there are other pieces on the board as well.

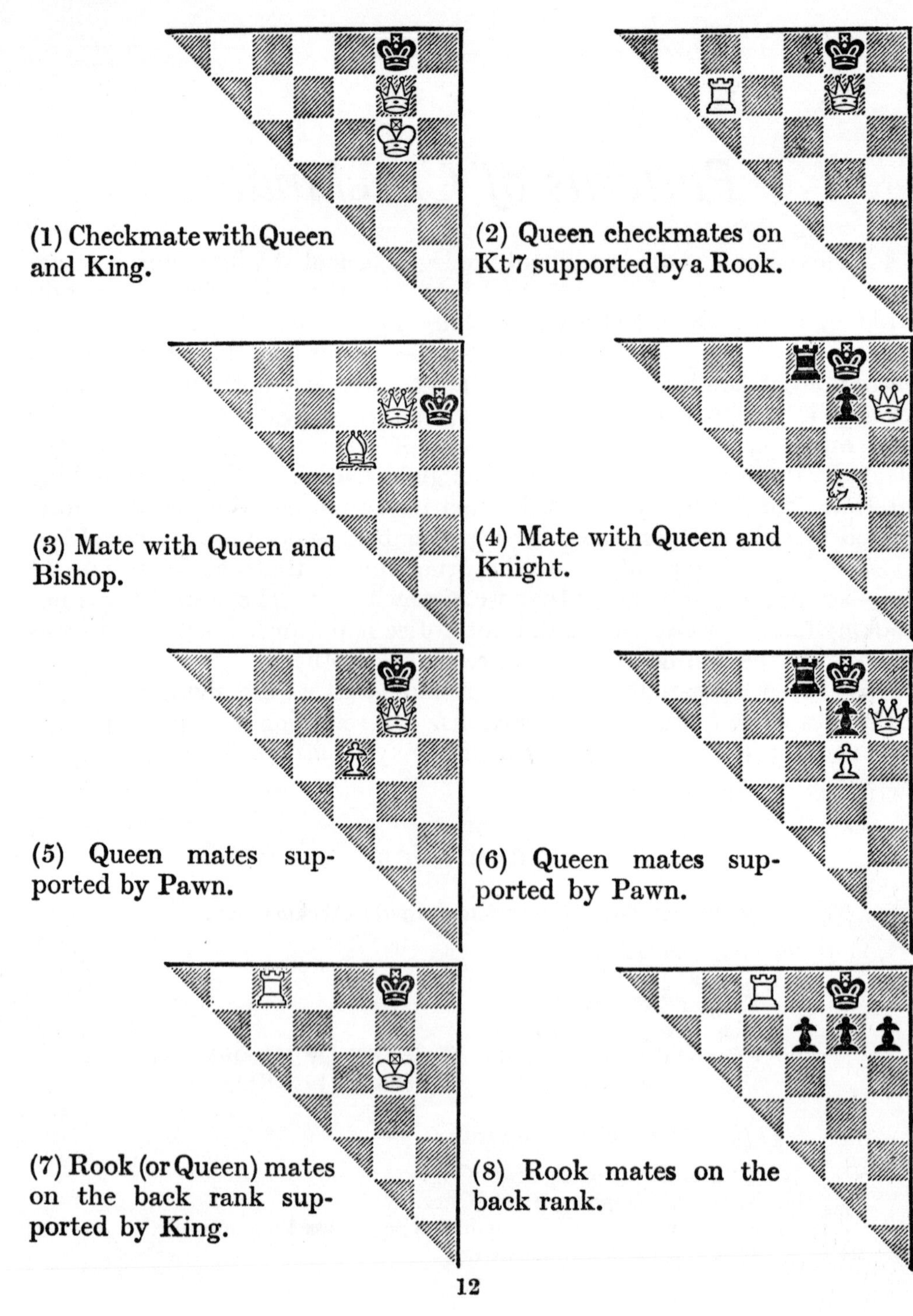

(1) Checkmate with Queen and King.

(2) Queen checkmates on Kt7 supported by a Rook.

(3) Mate with Queen and Bishop.

(4) Mate with Queen and Knight.

(5) Queen mates supported by Pawn.

(6) Queen mates supported by Pawn.

(7) Rook (or Queen) mates on the back rank supported by King.

(8) Rook mates on the back rank.

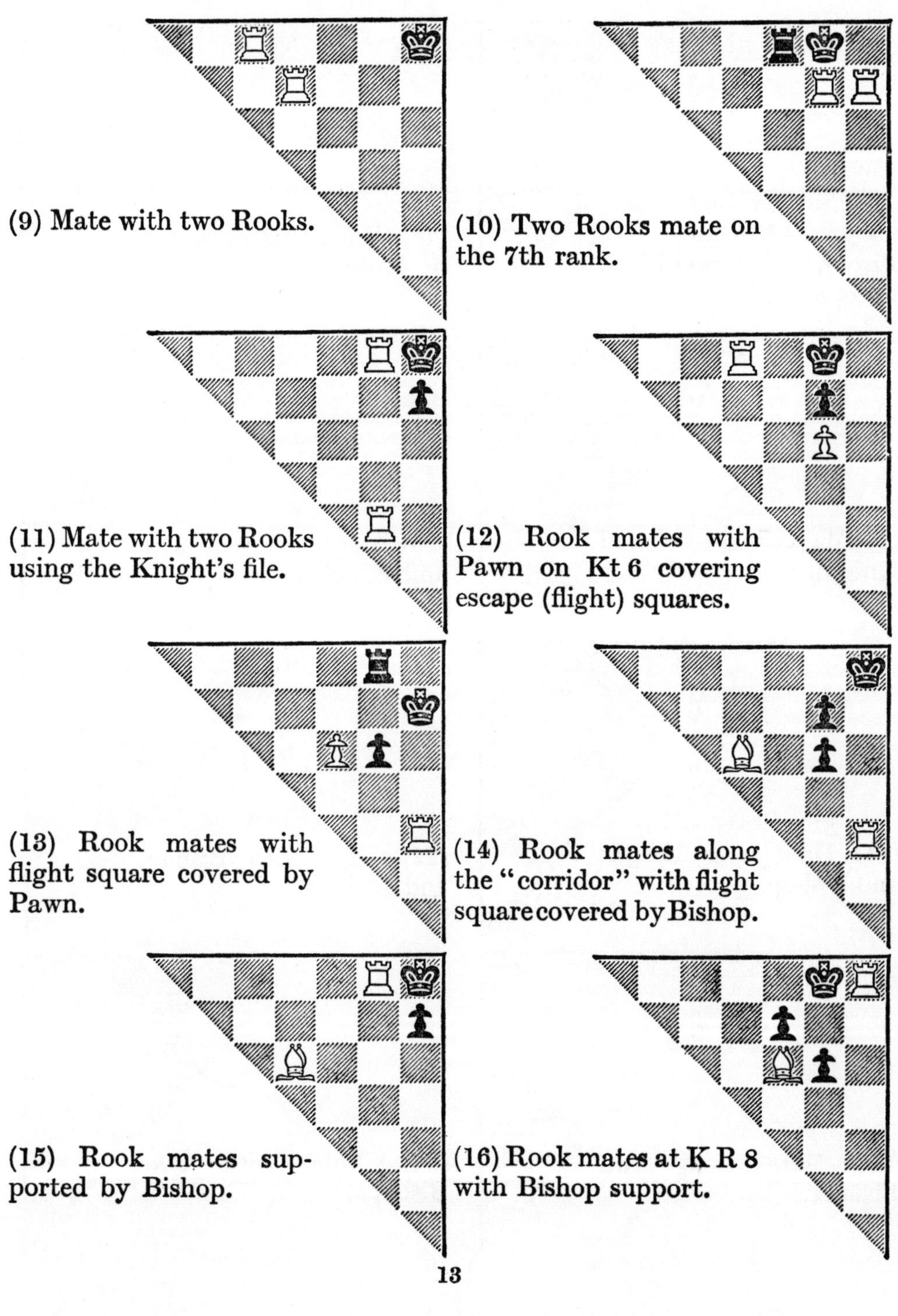

(9) Mate with two Rooks.

(10) Two Rooks mate on the 7th rank.

(11) Mate with two Rooks using the Knight's file.

(12) Rook mates with Pawn on Kt 6 covering escape (flight) squares.

(13) Rook mates with flight square covered by Pawn.

(14) Rook mates along the "corridor" with flight square covered by Bishop.

(15) Rook mates supported by Bishop.

(16) Rook mates at K R 8 with Bishop support.

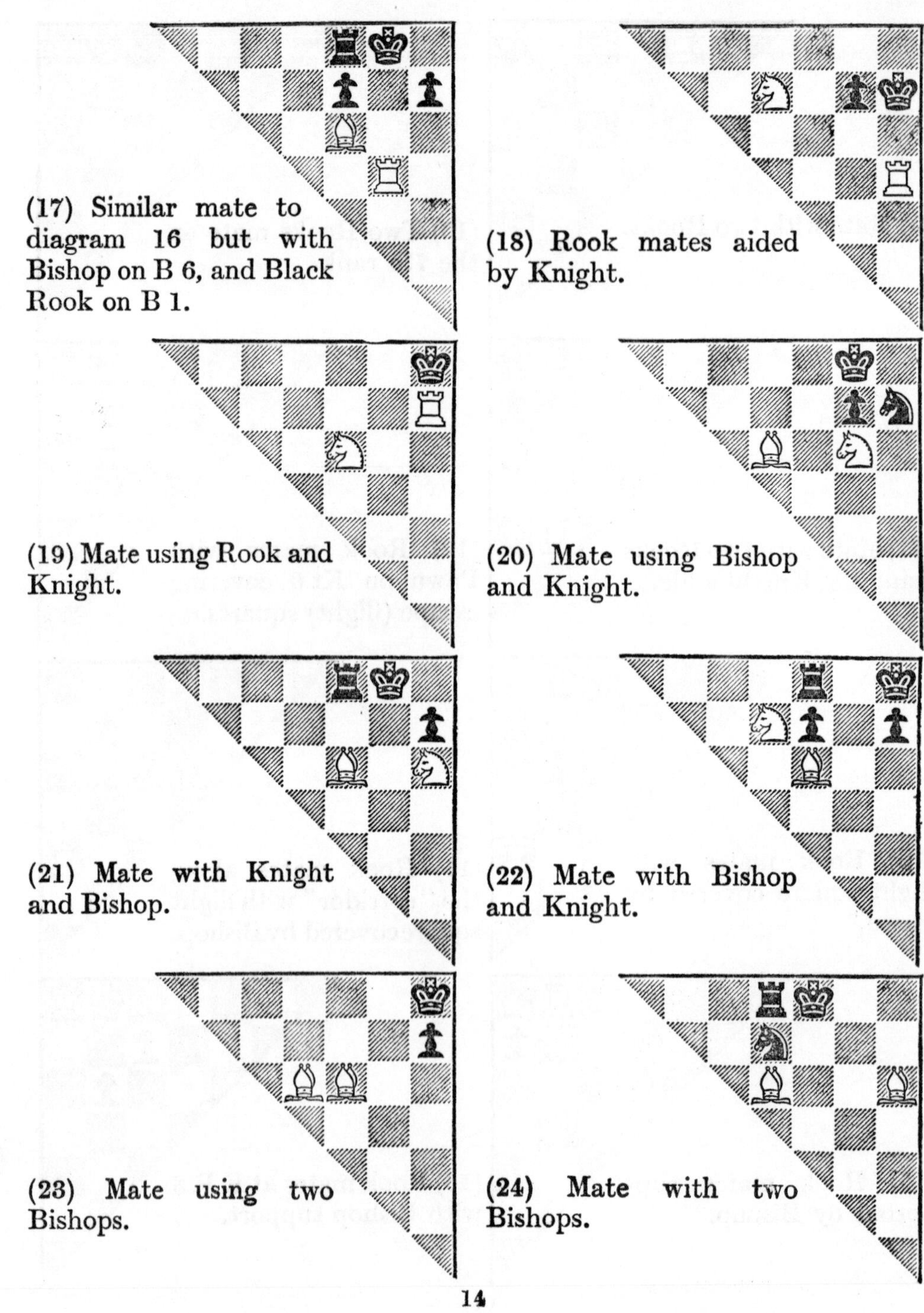

(17) Similar mate to diagram 16 but with Bishop on B 6, and Black Rook on B 1.

(18) Rook mates aided by Knight.

(19) Mate using Rook and Knight.

(20) Mate using Bishop and Knight.

(21) Mate with Knight and Bishop.

(22) Mate with Bishop and Knight.

(23) Mate using two Bishops.

(24) Mate with two Bishops.

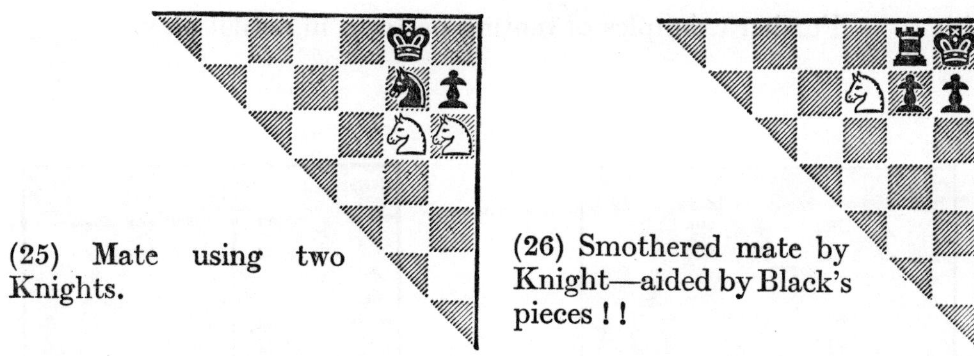

(25) Mate using two Knights.

(26) Smothered mate by Knight—aided by Black's pieces ! !

The mating patterns you have just seen only show the pieces necessary for the mates, so that the basic forms may be seen more clearly.

In the following positions we show examples of how the mating patterns, or variations of them, may be used in actual play.

It will help you to understand these and other positions in this book if you set them up on a chessboard when you are studying them.

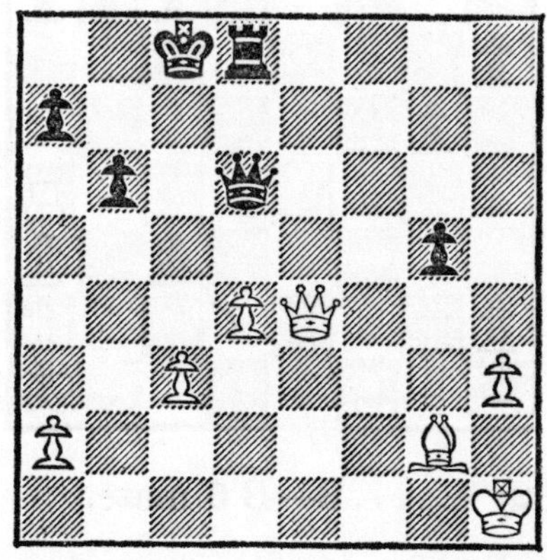

(27) White to play. Queen and Bishop strike down the long diagonal.

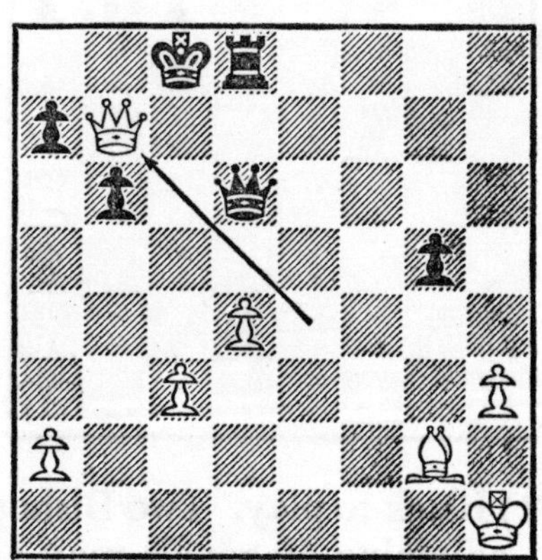

(28) 1. Q—Kt 7 checkmate !

Further examples of mating patterns in actual play.

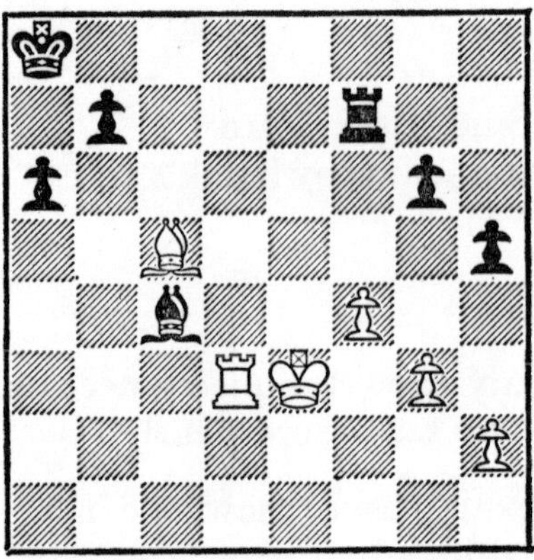

(29) White to play. Rook and Bishop are well placed to end Black's resistance.

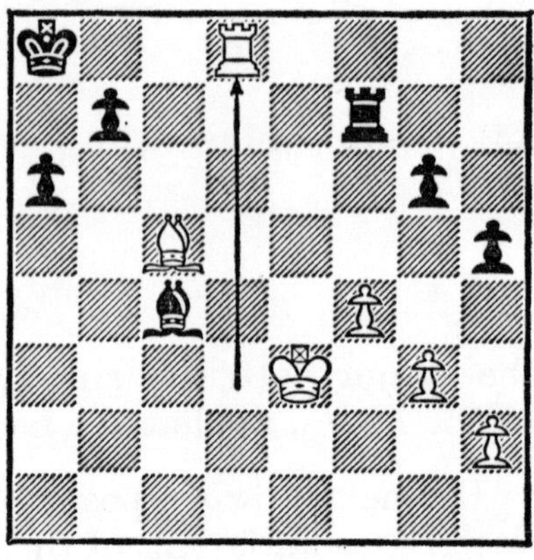

(30) 1. R—Q 8 mate, with White's Bishop covering flight square.

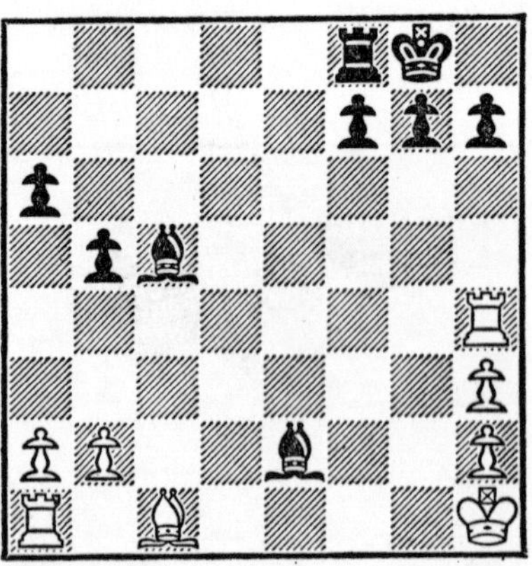

(31) Black to play. Two Bishops on adjoining diagonals may act with great power.

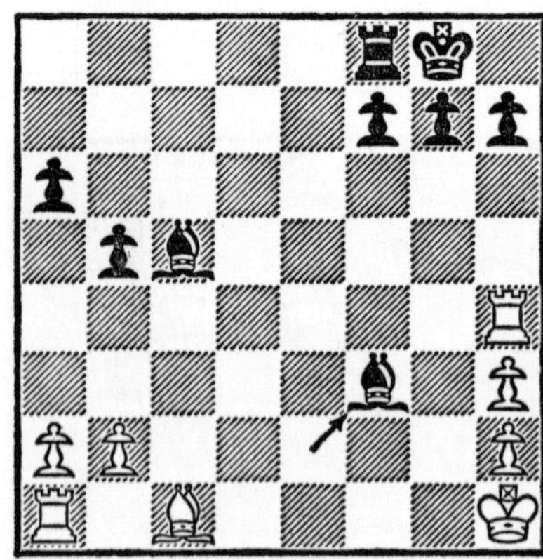

(32) 1. . . . . B—B 6 mate.

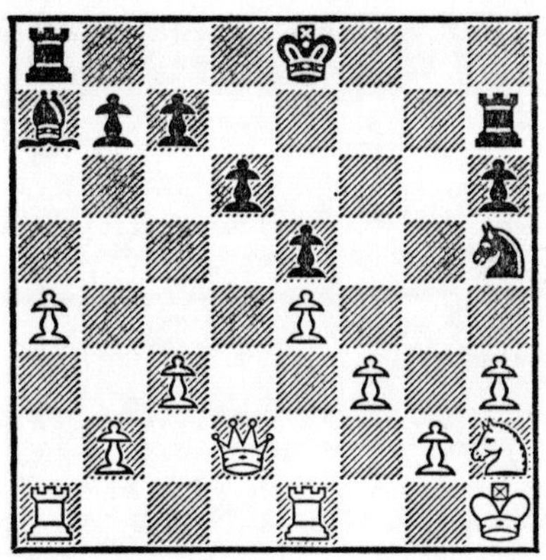

(33) Black to play. A duet with Knight and Bishop.

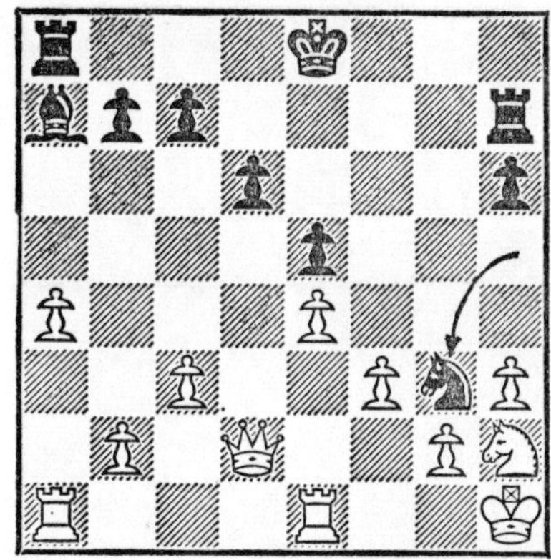

(34) 1. ....Kt—Kt 6 mate. Black's Bishop at Q R 2 prevents the King escaping to Kt 1.

White left many weak black squares which his opponent used effectively.

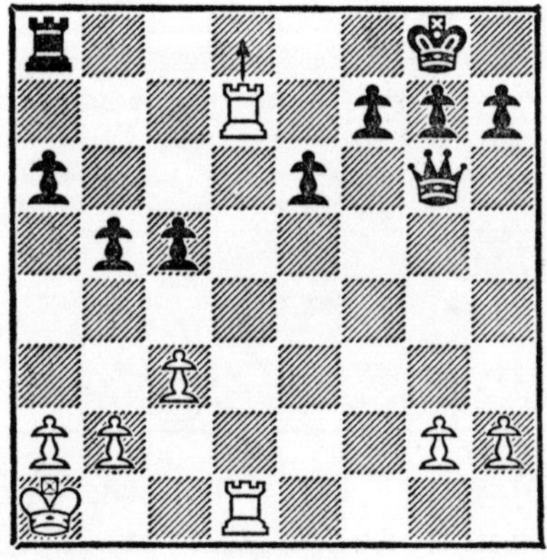

(35) White to play.
1. R—Q8 ch R × R (forced)

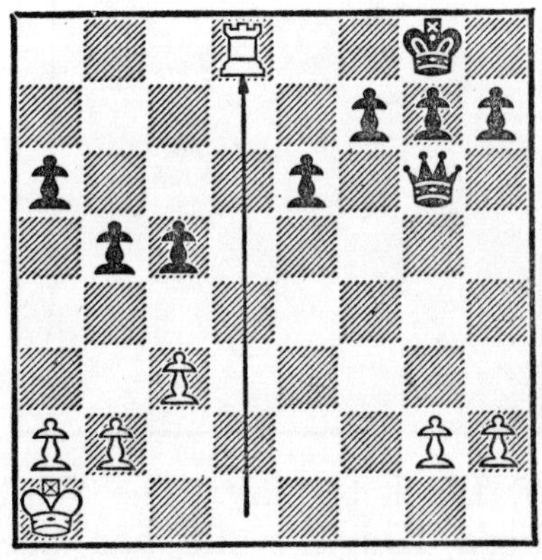

(36) 2. R × R mate. Black's back rank was inadequately defended.

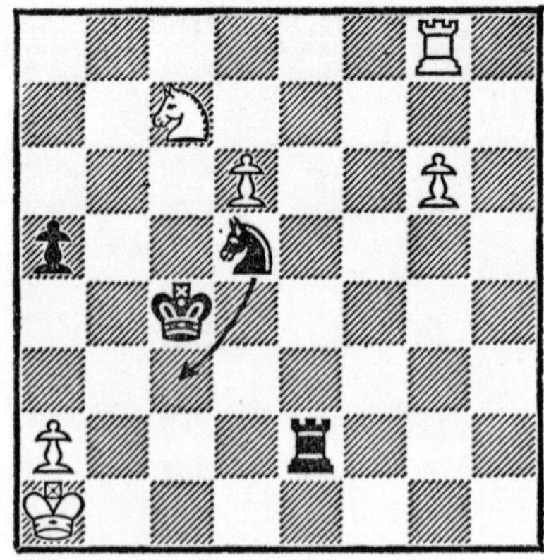

(37) Black to play.
1. . . . . Kt—B 6
threatening mate by
2. . . . . R × P

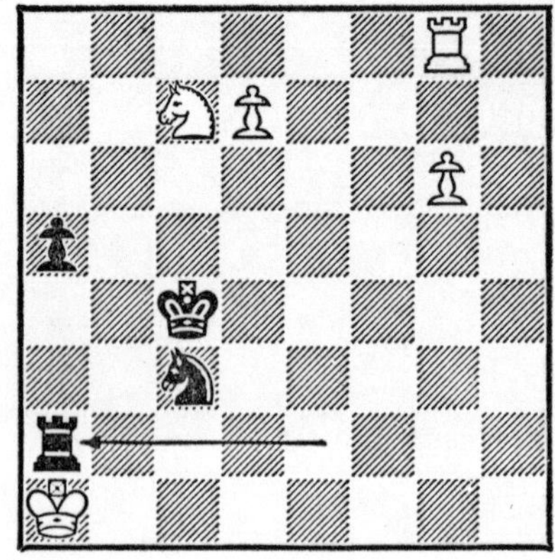

(38) We try 2. P—Q 7 and there follows 2. . . . . R × P mate.

Try any other move instead of 2. P—Q 7 and you will readily see that mate cannot be stopped.

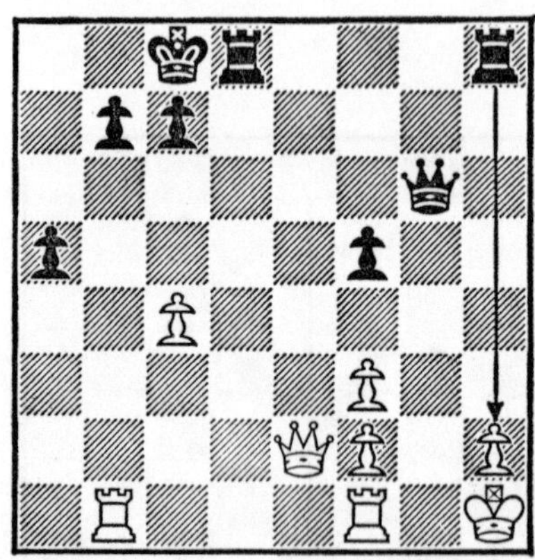

(39) Black to play. The White King's Knight's file has been opened up. This enables Black to make a Rook movement ending in mate on the Rook's file.
1. . . . . R × P ch
opening up the Rook's file by sacrificing a Rook.
2. K × R.

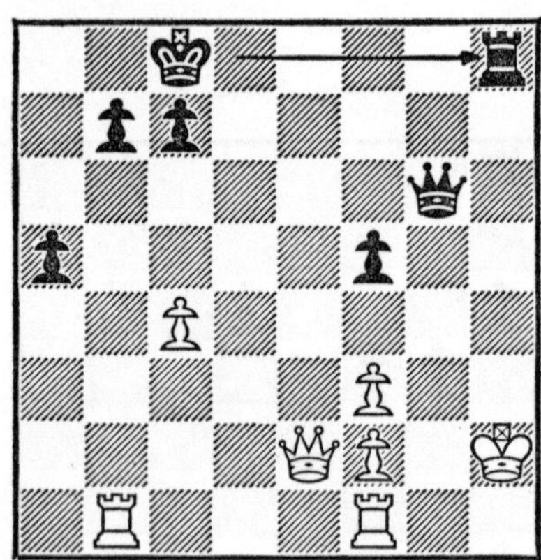

(40) 2. . . . . R—R 1 mate. Open files in front of a King are highly dangerous.

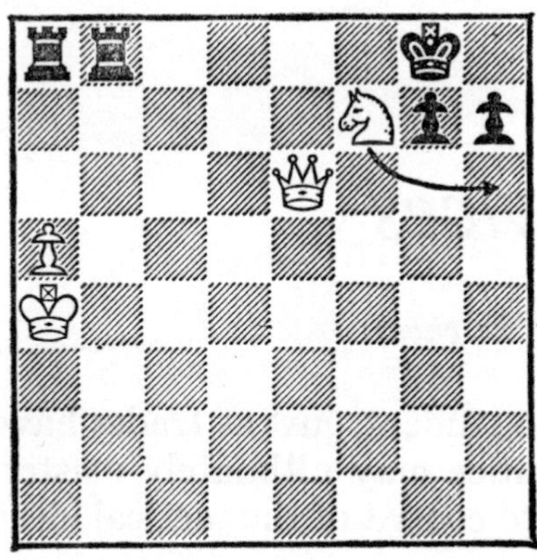

(41) White to play.
1. Kt—R 6 dble ch K—R 1
if K—B 1 then 2. Q—B 7 mate.
2. Q—Kt 8 ch R × Q

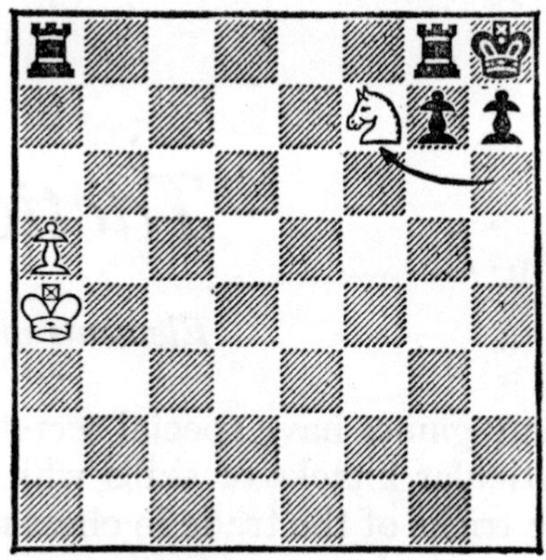

(42) 3. Kt—B 7 mate!

This checkmate commonly called "smothered mate" was recorded as long ago as 1496 by a Spaniard named Lucena. Easy to see why it has this name. The Black King is completely blocked up by his own pieces—no breathing space!

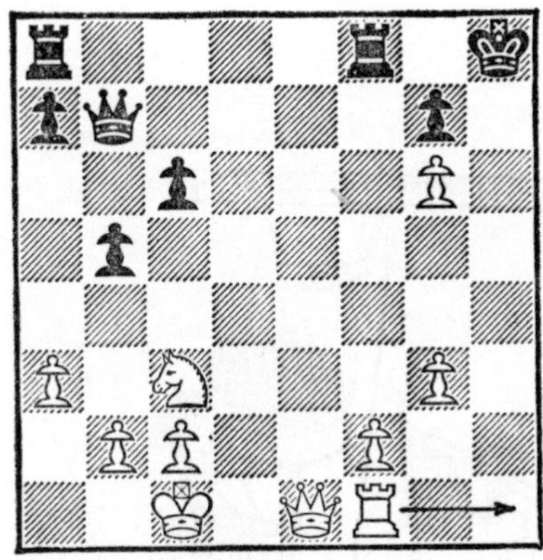

(43) White to play.
1. R—R 1 ch K—Kt 1
2. R—R 8 ch K × R
3. Q—R 1 ch K—Kt 1

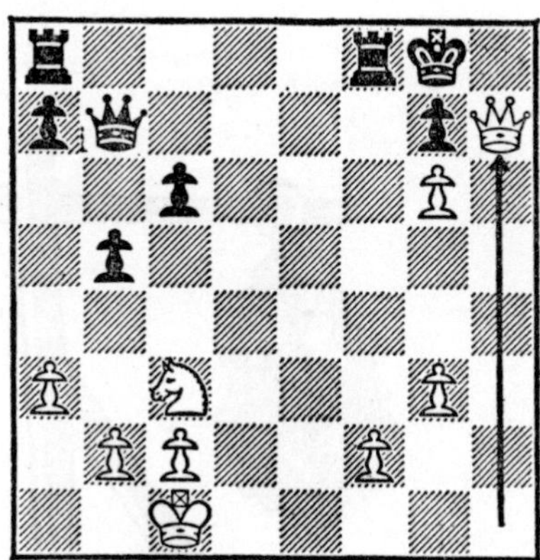

(44) 4. Q—R 7 mate.
All Black's moves were forced.

Tactical Devices

Elements of combination in chess

Many games have special secrets to offer the student, just as trades have particular knacks or skills which the apprentice may ultimately master. The tricks of the trade in chess may be said to consist of the tactical ideas known as *chess combinations*.

Many of these combinations of moves can be grouped in different classes and in this chapter we deal with the most common of them. Opportunities for using these tactical ideas occur in almost every game, and a study of, first, the Basic Patterns on pages 21-22, and then their application on pages 23-36, will assist you to *see* the opportunity as soon as it occurs—or even before ! We recommend that you practise the moves on the chessboard until you become thoroughly familiar with each particular idea. Patient study in this will bring a rich reward.

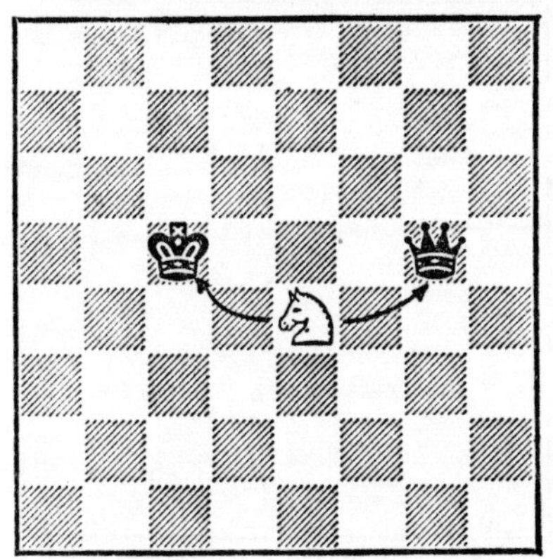

(45) Knight fork.

(46) Pawn fork.

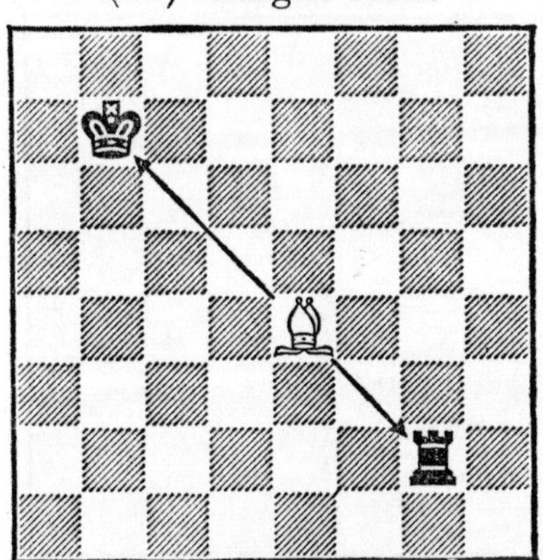

(47) Bishop fork.

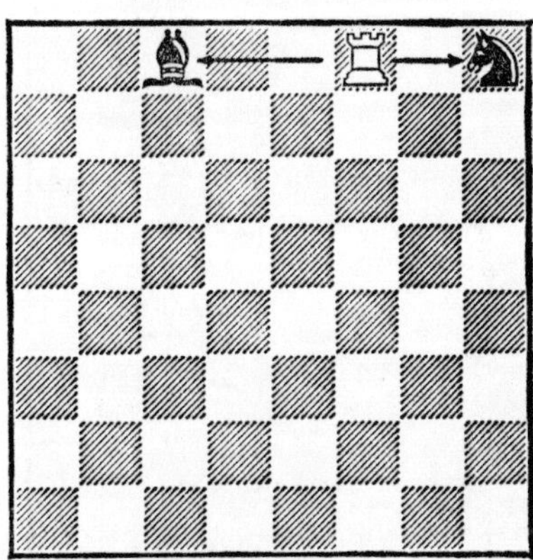

(48) Rook fork.

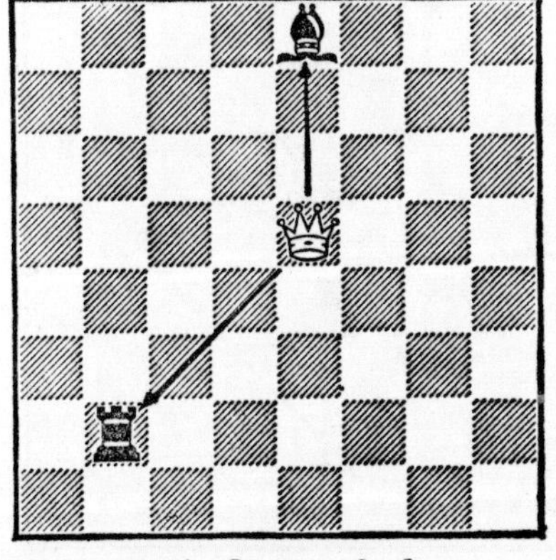

(49) Queen fork.

(50) Pin.

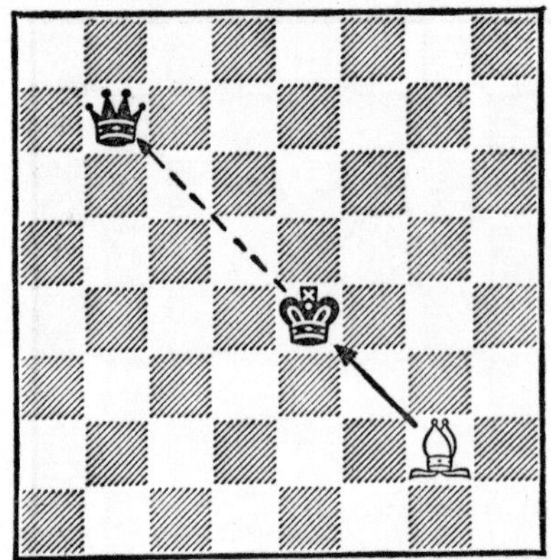

(51) Skewer.

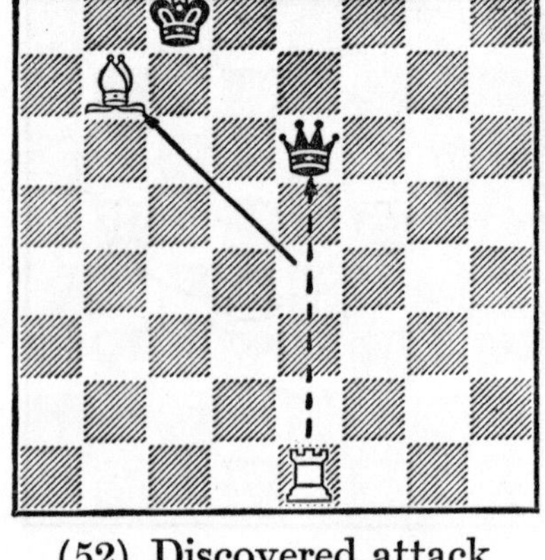

(52) Discovered attack.

(53) Discovered check.

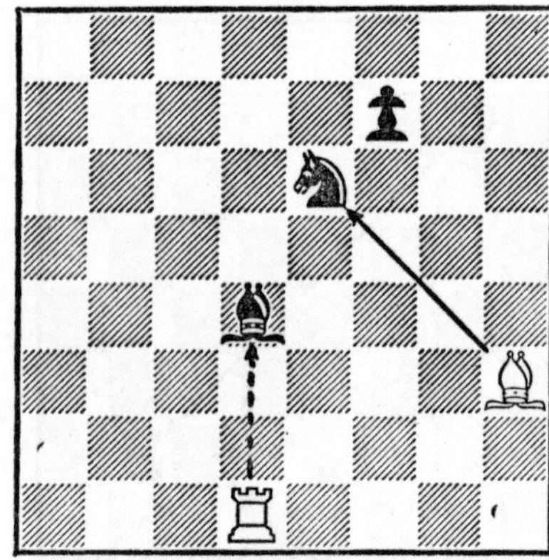

(54) Destroying the guard.

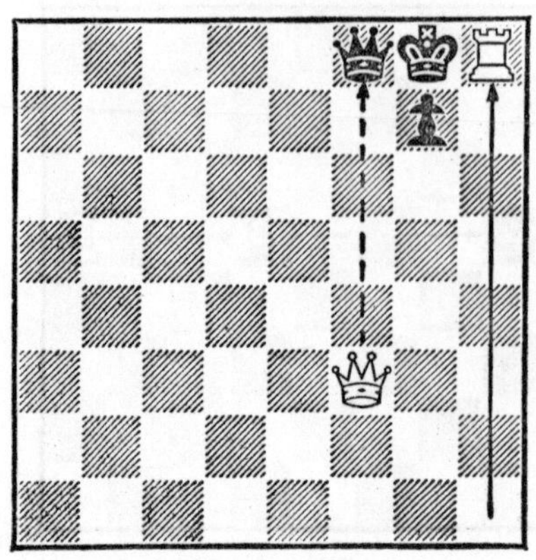

(55) Deflection.

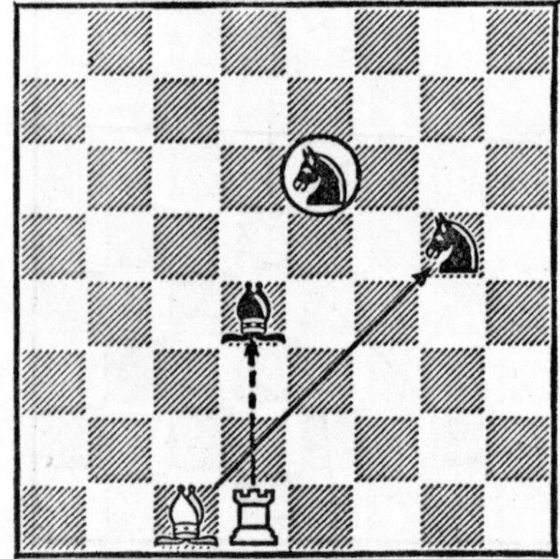

(56) Overworked piece.

KNIGHT FORK

A Knight fork is
a double attack
by a Knight

BASIC PATTERN

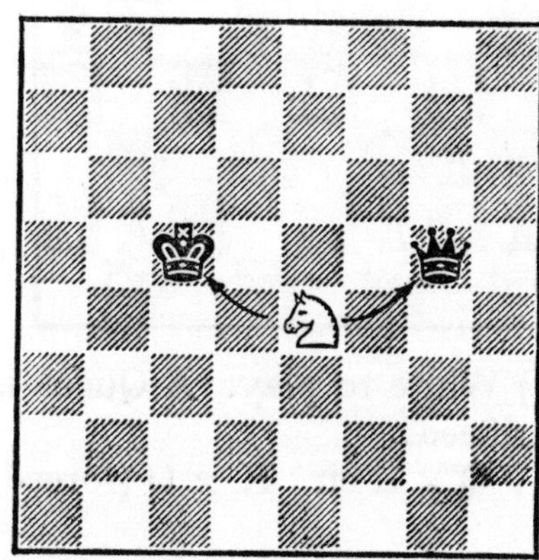

(57) Knight attacks King and Queen at the same time.

(58) White to play.

1. Q × R ch Q × Q

Did White blunder in giving up the Queen ?

(59) No ! There is no blunder for there follows :

2. Kt—B 6 ch forking the Black King and Queen. Black cannot stop 3. Kt × Q and White has won a Rook which gives him an easy win.

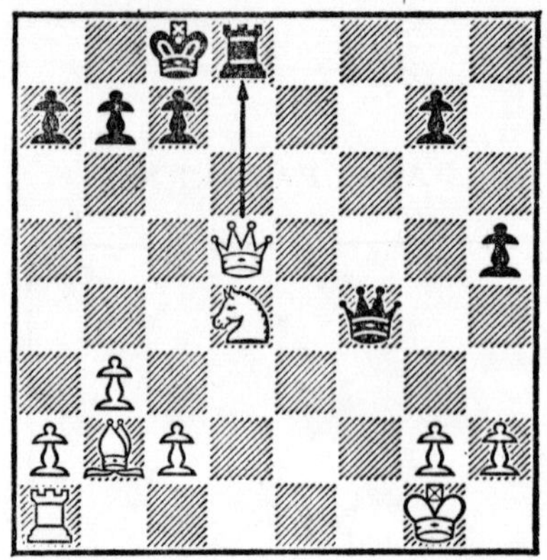

(60) White to play. A Queen is sacrificed.

1. Q × R ch K × Q (forced)

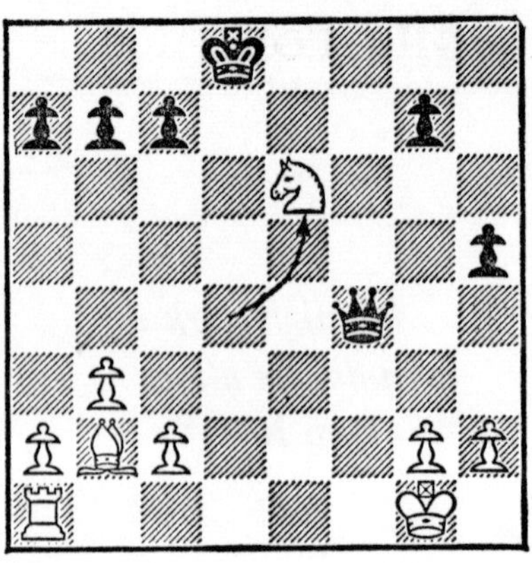

(61) 2. Kt—K 6 ch forking King and Queen. It is now seen that after 3. Kt × Q White gains a Rook.

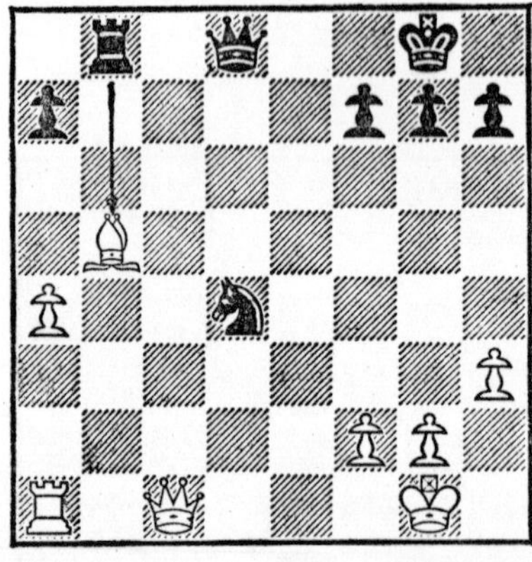

(62) Black to play. It is clear that were it not for the White Bishop, Black could fork the White King and Queen by .... Kt—K 7 ch. This gives the clue to Black's first move.

1. .... R × B!

White must give up the Bishop for if 2. P × R the White Queen is lost as follows:

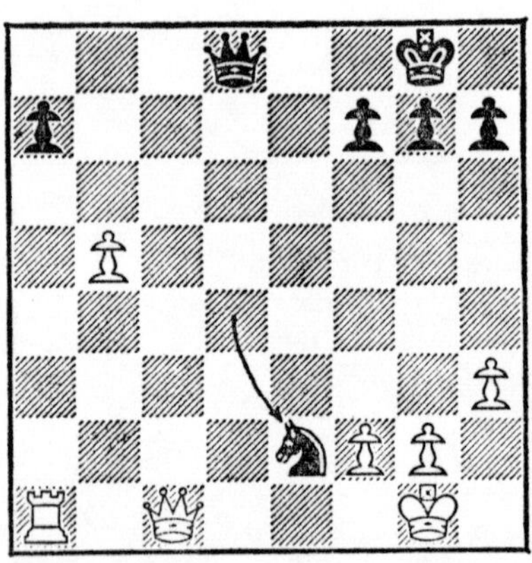

(63) 2. .... Kt—K 7 ch

The King must move—the Queen falls.

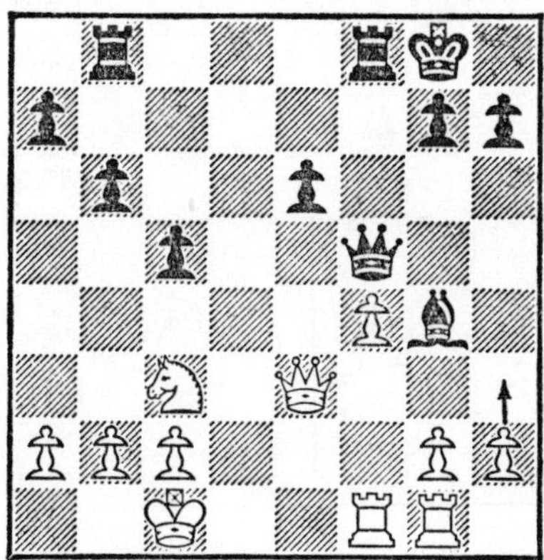

(64) White to play.
1. P—K R 3
The only square to which Black's Bishop may move without capture is K R 4—and even that square is unsafe.
1. . . . .   B—R 4

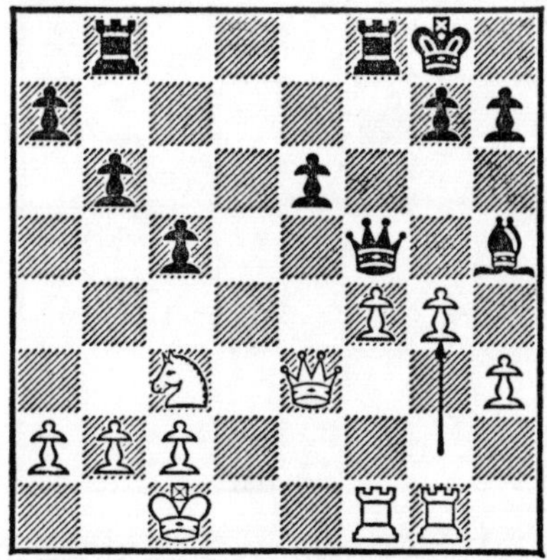

(65) White executes a Pawn fork.
2. P—K Kt 4 ! forking Queen and Bishop. The Bishop is lost.

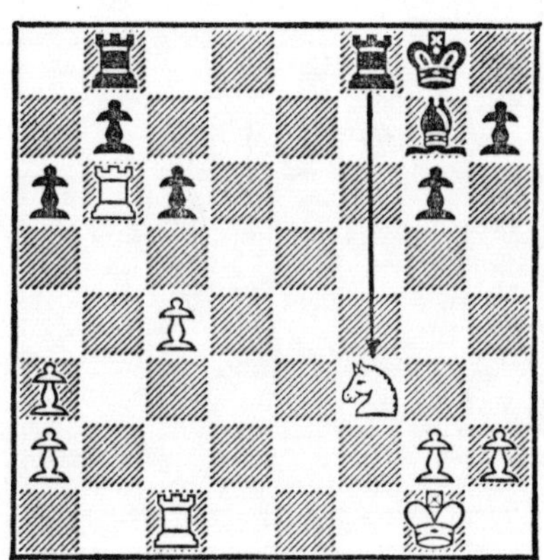

(66) Black to Play. You will notice that the Black Bishop could fork White's King and the Rook on Kt 6 but for the White Knight at B 3. The answer is clear :
1. . . . .   R × Kt

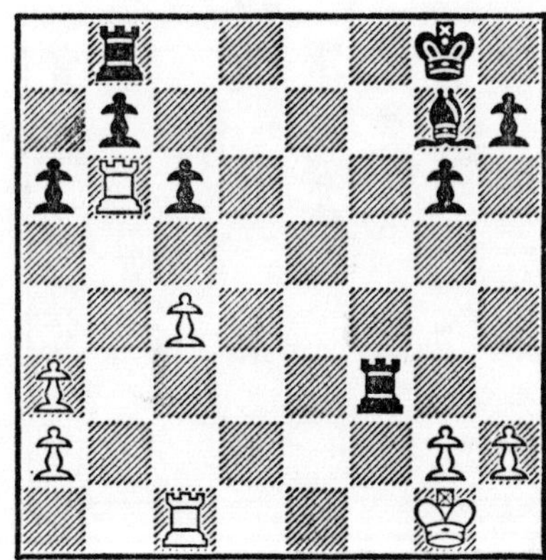

(67) The obstacle is removed. If now 2. P × R there follows 2. . . . . B—Q 5 ch and the White Rook must be given up.

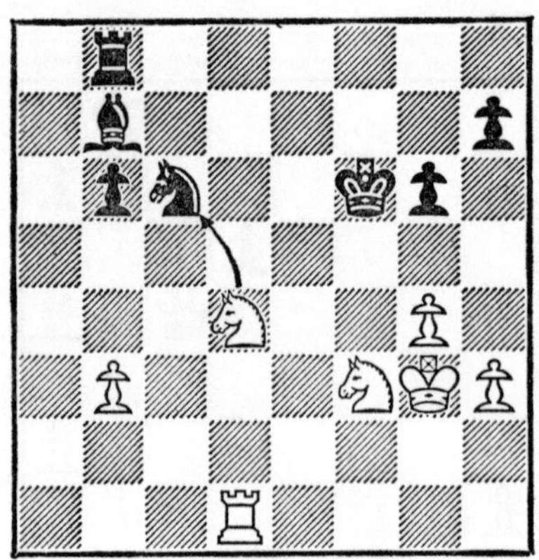

(68) White to play. The material is equal on both sides but White sees that his Rook can win a piece. The preliminary move is

1. Kt × Kt B × Kt

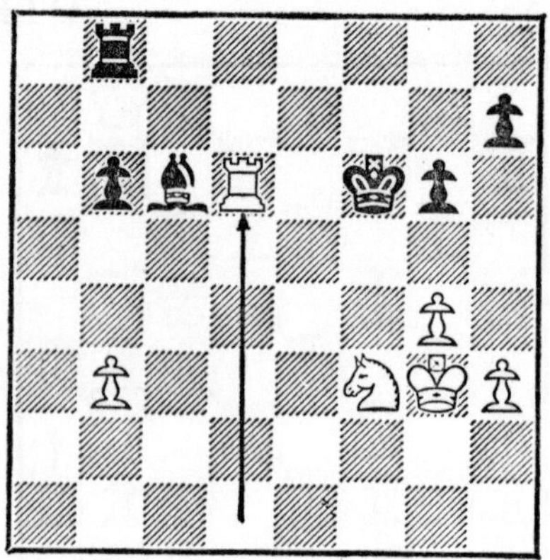

(69) Now comes the Rook forking King and Bishop.

2. R—Q 6 ch wins the Bishop, and White is a piece ahead.

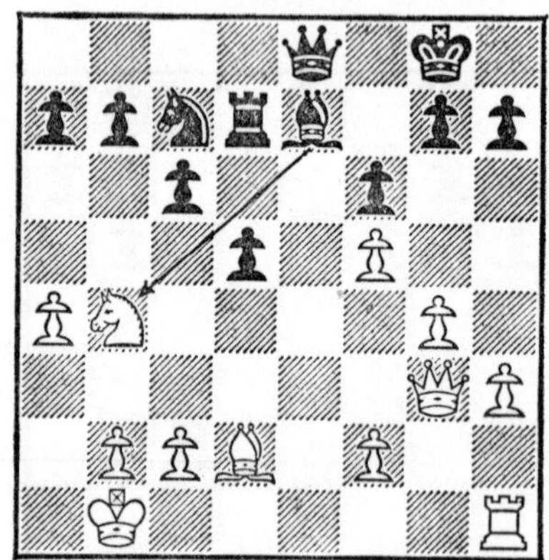

(70) Black to play.

1. .... B × Kt

White can do no better than recapture.

2. B × B

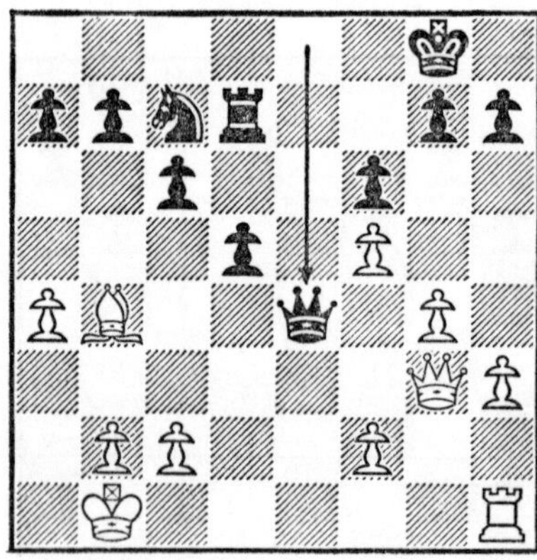

(71) 2. .... Q—K 5

The Black Queen now forks White's Rook and Bishop. If White moves the Rook to safety, the Bishop is lost.

PIN

A piece is said to be pinned when it is attacked along a line from which it cannot move without exposing a second piece to attack or capture.

BASIC PATTERN

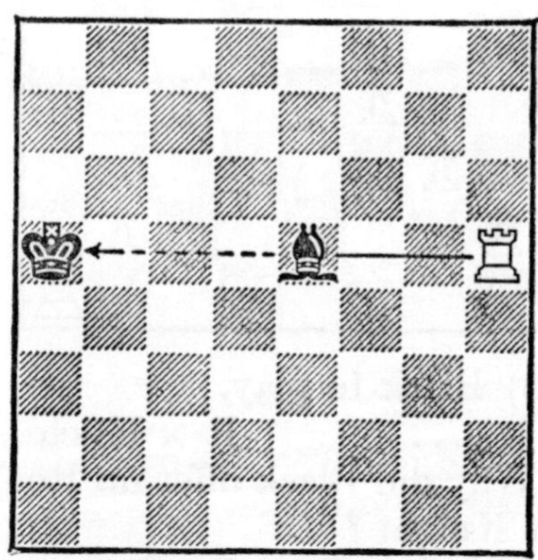

(72) The White Rook pins the Black Bishop which is in line with the Black King.

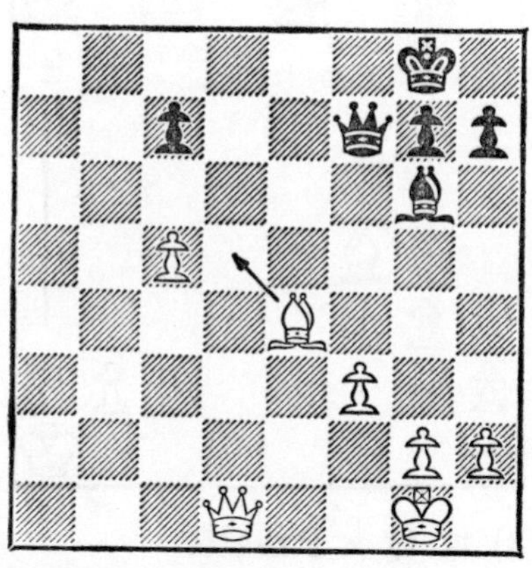

(73) White to play. The Black King and Queen share the same diagonal—not always a safe arrangement!

1. B—Q 5 attacking Black's Queen.

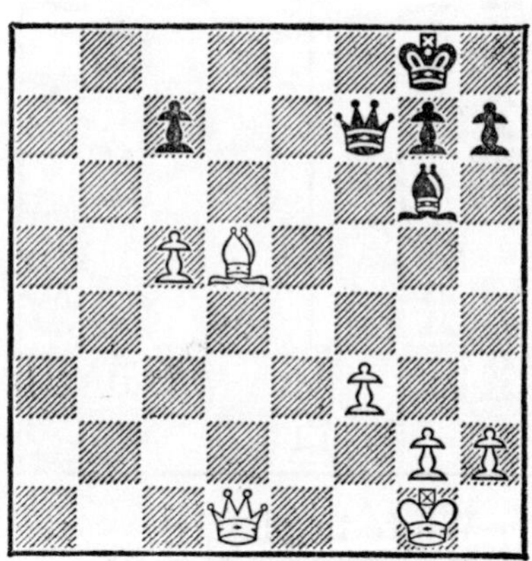

(74) The Queen is pinned and helpless, for to move it from the diagonal would expose the King to check. The Black Queen is lost and White has an easy win.

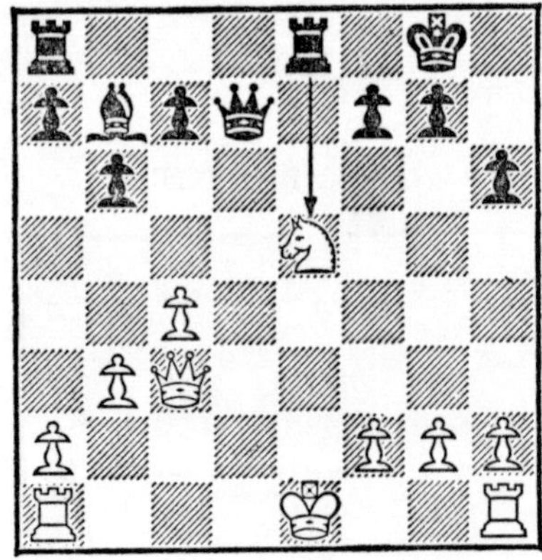

(75) Black to play.

1. .... R × Kt ch

Why did Black offer up Rook for Knight ?

If 2. Q × R R—K 1

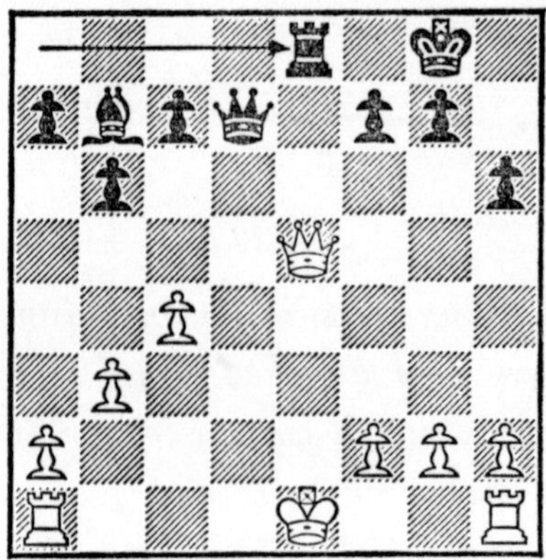

(76) Again we have a Queen pinned and paralysed. It cannot move off its file for behind it shelters the King. Best for White is 3. Q × R ch after which 3. .... Q × Q and Black has a clear advantage.

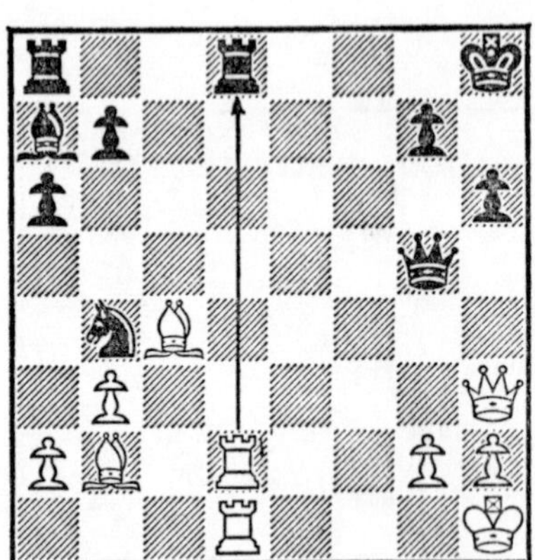

(77) White to play.

1. R × R ch R × R

2. R × R ch

If now 2. .... Q × R

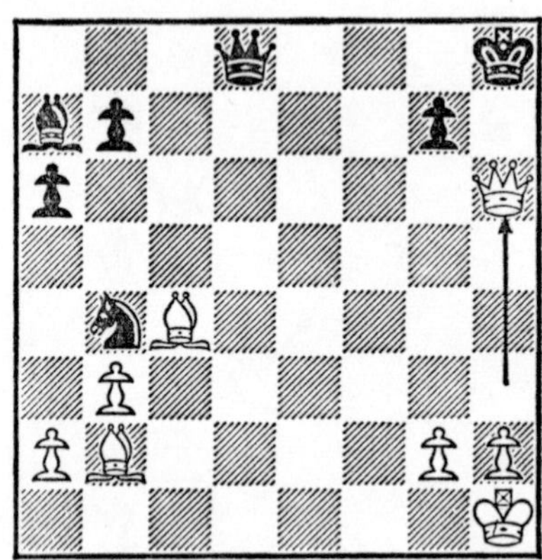

(78) 3. Q × P mate.

The White Queen cannot be taken, because Black's King's Knight's Pawn is pinned. Black must not play 2. .... Q × R for mate follows as shown and he has to be content with the loss of a Rook.

SKEWER

A skewer is an attack upon two pieces on the same line, where the piece nearest the attacker is compelled to move, leaving the other piece to be taken.

BASIC PATTERN

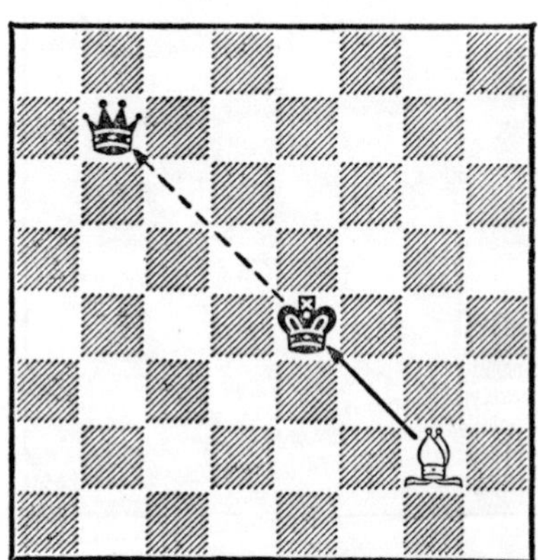

(79) The White Bishop checks the Black King which is forced to move away allowing the capture of the Black Queen.

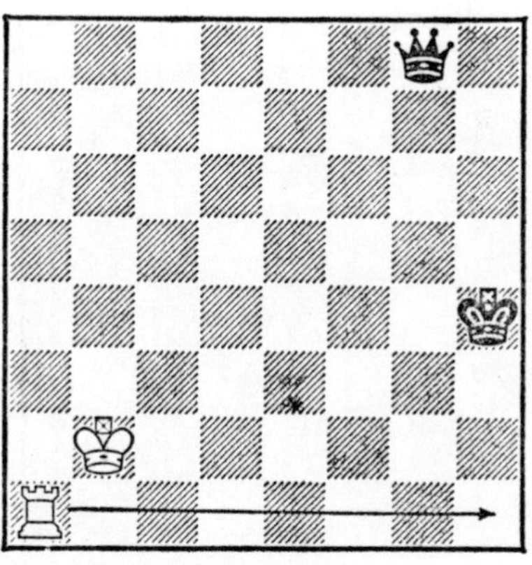

(80) White to play. Although there is no immediate skewer, one may be forced.

1. R—R 1 ch !

(81) The Black King is now forced to one of the squares shown, after which White plays

2. R—Kt 1 ch

and when the Black King moves out of check, the Queen is lost.

Here White may choose between being skewered on file or diagonal!

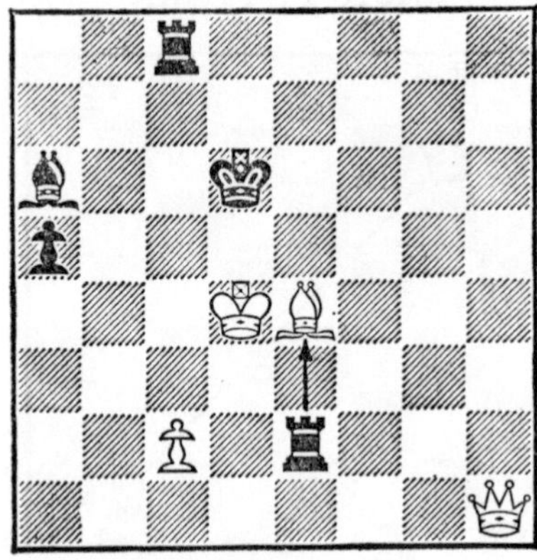

(82) Black to play.

1.	R × B ch
2. Q × R	

(83)

2.	R—B 5 ch
3. K—Q 3 (or K 3)	R × Q

4. K × R and Black's win is ensured.

(84) If, instead of 2. Q × R White decides to play 2. K × R, Black skewers on the diagonal.

(85) 2. .... B—Kt 2 ch and White's position is black indeed!

DISCOVERED ATTACK

A discovered attack occurs when one piece moves in order to uncover the attacking action of another piece of its own colour.

BASIC PATTERN

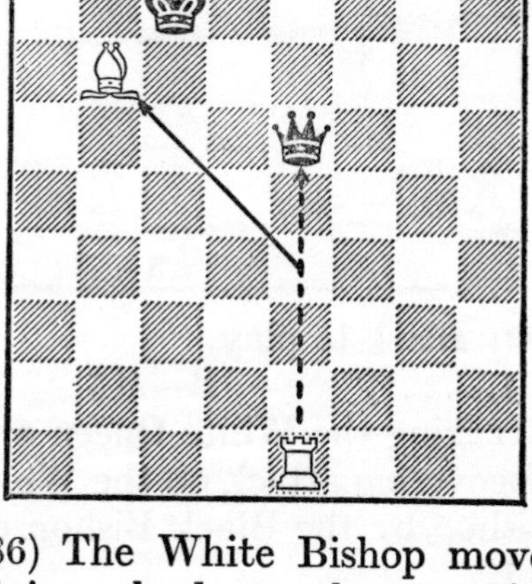

(86) The White Bishop moves giving check to the opposing King, at the same time exposing Black's Queen to attack by the Rook.

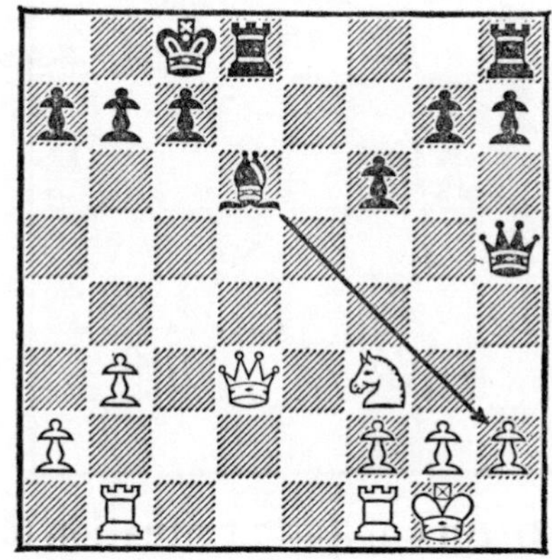

(87) Black to play.
1. . . . . B × P ch
discovering attack on the White Queen by the Black Rook on Q1.
2. Kt × B

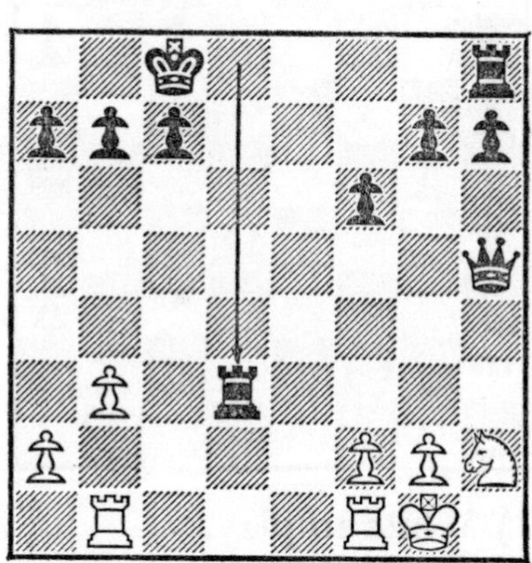

(88) 2. . . . . R × Q
NOTE—If White plays 2. K—R 1 instead of 2. Kt × B the Queen is lost just the same.

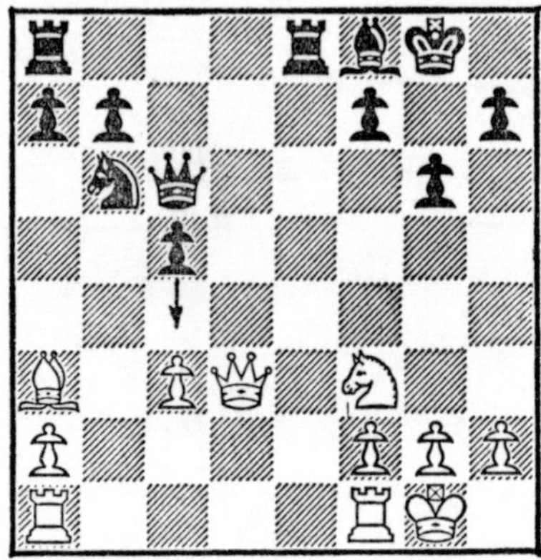

(89) Black to play.

1. . . . . P—B 5

attacking the White Queen and discovering attack on the White Bishop by the Black Bishop on B 1.

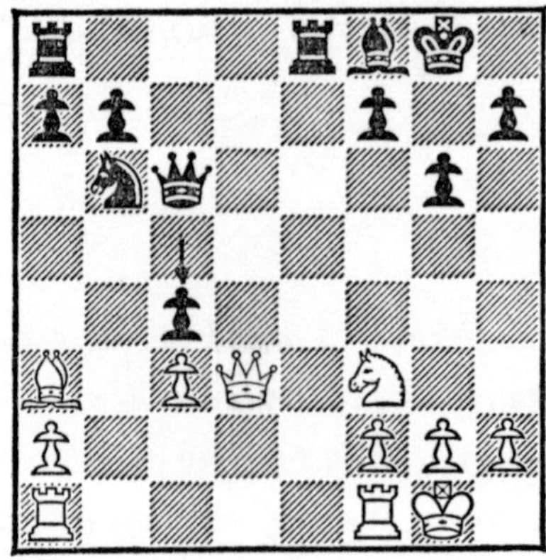

(90) It will be seen that the White Queen cannot move to any square where it protects the attacked Bishop, which is thus lost.

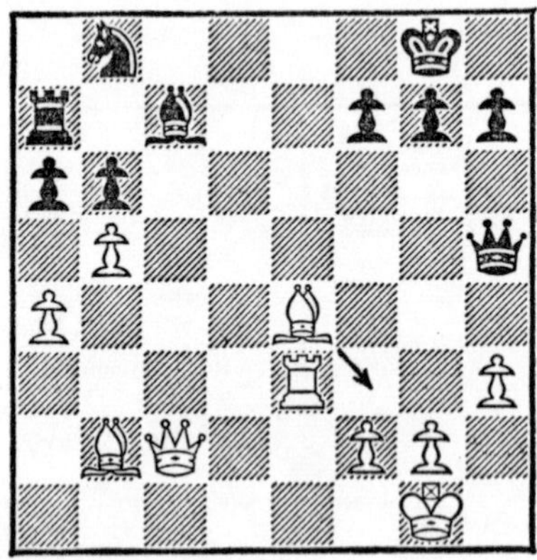

(91) White to play.

1. B—K B 3

This move attacks the Black Queen and at the same time threatens mate by R—K 8.

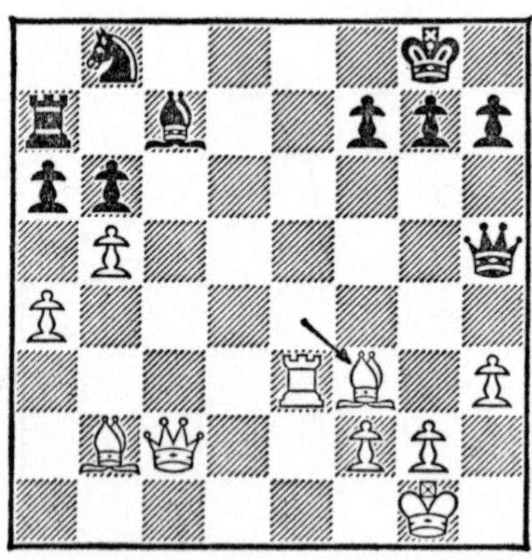

(92) An unpleasant situation for Black as he has to play a move to avoid mate. The Queen must be given up.

DISCOVERED CHECK

A discovered check happens when one piece is moved 'uncovering check' by another piece.

BASIC PATTERN

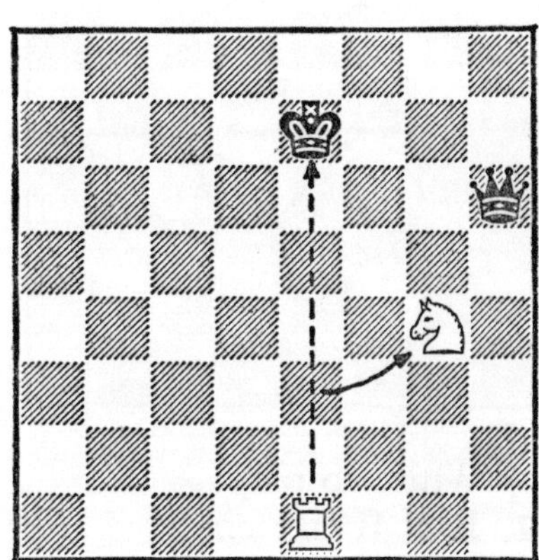

(93) The White Knight has moved attacking the Black Queen and uncovering check by the White Rook.

(94) Black to play and win a Rook.

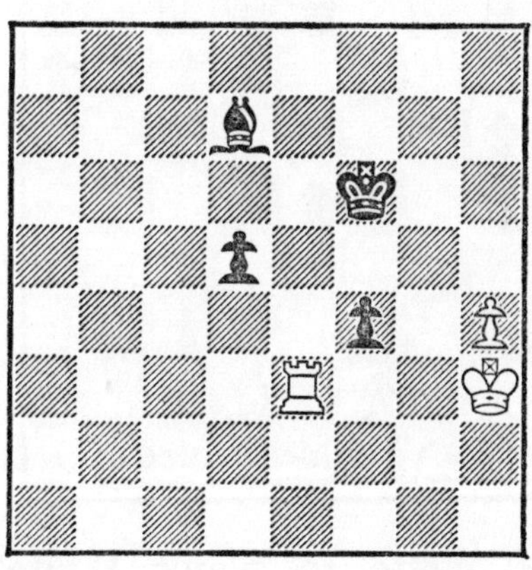

(95) 1. . . . . P—B 5 disc ch! White must deal with the check and the Rook falls.

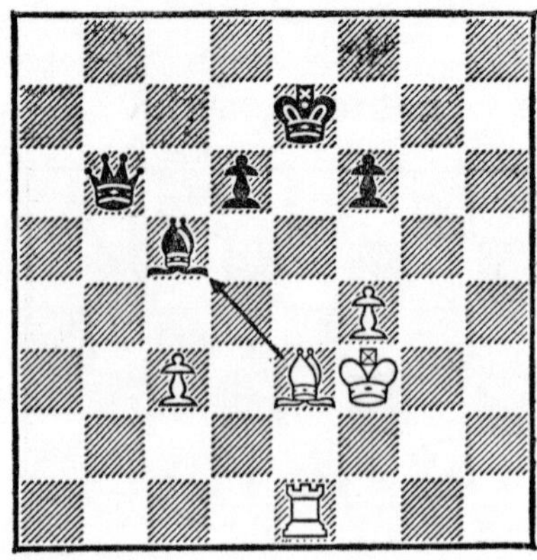

(96) White to play.
1. B × B disc ch

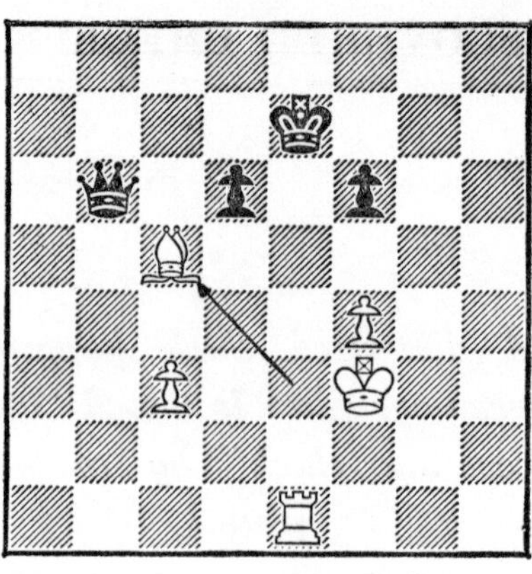

(97) It is clear that the Black King is forced to move out of check as no piece can interpose to block the attack. Black cannot stop 2. B × Q and White has an easy win.

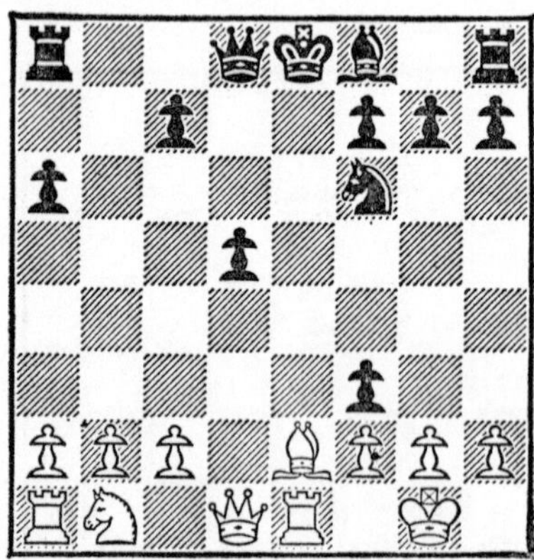

(98) White to play. White's Rook is on the same file as the Black King. You will notice that White can play 1. B × P disc ch, but there is a better move.

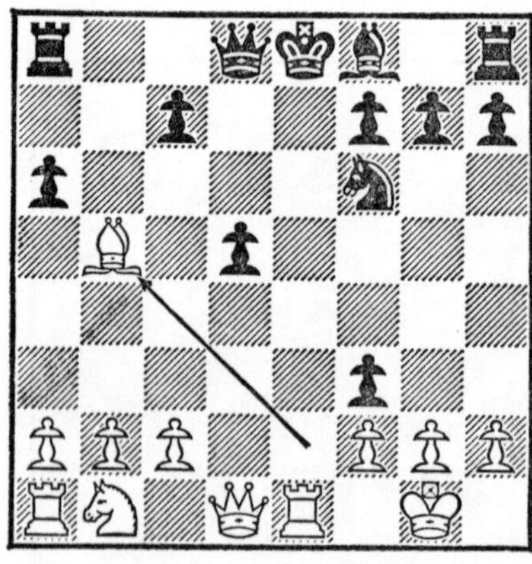

(99) 1. B—Kt 5 double checkmate !

REMOVING THE DEFENDER

Removing the defender can take three forms:

(*a*) *destroying the guard*

(*b*) *deflection*

(*c*) *overworked piece*

We will show you an example of each.

BASIC PATTERN

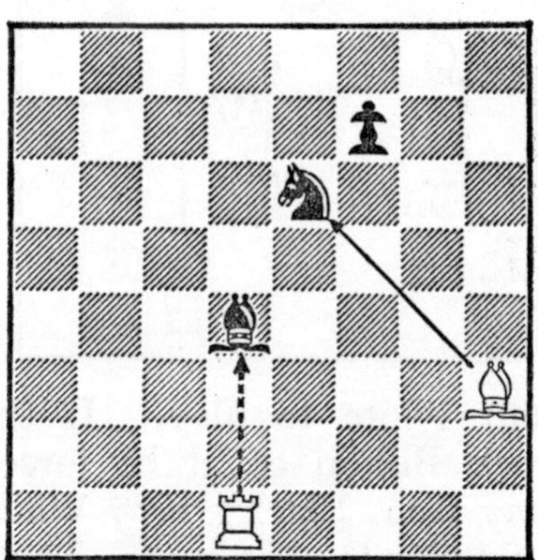

(100) The Black Bishop is attacked by the Rook and defended by the Knight. The White Bishop removes the Knight and Black loses a piece.

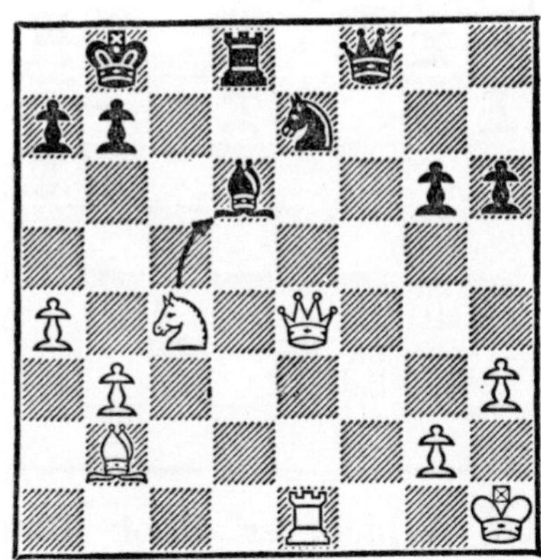

(101) White to play. Black's Queen and Bishop defend the Knight.

White therefore *destroys* one of the defenders by

1. Kt × B R × Kt

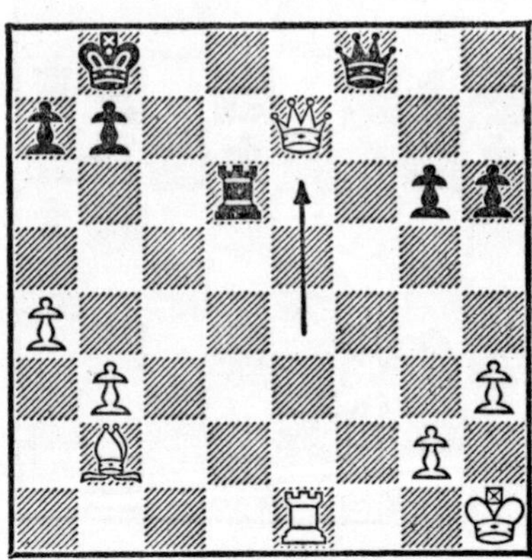

(102) Now we see the Black Knight having only one defender, is lost.

2. Q × Kt

and White has won a piece.

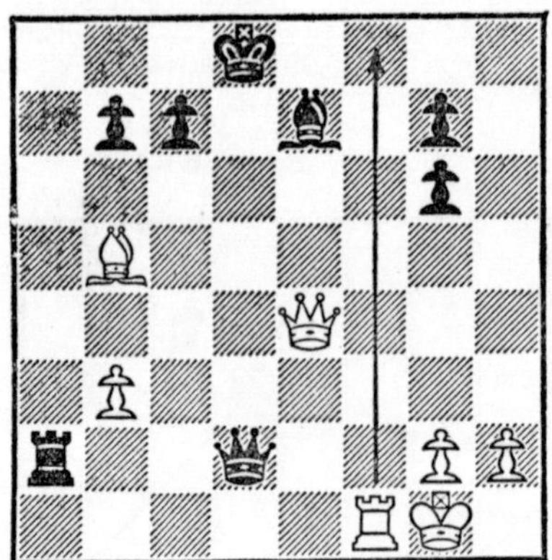

(103) White to play. If the Black Bishop could be forced away from Black's K 2, White could play Q—K 8 mate. There *is* a way to *deflect* this Bishop from its square!

1. R—B 8 ch!

Black's reply is forced.

1. .... B × R

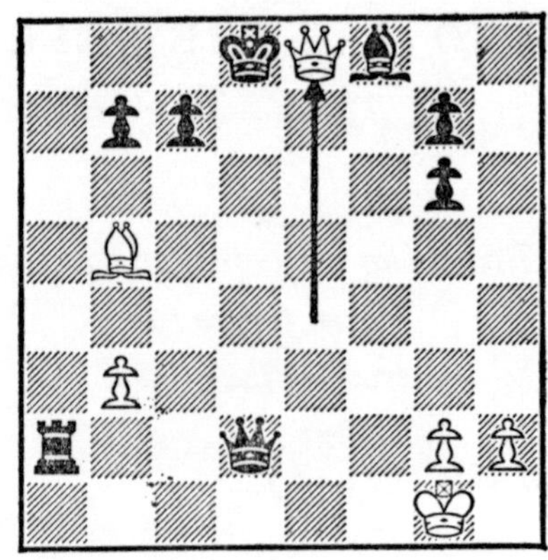

(104) 2. Q—K 8 mate.

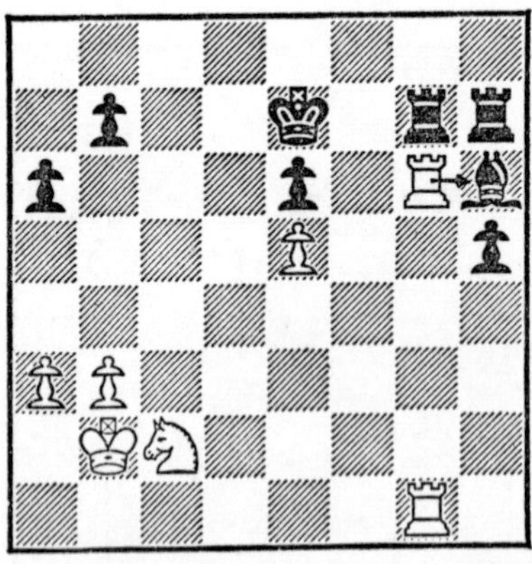

(105) White to play. Black's Rook at K R 2 has two tasks to perform. It protects the other Rook at Kt 2 and the Bishop. White plays

1. R × B

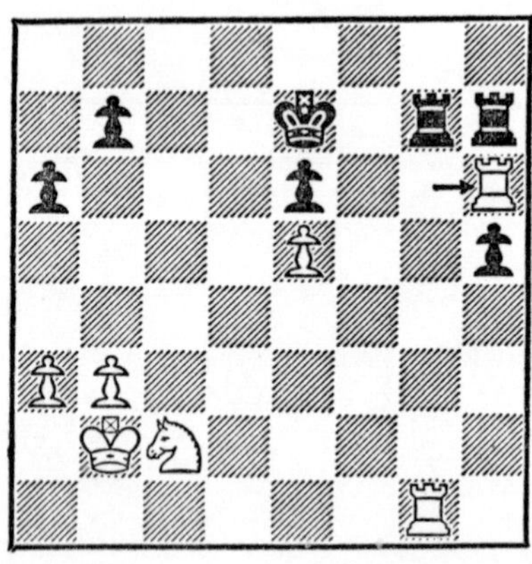

(106) Whichever Rook Black chooses to capture, White captures a Rook with the other. The Black Rook on K R 2 is only able to perform one of its tasks, and is clearly *overworked.* The result is that White gains a piece.

QUIZ ON "TACTICAL DEVICES"

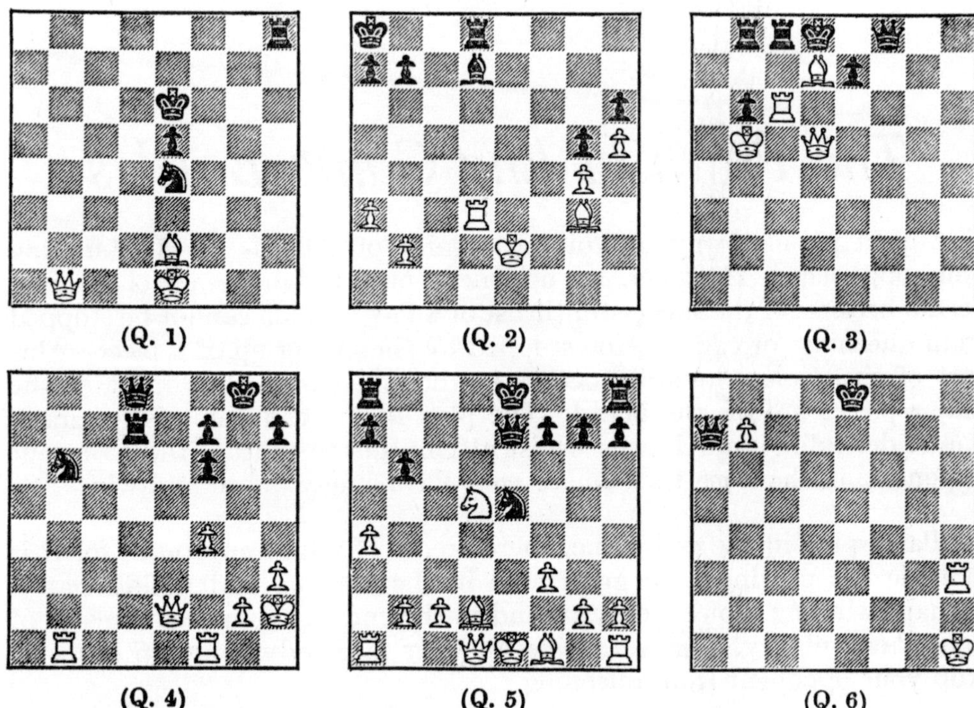

(Q. 1) (Q. 2) (Q. 3)

(Q. 4) (Q. 5) (Q. 6)

(Q.1) Black to play.
How can Black sacrifice a Rook for Bishop in order to win White's Queen ?

(Q.2) Black to play.
White's King and Rook are on the same diagonal. Is this a weakness in this position ? If so how can Black take advantage of it ?

(Q.3) White to play.
Can you find a discovered check assisting White to mate in two ?

(Q.4) White to play.
The Black Queen is overworked as it has the task of protecting both Knight and Rook as well as the back rank. Suggest how White may win a piece as a result of this.

(Q.5) Black to play.
Although Black's Queen is *en prise* (attacked) Black has no need to protect it for he has a devastating move at his disposal. What is it ?

(Q.6) White to play.
The Pawn on Kt 7, although near to queening, is unprotected. What is White's best move in this position ?

Answers to Quiz on "Tactical Devices" on page 193.

The Pawn in End Game Battles

THE most popular way of winning a game of chess is by checkmating your opponent! However, an opponent may resign before checkmate occurs because of the successful thrust of a Pawn which cannot be stopped from queening, or can only be stopped by the giving up of a piece. This sort of situation commonly occurs in the end game when most of the major pieces are off the board. The plan in the end game is generally one of defending your Pawns whilst attempting to capture those of your opponent, in the hope that one of *your* Pawns may queen and win.

Pawn play in the end game, therefore, is of vital importance for it is of little use playing with great skill in the opening and middle game, perhaps winning a piece, only to find in the end game that as a result of poor Pawn play you have to give up your piece advantage in order to stop your opponent from queening.

Pawns may be said to be the tin soldiers of the chessboard but in the end game they are worth their weight in gold!

1. PROMOTING A PAWN

The positions which follow show the passed Pawn in its most powerful form—on the 7th rank and about to queen. A protected, advanced, passed Pawn in the end game often brings victory with it, and it is well to remember this in the opening and middle game when making exchanges which alter Pawn formations. To allow your opponent to create a passed Pawn in the early stages of the game may not appear important, but to find it still there in the end game is very often to have a serious problem on your hands.

Although some games of chess are concluded without the queening of a Pawn, many are decided as a result either of queening or the threat of queening an advanced, passed Pawn.

A player often prefers to capture a Pawn that is about to queen, even if it means giving up a piece. After all, it is better to lose a Bishop, Knight or Rook than be faced with a new enemy Queen!

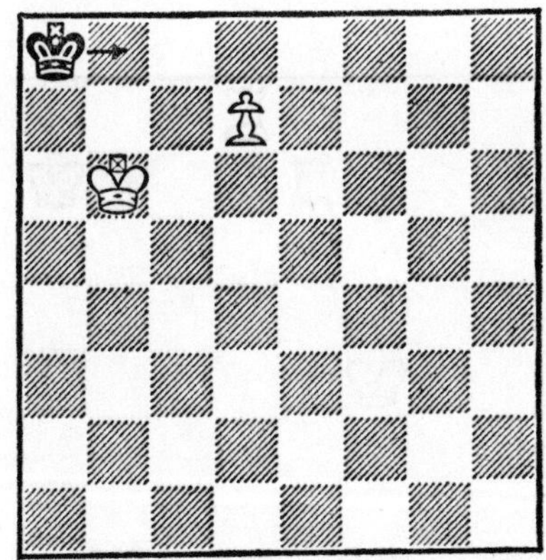

(107) Passed Pawn on the 7th rank. The Black King's move is forced

1. .... K—Kt 1

(108) The Pawn reaches the eighth rank—a Pawn no longer!

2 P—Q 8 = Q mate

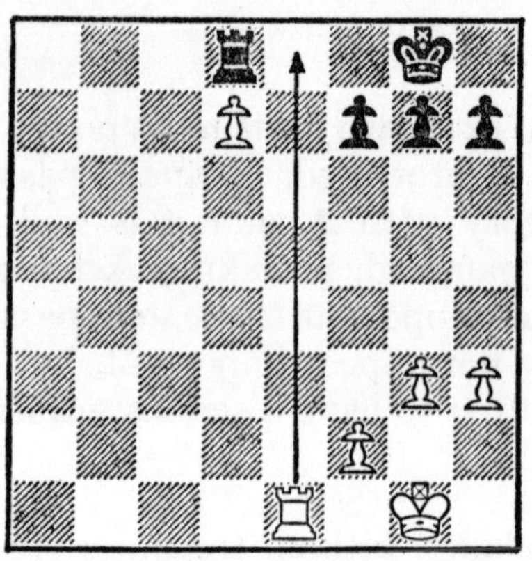

(109) White plays **1. R—K 8 ch!** The Pawn on the 7th rank needs no protection, although it is attacked by a Rook. Black's reply is forced.

1. . . . . **R × R**

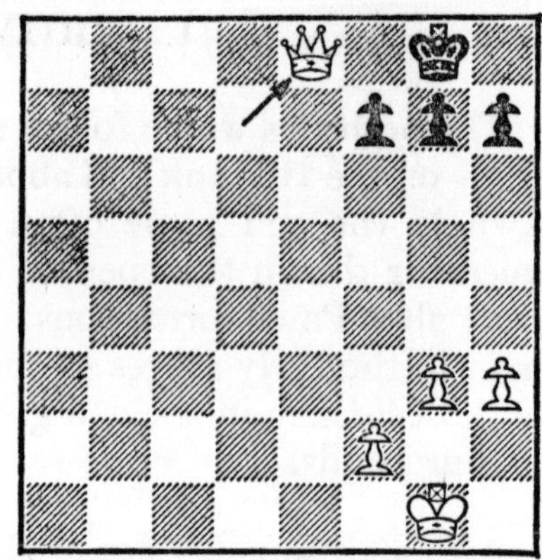

(110) **2. P × R = Q mate!** Black had to face not only an advanced passed Pawn but also the weakness of having no flight square for his King.

In diagram **111** *you will see the Black King is not exposed to a check on the back rank, which in the previous example forced the Pawn home.*

(111) If White plays **1. R—K 8** now, he simply wastes his valuable passed Pawn. Black is not now compelled to take the Rook.

(112) **1. . . . .** **R × P**
It is clear that White should have protected the Pawn with **1. R—Q 1**, and brought the King up to support the Pawn.

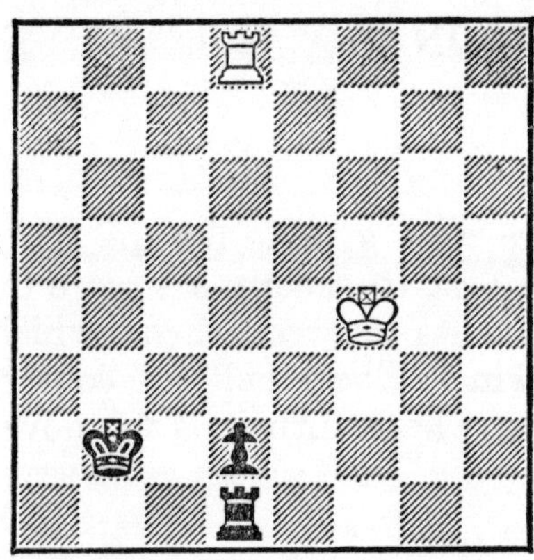

(113) Here is a Pawn on the 7th rank again. It is attacked once and defended once. Can Black move his Rook out of the Pawn's path in such a way that it may queen ? Yes. There is a way.

1. .... R—B 8 ch

White moves out of check—he cannot capture the Pawn.

2. K—K 3

(114) Now the way is clear.

2. .... P—Q 8 = Q

Clearly the Queen may be captured but after 3. R × Q, R × R; Black has an easy win.

NOTE—It was the check on Black's first move which was decisive.

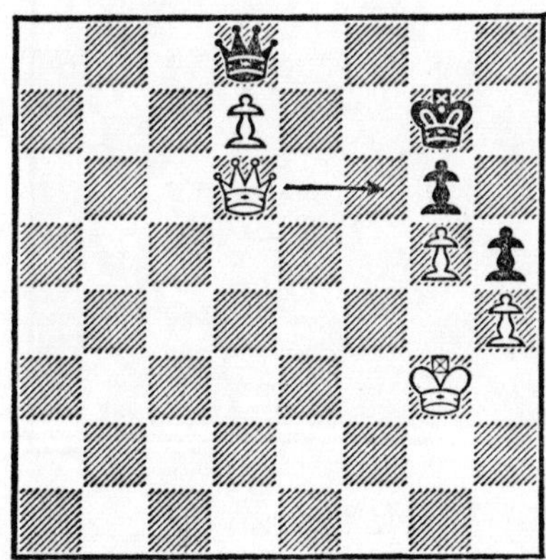

(115) White deserts his Pawn on the 7th rank in order to make sure it queens !

1. Q—B 6 ch ! Q × Q

(116) 2. P × Q ch and Black is unable to stop 3. P—Q 8 = Q

NOTE—Here the queening path was cleared by the forced exchange of Queens.

2. THE OPPOSITION

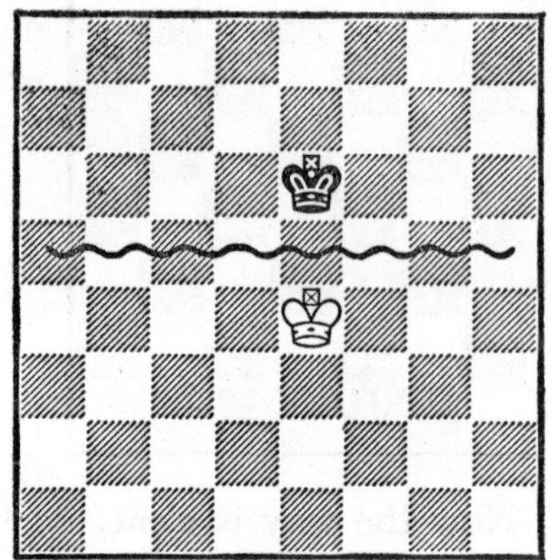

(117) If there were a prize for the King who was the first to occupy a square on the rank that lies between them, which one would win? The result, of course, depends upon whose turn it is to move.

In this race it is he who starts *last* who will be the winner. This may sound strange but the situation arises because the rules of the game do not allow Kings to occupy adjoining squares. In the following two diagrams we will examine what would happen if it were White to move, and then if it were Black to move first.

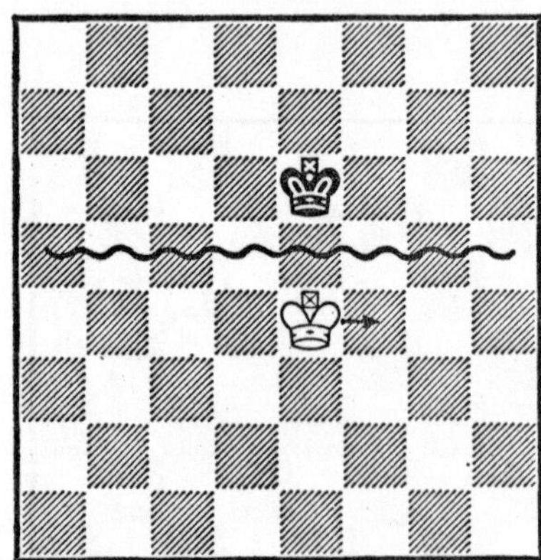

(118) White to move.

1. K—B 4 K—Q 4

and Black occupies the intervening rank first.

If 1. K—Q 4, K—B 4; Black still advances to the next rank first.

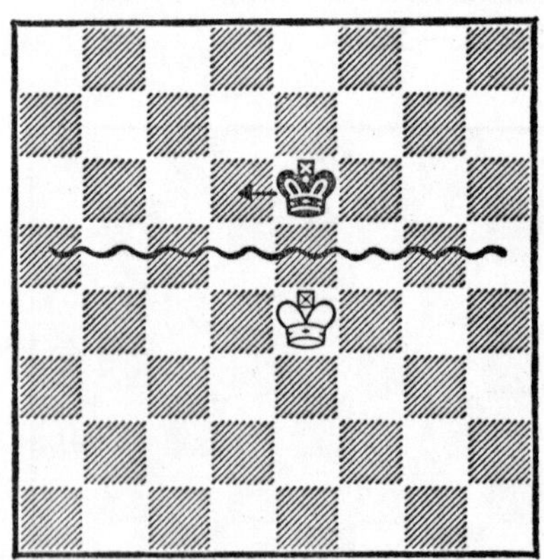

(119) Black to move.

1. .... K—Q 3

2. K—B 5 and White reaches his 5th rank first.

If 1. .... K—B 3.

2. K—Q 5 and White again advances to his 5th rank.

When the two Kings are facing each other with one square separating them, if White is able to force the Black King to move so that the White King occupies a square on the rank or file between them, then White is said to have the opposition. If Black, instead, is able to do the forcing, then Black is said to have the opposition.

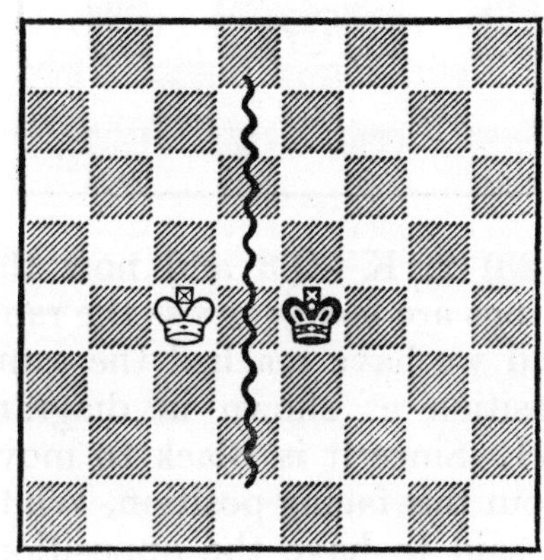

(120) File opposition. Facing each other across the file.

If Black to move—White has the opposition.

If White to move—Black has the opposition.

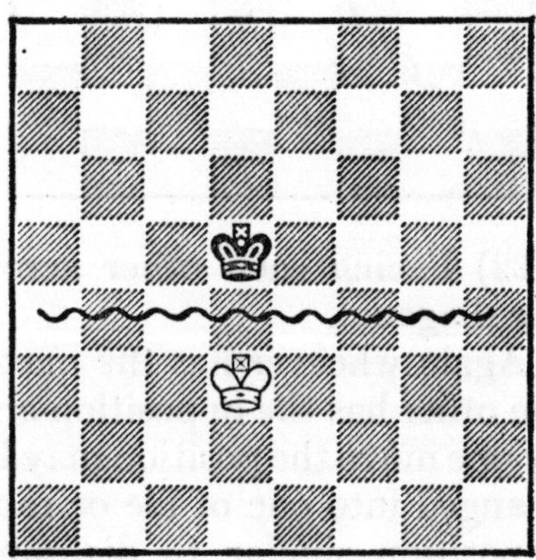

(121) Rank opposition. Facing each other across the rank.

Whoever has the move, the other has the opposition!

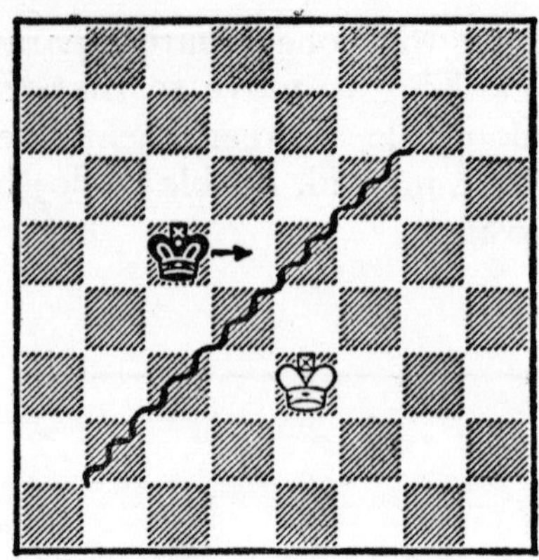

(122) Facing each other across the diagonal.

Again whoever has the move, the other has the opposition and by one move the position may be changed into one of file or rank opposition similar to diagrams 120 and 121.

Suppose it is Black to move.

1. . . . . K—Q 4

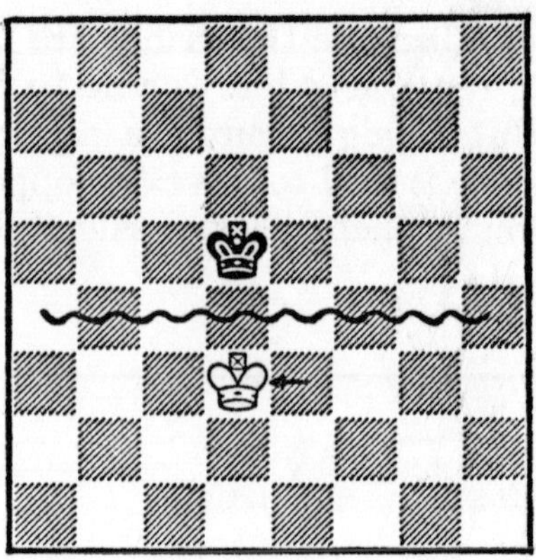

(123) 2. K—Q 3 and now the Kings are facing across the rank and we have reached the same position as shown in diagram 121. Since it is Black to move from this facing position, White is said to have the opposition. Had Black played 1. . . . . K—B 5 then 2. K—K 4 and we again have the facing position, with Black to move. White still has the opposition.

We now consider some examples where the knowledge of the opposition is used with King and Pawn against King—when the opposing King blocks the way.

If you wonder why we consider the opposition important, then look at the following position and you will see, then, that the opposition is sometimes worth a Queen ! !

(124) Black to move. He is in the facing position. As White therefore has the opposition White is able to win.

1.	K—K 1
2. P—K 7	K—Q 2 (fcd.)
3. K—B 7 and Pawn must queen.	

If 1. ....K—Kt 1; 2. P—K 7 and the Pawn queens next move.

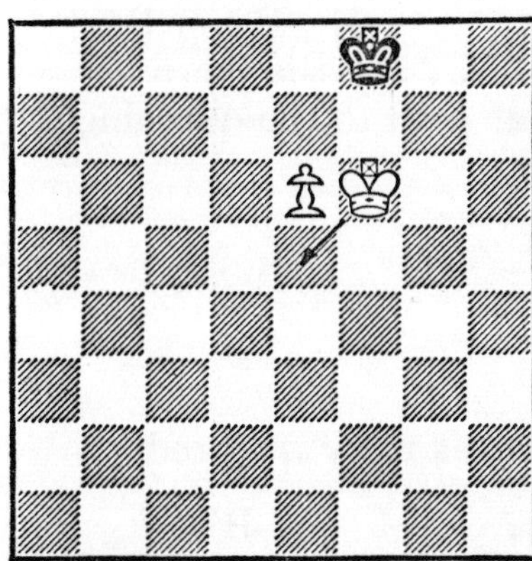

(125) If it is White to move Black has the opposition and the game may be drawn :

1. K—K 5	K—K 2
2. K—B 5	K—K 1

Not 2. ....K—Q 1 or B 1 as White then plays 3. K—B 6 gaining the opposition. 3. ....K—K 1, and 4. P—K 7 and wins.

3. K—B 6	K—B 1

and we are back to where we were.

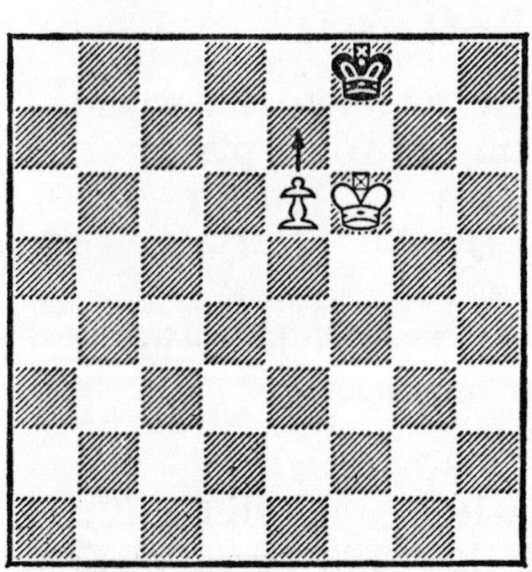

(126) If, instead of 1. K—K 5, White plays 1. P—K 7 ch then 1. ....K—K 1.

(127) 2. K—K 6 stalemate. Any other move except this loses the Pawn, of course.

In the position shown in diagram 128 White may win whether he has the move or not. The position, therefore, is of special importance in this type of ending.

(128) White to move.

1. K—K 6	K—K 1
2. P—Q 6	K—Q 1
3. P—Q 7	

NOTE—If 1.....K—B 1 or B 2; 2. K—K 7 and the Pawn has a clear path to the queening square.

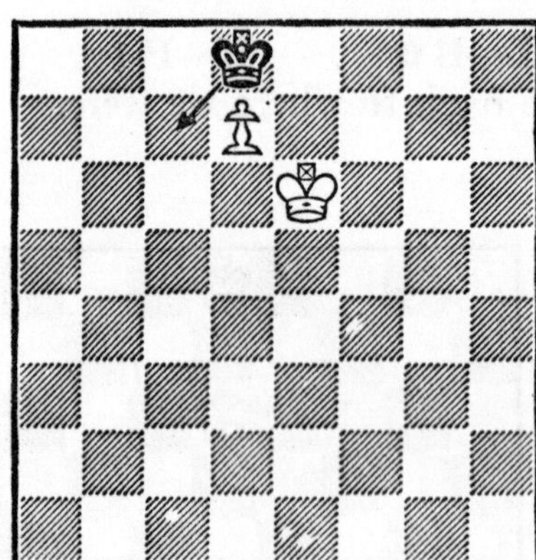

(129) Black's reply is forced.

3.	K—B 2

4. K—K 7 and Black cannot stop 5. P—Q 8 = Q

If in the position shown in diagram 128 White plays:

1. K—B 6	K—B 1
2. P—Q 6	K—Q 1
3. P—Q 7	K—K 2

4. K—B 7 and White wins in a similar manner.

Or

1. K—B 6	K—K 1 or K 2

2. K—B 7 wins even more quickly.

(130) Position as in diagram 128 but with Black to move.

1. . . . . K—K 1
2. K—B 7 (not K—K 6 ?) shepherding the Pawn home to its queening square.

If 1. . . . . K—B 1, then White plays 2. K—K 7 and wins in much the same way.

(131) Look again at the position reached after 1. . . . . K—K 1.

If White makes a poor plan Black may force a draw.

2. K—K 6 ?	K—Q 1
3. P—Q 6 ?	K—K 1
4. P—Q 7 ch	K—Q 1
5. K—Q 6 stalemate	

NOTE—If the Pawn checks on the 7th rank when the supporting King is on the 6th rank the lone King draws.

In endings with King and Pawn *v* King, the King on the 6th rank in front of its Pawn should always win, except in the case of a Rook's Pawn.

The Rook's Pawn is a special case however. This may be prevented from queening if the opposing King is able to reach the queening square, whether the player having the Pawn possesses the opposition or not.

Look at the following moves :

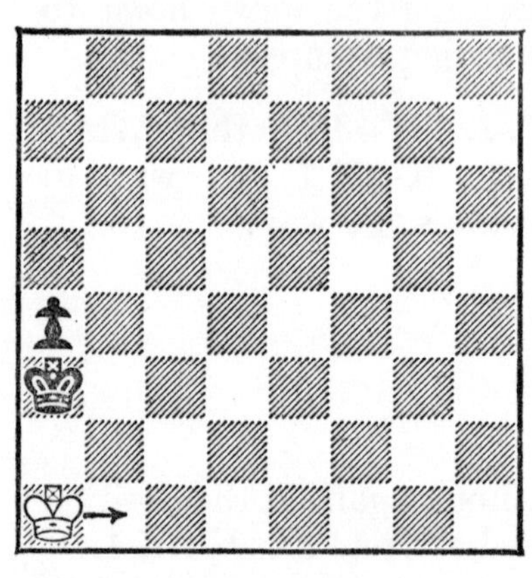

(132) White to play.
1. K—Kt 1

(133) 1. . . . .   K—Kt 6
2. K—R 1

(134) 2. . . . .   P—R 6
3. K—Kt 1

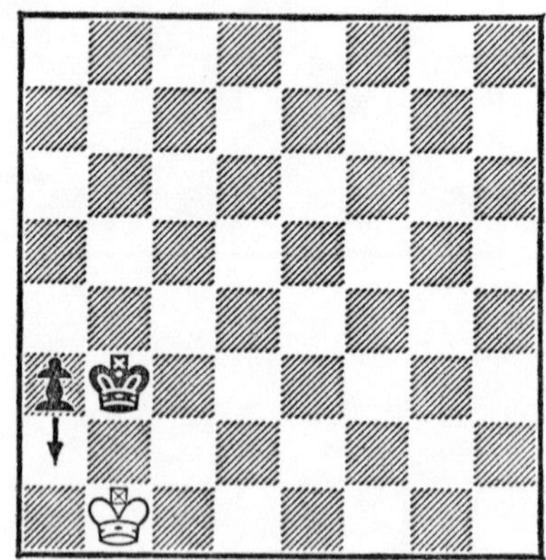

(135) Black to play.
If 3. . . . .   P—R 7 ch
4. K—R 1   K—R 6 stale-mate

The White King controls the Rook's Pawn's queening square. The Pawn cannot queen.

3. COUNTING AND QUEENING

(136) White to play.

Looking at this position it is clear that White easily queens the Pawn before the Black King can move across to prevent it.

(137) White to Play.

In this example it is not so obvious. Each square on the route to the queening square has been numbered and it can be seen that when both White Pawn and Black King have made two moves the White Pawn will queen on its next move.

(138) Here we see White making his third move. The Black King is too late!

(139) Black to play.

Now examine the same position as diagram 137 but with the important difference that *Black* moves first.

(140) Black to play.

Here we see the position after both have made two moves. Black's next move will be as shown and he catches the Pawn in time. If it queens he can capture it.

Providing there are no other pieces to hinder the race between the two, there is a simple rule which will help you to discover quickly whether the King can reach the queening square in time.

> *When it is the Pawn to move, if the opposing King can reach the queening square in the same number of moves or less than the Pawn, then the King is successful and the Pawn will be stopped, or captured on the queening square.*

Let us see how this rule works.

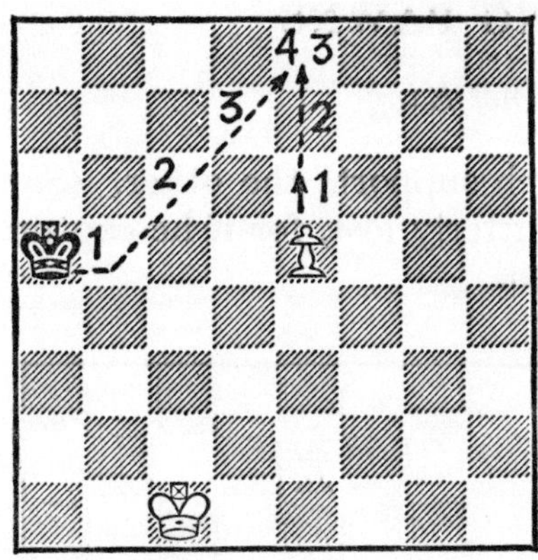

(141) White to play.

Here White queens on his third move. The Black King is too late even to make his third move towards the queening square.

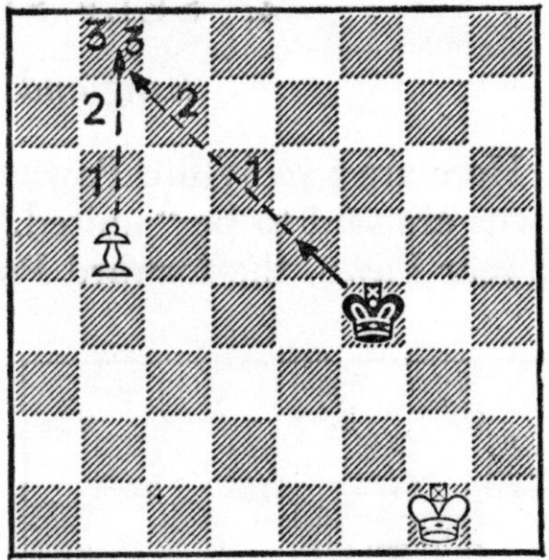

(142) Black to play.

Keeping to the rule, we must count from a position where the Pawn has first move. So the Black King moves to K 4 as shown. Then it would be the Pawn's turn to move and the counting rule applies. Three moves needed; the same as the Black King. Thus the Black King succeeds.

The rule again—*with Pawn to move, the opposing King succeeds if he has the same or less number of moves to make to arrive on the queening square.*

4. SELF-SUPPORTING PAWNS

King and 2 Pawns against King

Here are two White Pawns, one of which supports the other. (Such Pawns are said to be "united.") Black is utterly lost, for if he captures the rear Pawn, the forward Pawn can queen.

(143) Black to move.
1. .... K × P

(144) 2. P—Q 7

Using our counting rule we can see that the White Pawn has made one of its *two* moves required to reach the queening square. The Black King needs *three* moves, and therefore must fail.

(145) 2. .... K—B 3
A fruitless chase.

(146) 3. P—Q 8 = Q
The Pawn queens in safety.

Correct play for White if the Black King does not capture the rear Pawn, is to bring up his King in support. One of the Pawns will then queen quite easily.

Here is another example of self-supporting Pawns

(147) White to play.
In this position if White plays
1. P—Q 4
the Black King cannot capture the Knight's Pawn without allowing the other Pawn to queen.

(148) Similarly if the opposing King is in front of the other Pawn then
1. P—Kt 4
We have this position. If now
2. . . . . K × P the Knight's Pawn will queen.

In these examples of self-supporting Pawns it is seen that although the Black King is in a position to halt the advance of the Pawns, he cannot safely capture either. White brings up his King to assist and will queen with little difficulty. Pawns more widely separated make it even more difficult for the opposing King—he cannot be in two places at once.

If the Pawns are as far advanced as the 6th rank there is no need to wait for the opposing King to capture; the free Pawn may move to the 7th rank and will queen whether the King captures the other or not.

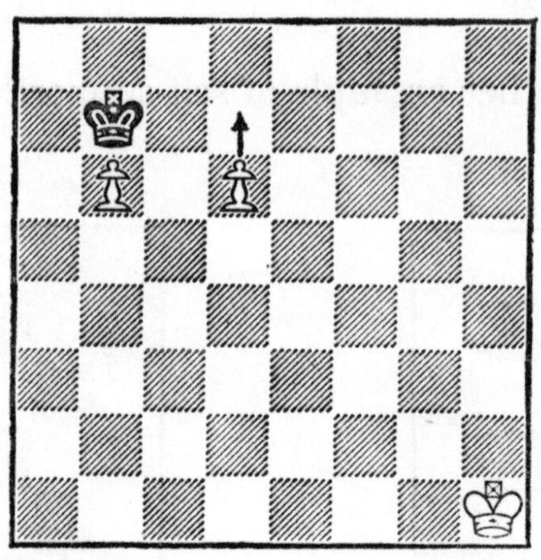

(149) White to play. In this position 1. P—Q 7 must queen the Pawn.

1. .... K × P
2. P—Q 8 = Q ch

or

1. .... K—Kt 1
2. P—Q 8 = Q ch

5. PAWN BREAKTHROUGH

Here are an equal number of Pawns confronting each other. The fact that White's Pawns are more advanced than those of Black, allows White to win by an instructive sacrifice.

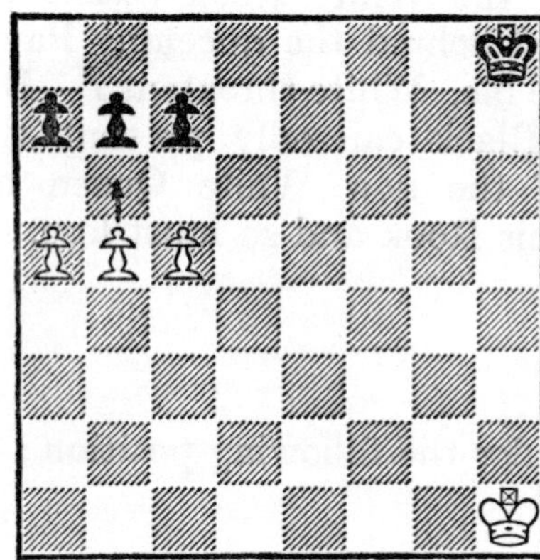

(150) White to play.
1. P—Kt 6 ! B P × P

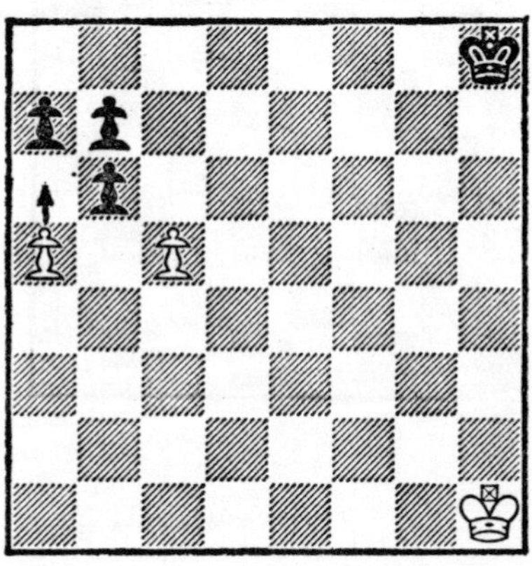

(151) If Black's Pawn at Kt 2 were removed, White's Bishop's Pawn would have a clear path to its queening square.
2. P—R 6 ! P × R P

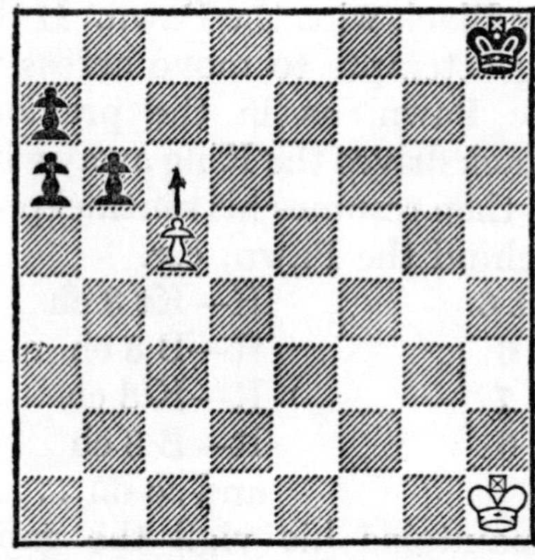

(152) 3. P—B 6 and White will queen in *two* more moves, whereas Black would take *five* moves to queen if allowed.

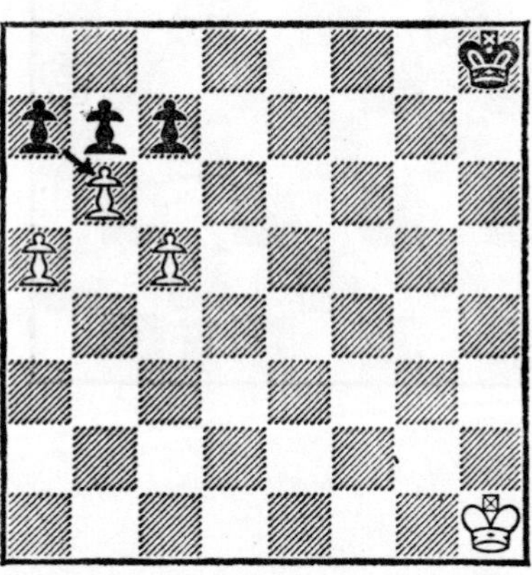

(153) If instead of 1. . . . . BP × P Black plays 1. . . . . R P × P then 2. P—B 6, P × B P; 3. P—R 6 and queens first.

6. ROOKS AND PAWNS

(154) White to play.
The White King guards the queening square and the White Rook assists by being placed behind the queening Pawn on the same file. White threatens P—B 8 = Q and Black can only prevent the survival of the new White Queen by sacrificing his Rook and so must lose.

Now consider the following position :

(155) White to play.
White has a Pawn on the 7th rank—one square to go ! But the White Rook is not placed *behind* the Pawn. The Black Rook enjoys that situation. If the White Rook moves away Black wins the Pawn. If the White King attempts to move across to support the Pawn, as in the previous example, Black drives the King away with checks, and then resumes his sentinel post at K B 8 behind the Pawn, e.g.

1.	K—Kt 6	R—Kt 8 ch
2.	K—B 6	R—B 8 ch
3.	K—K 7	R—K 8 ch
4.	K—B 6	R—B 8 ch
		and so on .... !

If Black maintains his vigil the game should be drawn. Any other plan by White is countered by keeping the Black Rook on the King's Bishop file at a respectful distance from the White King.

(156) Black must be careful though. Here is the same position again and if it were Black's move and the King moved off the 2nd rank on to any of the squares marked *, White could win by moving the Rook giving check. (This is similar to the position in diagram 113.)

(157) Here we see this has taken place. The Black King must move out of check, and next move White plays P—B 8 = Q, and the Queen and Rook protect each other.

(158) Then again the Black King must not move along the rank away from contact with the Queen's Rook's file. In this position you will see the Black King is on Q B 2 so White plays

1. R—Q R 8 as shown.

Now the White Pawn threatens to queen next move and if Black plays 1. . . . . R × P, White wins by a killing skewer.

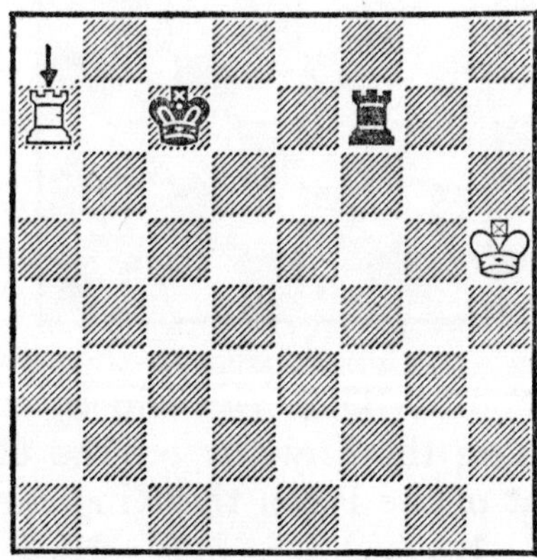

(159) 2. R—R 7 ch

The Black King must move away and White can then play

3. R × R!

Now let us consider a similar situation. Black has a Pawn on the 6th rank of the Rook's file.

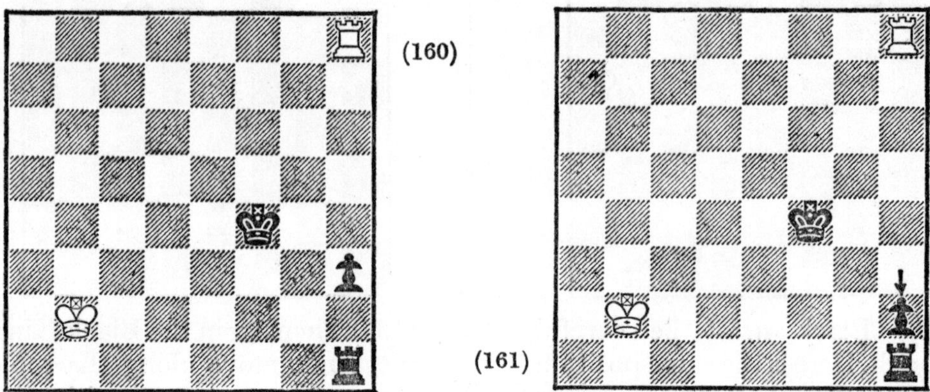

(160) (161)

The enemy Rook is behind the Pawn and the assisting Rook occupies the queening square (160). If Black plays ....P—R 7 the game can be drawn by keeping the White Rook behind the Pawn (161). If the Black King moves to aid the Black Rook it can be driven away by checks.

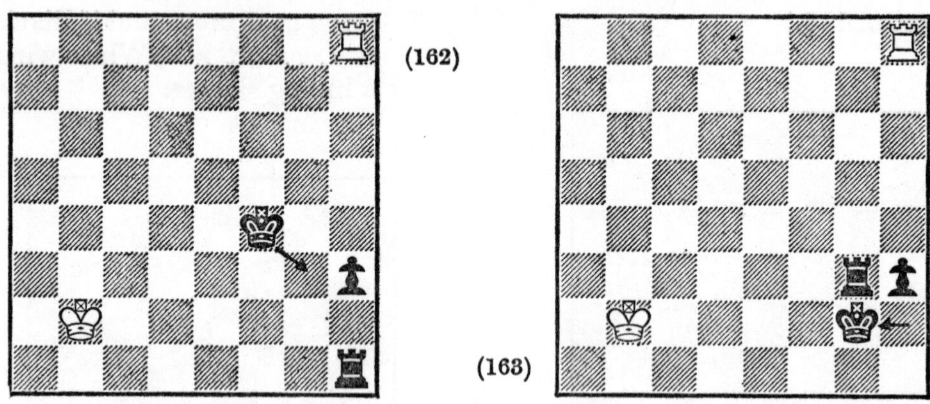

(162) (163)

(162) But Black can win by bringing the King to the Pawn's aid, and because the Pawn is on the 6th rank and there is a vacant square in front of the Pawn the King can find shelter from a checking storm.

1.	K—Kt 6	4. R—K R 7	R—Kt 6
2. R—Kt 8 ch	K—R 7	5. R—K R 8	
3. R—Kt 7	R—K Kt 8		

(163) 5. .... K—Kt 7! and now White would have to give up his Rook to stop the Queen and so must lose.

The situation is much easier for queening the Pawn when the Rook supports from behind it. Consider the following:

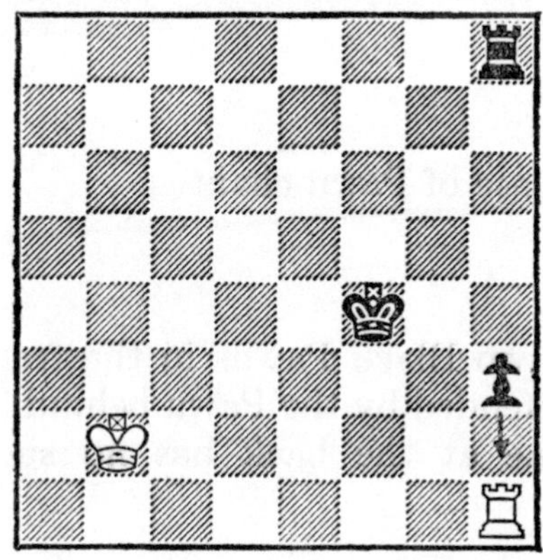

(164) This time the Black Rook is behind the Pawn and after

1.	P—R 7
2. R—K B 1 ch	K—Kt 6
3. R—K R 1	

(165) 3. . . . . K—Kt 7
the Black Pawn queens unless the Rook gives itself up. The only other choice after Black has moved his Pawn to the 7th rank is a King move.

(166) For example:

2. K—B 2	K—Kt 6
3. K—Q 2	

(167) 3. . . . . K—Kt 7
and again the Black Pawn queens.

You can usually help your advancing passed Pawns by placing your Rooks behind them and using your King to assist.

When there are a number of linked Pawns on the board it is best to try to attack the weakest Pawn in your opponent's Pawn chain.

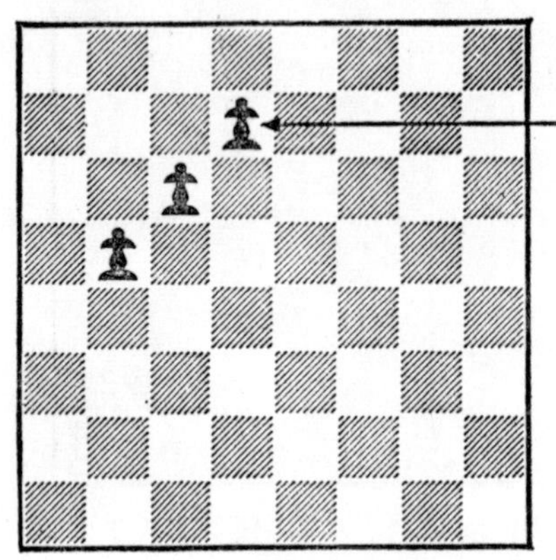

weak base of Pawn chain

(168) The two Black Pawns in the front are each defended by the Pawn behind it, but the one at the back has no such defence.

Look at the following situation :

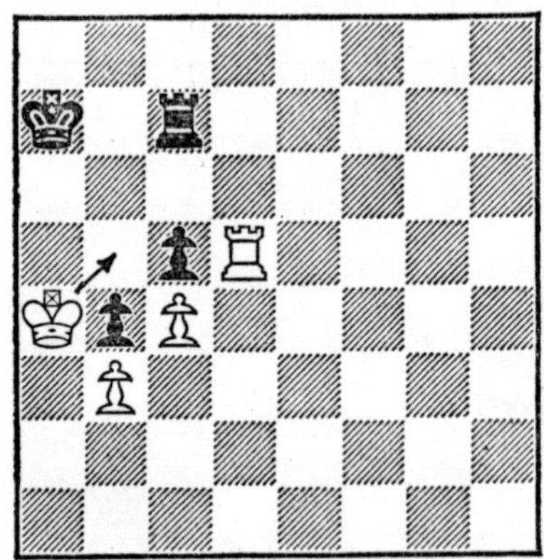

(169) White to play.
White's Rook is better placed, attacking the backward Black Pawn. 1. K—Kt 5 now doubly attacks the weak Pawn. If now
1. . . . . R—Kt 2 ch

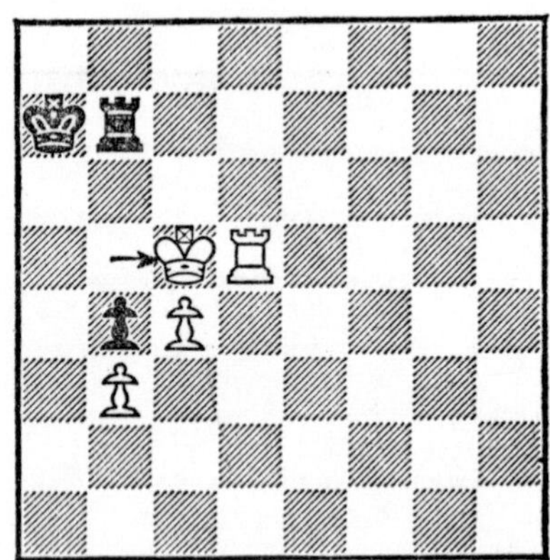

(170) 2. K × P and White should win with the extra Pawn. Any other move by Black still results in the loss of the Pawn, as a result of the attack on the weak base.

QUIZ ON "THE PAWN IN END GAME BATTLES"

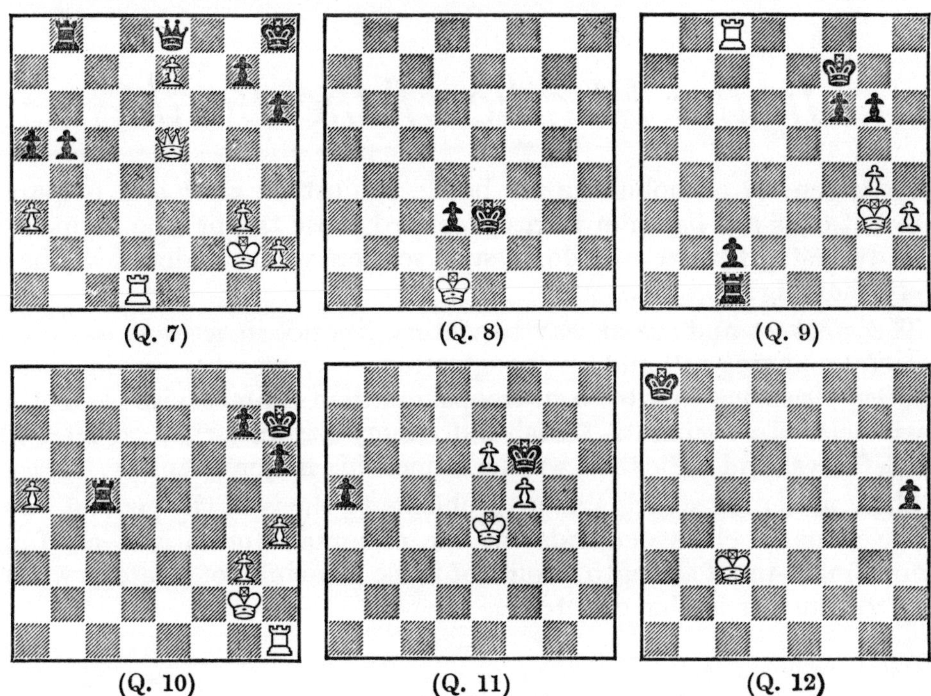

(Q. 7) (Q. 8) (Q. 9)

(Q. 10) (Q. 11) (Q. 12)

(Q.7) White to play and win.
There is a combination in which White's Pawn on the 7th rank plays a vital part. Can you find it ?

(Q.8) Two questions about this position :

(*a*) White to play.
What should White play and what would be the result ?

(*b*) Suppose it is Black to play.
What should Black play and what would be the result ?

(Q.9) Suggest a move for Black to win.

(Q.10) White to play.
Black threatens White's Queen's Rook Pawn. Should this attack be met by P—R 6 or R—R 1 ?

(Q.11) White to play.
The White King is guarding his two Pawns but he sees that Black's Rook's Pawn is marching to its queening square. What general plan do you suggest for White ?

(Q.12) White to play.
By counting, decide whether the Pawn may queen safely.

Answers to Quiz on " The Pawn in End Game Battles " on page 193.

In the Middle of the Battle

WHEN a general is mobilising for battle against an alert and prepared enemy, it does not pay him to rush forward those troops who happen to be ready first. If he were to do so, such soldiers would undoubtedly have a very short fighting life.

The quickest and surest way to victory lies not in reckless haste but in careful planning to build up enough strength to smash open the enemy defences. Ensuring that his own troops maintain contact with each other he will seize strong points, search out enemy weaknesses, look after his own defences, and only then will he launch his major offensive.

Chess presents us with similar problems to those of the general. The middle game in chess demands the use of mobile forces in a carefully planned build-up of strength. Some of these principles of strategy we are going to consider in this chapter.

1. CHECKMATE IN THE MIDDLE GAME

The examples which follow are taken from actual games and illustrate how well-placed attacking pieces take final decisive advantage of enemy weaknesses.

Berlin, 1933

RICHTER *v* SAMISCH

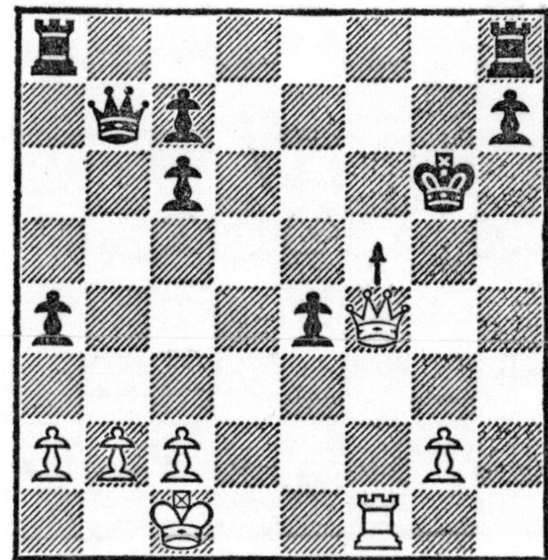

(171) White to play.
Black's extra Rook is of no use to him. His exposed King has no pieces suitably placed to help.

1. Q—B 5 ch   K—Kt 2
2. Q—B 6 ch   K—Kt 1

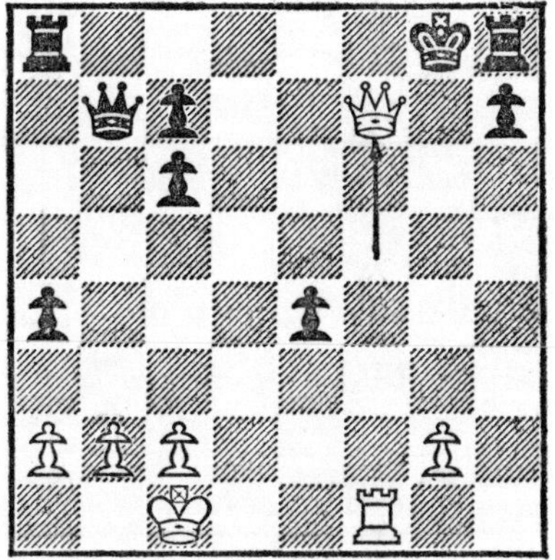

(172) 3. Q—B 7 mate.
Black could have been mated one move quicker by

1. Q—Kt 4 (or Kt 3) ch
1.....   K—R 3
2. R—R 1 mate!

Birmingham, 1937

SILVERMAN *v* ELISKASES

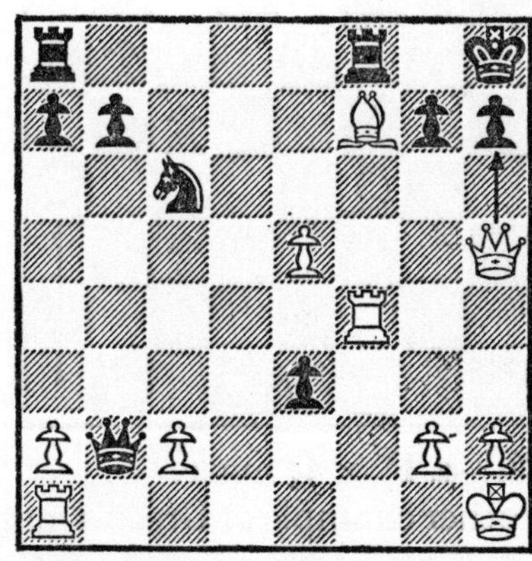

(173) White to play.
Black threatens Q × R ch with mate to follow, but has no time to carry out this plan.

1. Q × P ch   Resigns

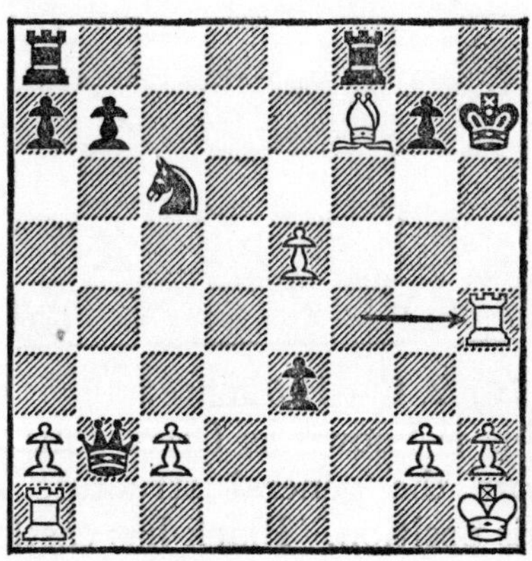

(174) for after

1. ....   K × Q
2. R—R 4 mate.

Amsterdam, 1851

HEIJMANS *v* VAN PRAAG

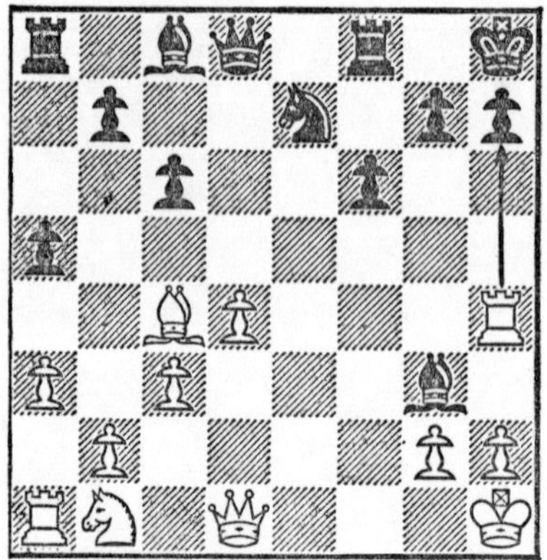

(175) White to play.

White breaks open Black's K R file.

1. R × P ch K × R (fcd.)

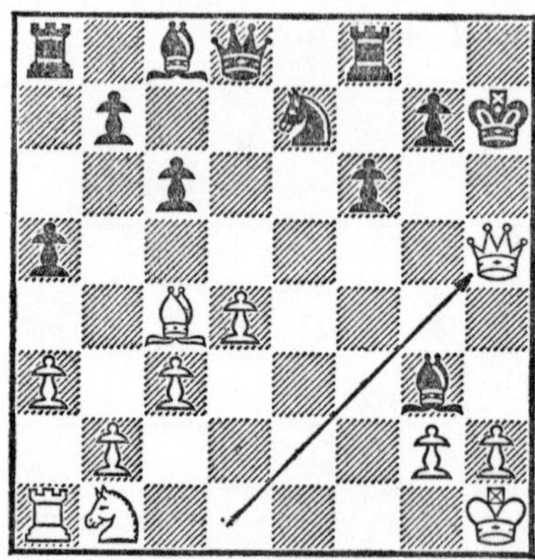

(176) 2. Q—R 5 mate !

This is known as Greco's mate. Note the general structure of this position. Black has castled behind an advanced K B Pawn, and White controls the diagonal Q R 2—K Kt 8, particularly the square K Kt 8. Then the K R file is opened up.

Chicago, 1899

JOHNSON *v* MARSHALL

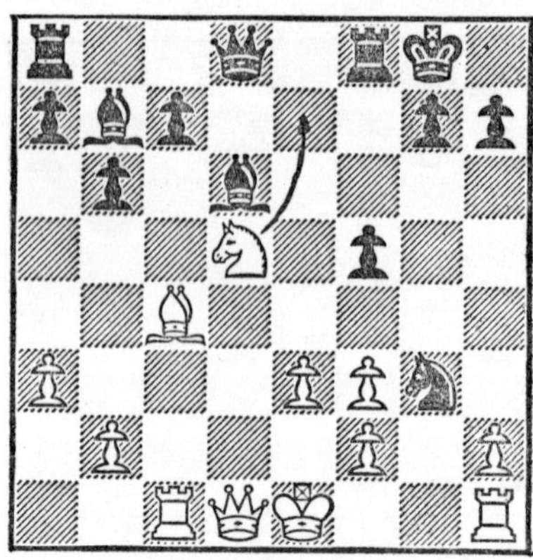

(177) White to play.

A brilliant manœuvre is initiated by a double check.

1. Kt—K 7 dble ch K—R 1
2. Kt—Kt 6 ch P × Kt
3. R P × Kt disc ch Q—R 5

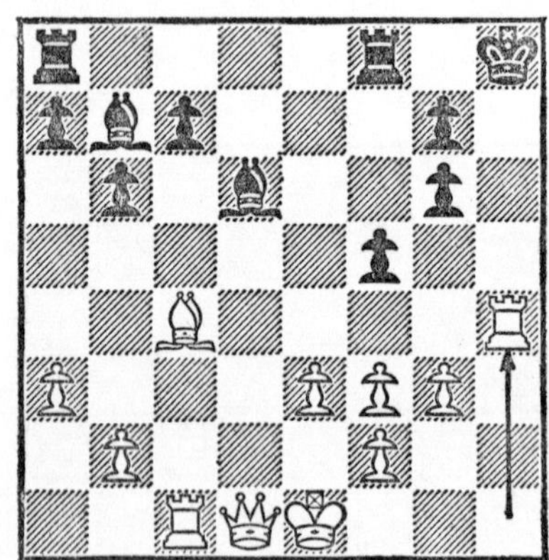

(178) 4. R × Q mate.

Another example of Greco's mate

Greco was a famous Italian player of the early 17th century.

Note all Black's moves were forced.

Ljusne, Sweden, 1927

HAGLUND *v* ERDMAN

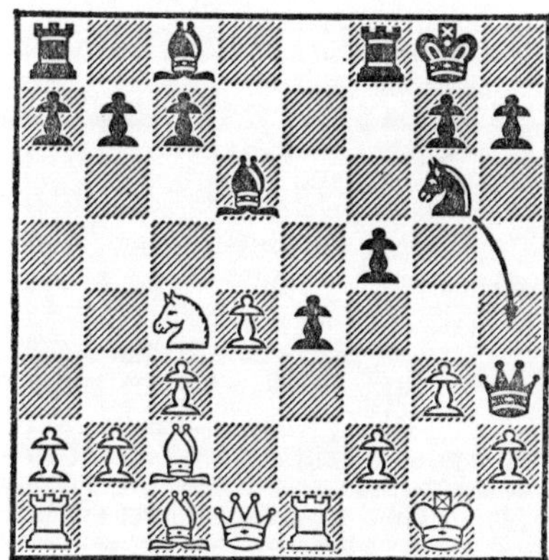

(179) Black to play.

1. . . . . Kt—R 5 threatening mate next move by 2. . . . . Q—Kt 7. White has no choice but to play

2. P × Kt

This has the effect of allowing Black's King's Bishop to enter the attack.

2.	B × P ch
3. K—R 1	B—Kt 6 disc ch
4. K—Kt 1	Q—R 7 ch
5. K—B 1	

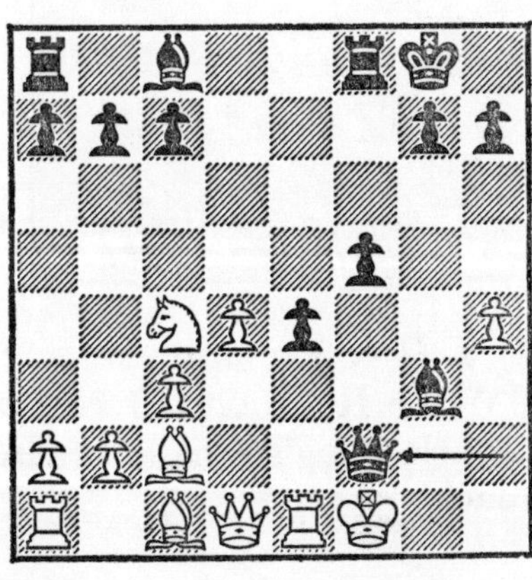

(180) 5. . . . . Q × P mate!

New Zealand correspondence match, 1935

ABBOT *v* BARNES

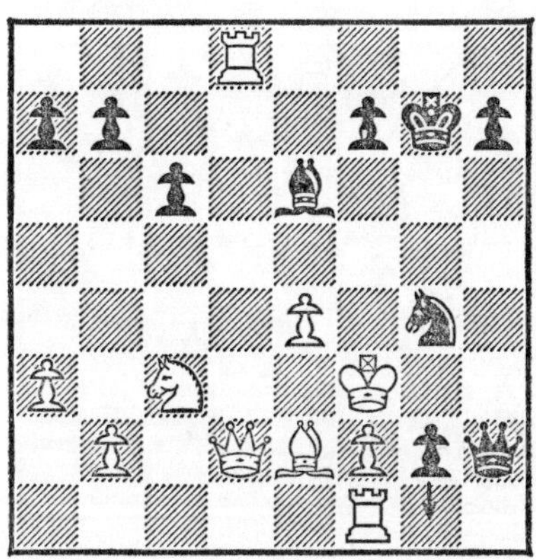

(181) Black to play.

Here is an example where a Pawn is promoted not to a Queen but to a minor piece.

1. . . . . P—Kt 8 = Knight ch clearing the rank for an attack by the Queen on White's K B 2, and compelling the White Rook to move away from the defence of this square.

2. R × Kt (forced.)

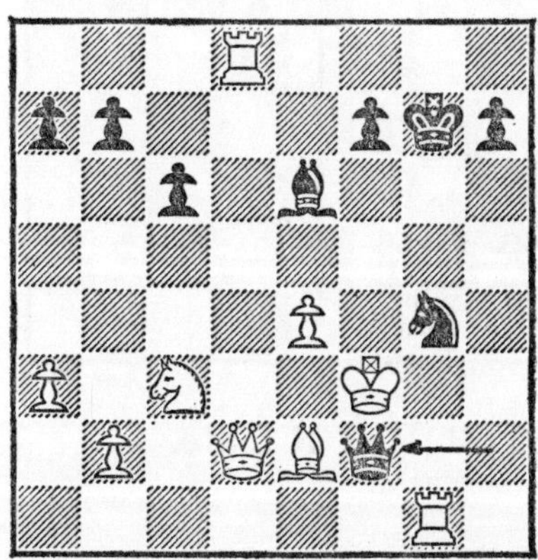

(182) 2. . . . . Q × P mate.

ANDERSSEN *v* WYVILL
London, 1851

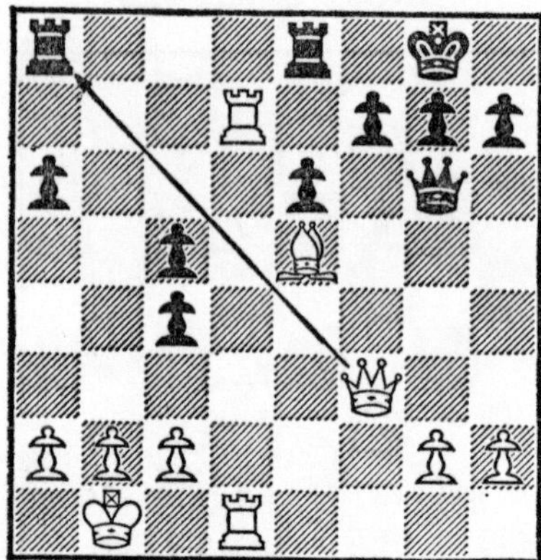

(183) White to play.
White controls the open file with doubled Rooks and, with the aid of the Queen, decisively weakens Black's back row defences.

1. Q × R R × Q
2. R—Q 8 ch R × R

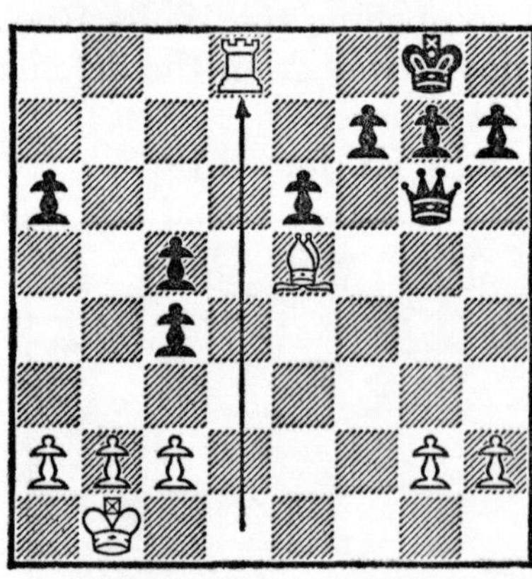

(184) 3. R × R mate.

BLEDOW *v* BILGUER
Berlin, 1838

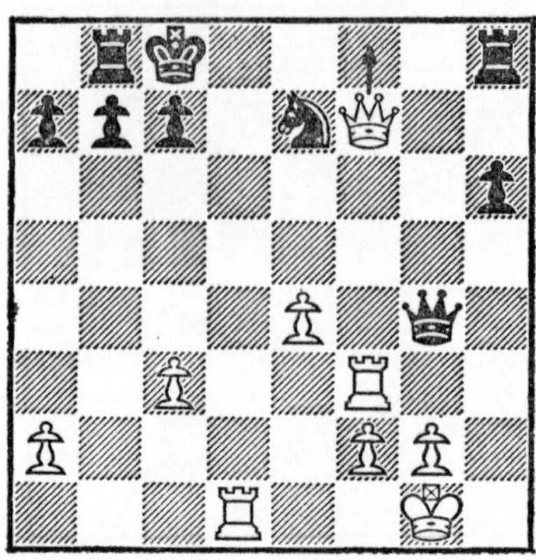

(185) White to play.
With open Queen's file and K B file doubly controlled, White plays

1. Q—B 8 ch R × Q

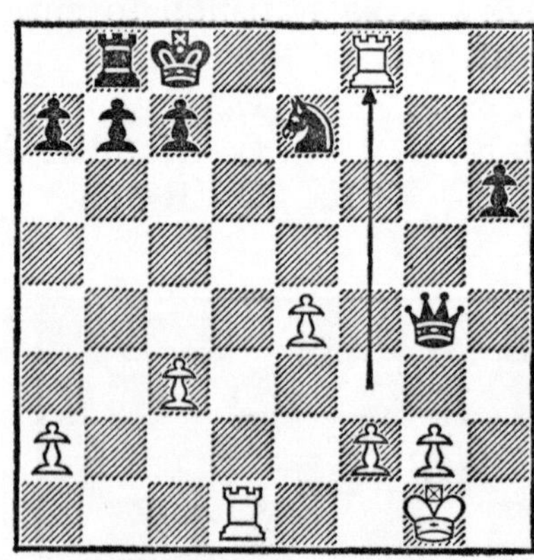

(186) 2. R × R mate.
The White Rook on Q 1 covers the Black King's escape square at Black's Q 2.

Rio de Janeiro, 1900

CALDAS VIANNA *v* SILVESTRE

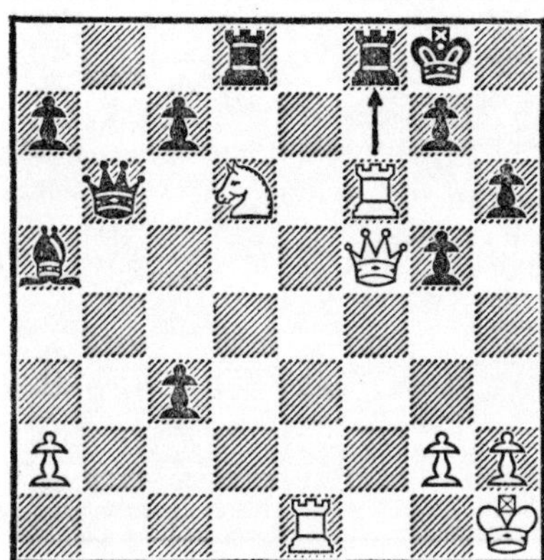

(187) White to play.

1. R × R ch R × R
2. Q × R ch K × Q

This combination by White draws the Black King away from an escape square on K R 2.

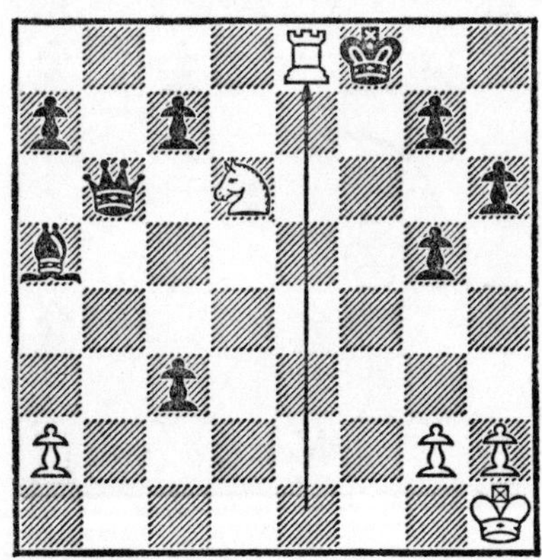

(188) 3. R—K 8 mate.

Reykjavik, 1931

ALEKHINE *v* ASGEIRSSON

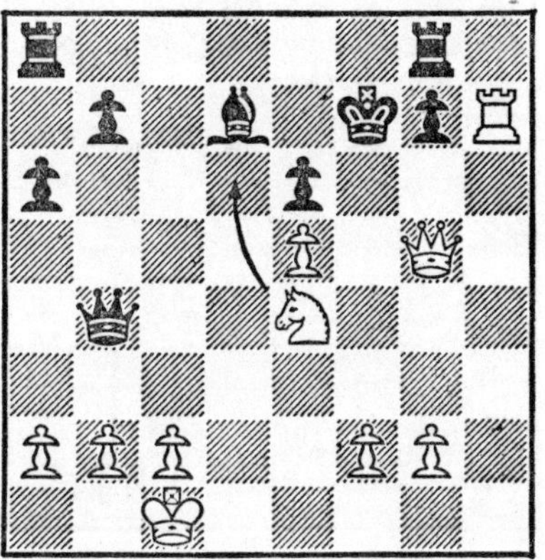

(189) White to play.

1. Kt—Q 6 ch K—B 1

The only other choice for Black would have been to give up Queen (1. . . . . Q × Kt; 2. P × Q).

2. Q—B 6 ch

Sacrificing the Queen in order to allow the Rook to penetrate along the 7th rank.

2. . . . . P × Q

(190) 3. R—B 7 mate.

Meran, 1926

PRZEPIORKA *v* PATAY

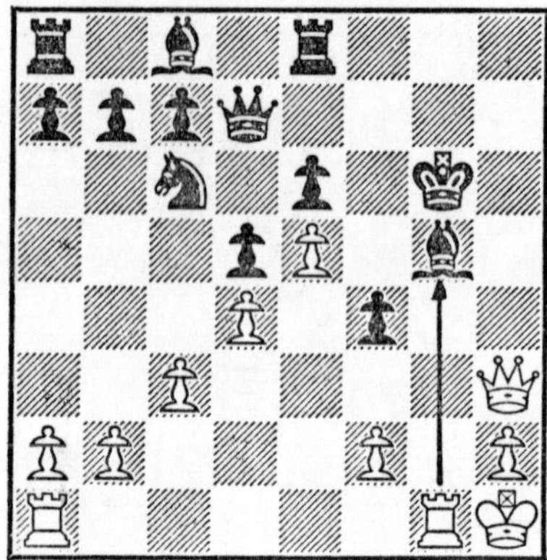

(191) White to play.
White has given up two minor pieces in order to open up the Black King's position.

1. R × B ch ! K × R

if 1. . . . . K—B 2 then White plays 2. Q—R 7 ch and wins).

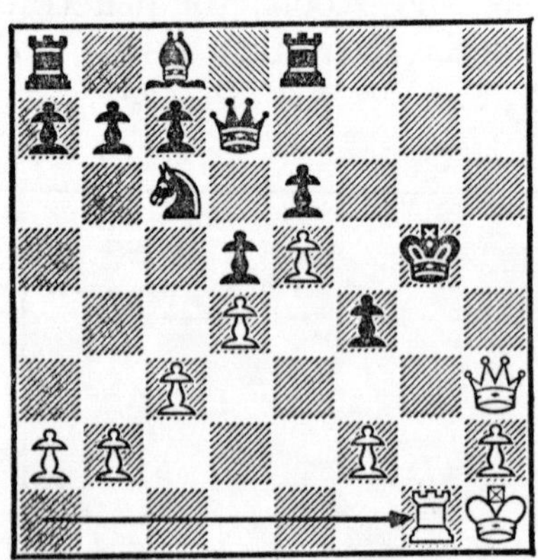

(192) 2. R—K Kt 1 mate.

Sitges, 1934

DR. TICOULAT *v* LILIENTHAL

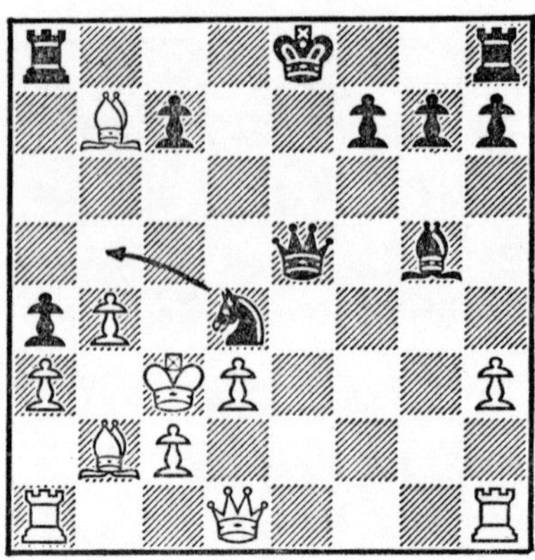

(193) Black to play.
The White King has been forced out into the open.

1. . . . . Kt—Kt 4 dble ch
2. K—B 4 (fcd)

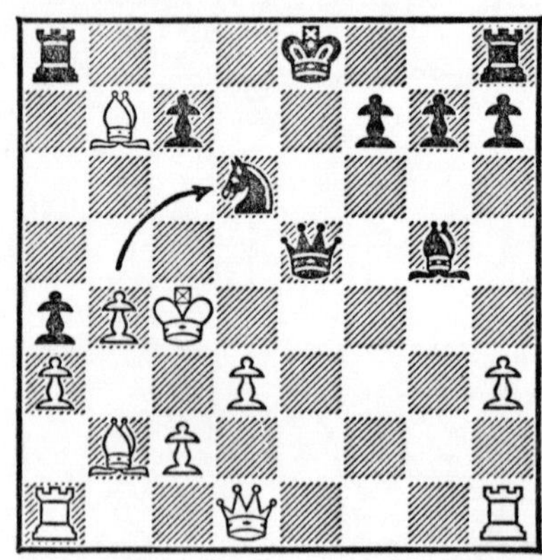

(194) 2. . . . . Kt—Q 3 mate

Breslau, 1880

TARRASCH *v* VON SCHERE
(when 17)

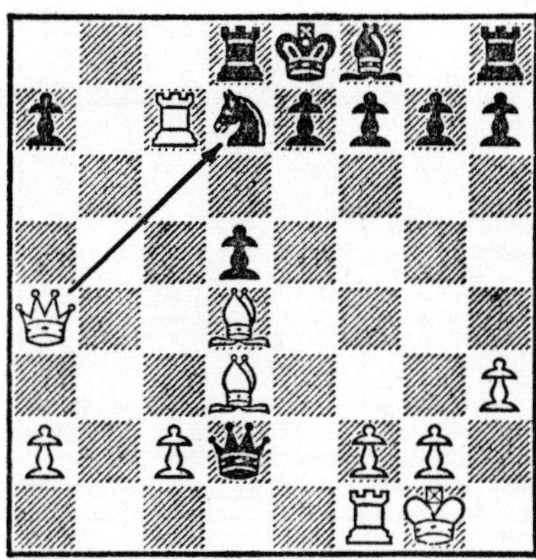

(195) White to play.

1. Q × Kt ch	R × Q
2. R—B 8 ch	R—Q 1

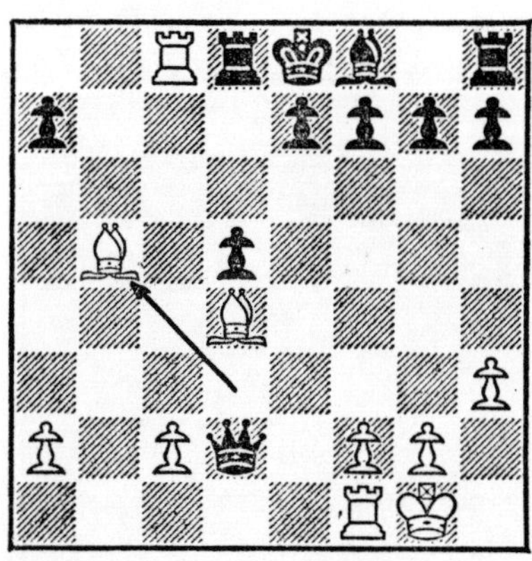

(196) 3. B—Kt 5 mate.
The Black Rook on Q1 is pinned.

Sweden, 1933

KINMARK *v* JOHANSSON

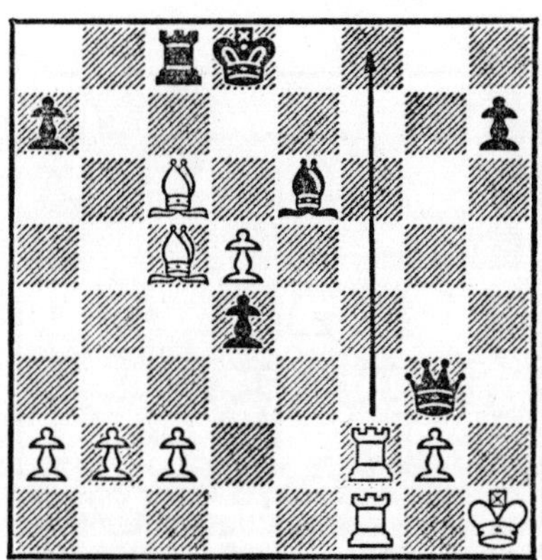

(197) White to play.
This game was awarded a brilliancy prize.

1. R—B 8 ch	K—B 2
2. R(B 1)—B 7 ch	B × R
3. R × B ch	K—Kt 1

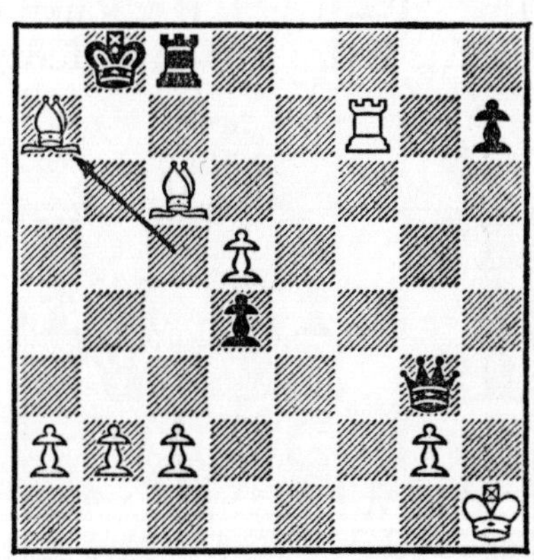

(198) 4. B × P mate.
Black could have lasted a little longer by playing 3. . . . . K—Q 1. Then follows 4. R—Q 7 ch, K—K 1; 5. R—Q Kt 7disc ch, K—Q 1; 6. B—K 7 mate.

Played by correspondence, 1932

KERES *v* FOLDSEPP

(when 16)

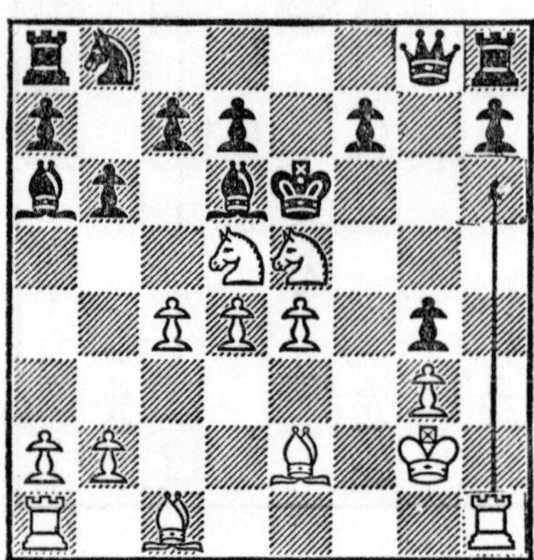

(199) White to play.

Keres has sacrificed his Queen in order to bring Black's King out into the open.

1. R—R 6 ch Q—Kt 3

If 1. . . . . P—B 3; 2. R × P mate!

2. B × P ch P—B 4 (fcd.)

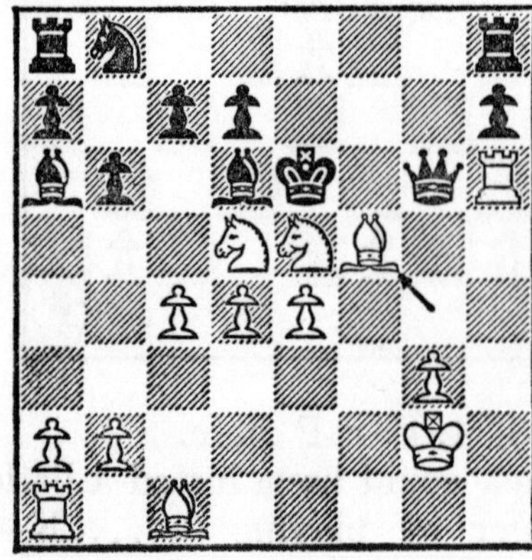

(200) 3. B × P mate.

The Black Queen is pinned!

Simultaneous display, 1934

CANAL *v* AMATEUR

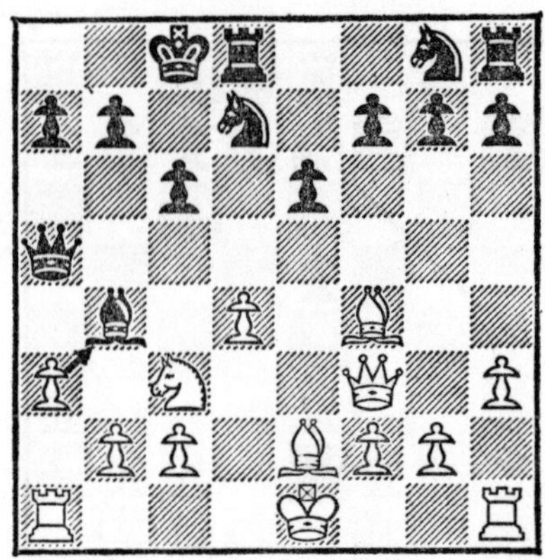

(201) White to play.

Giving up two Rooks and Queen in exchange for Bishop!

1. P × B	Q × R ch
2. K—Q 2	Q × R
3. Q × P ch	P × Q

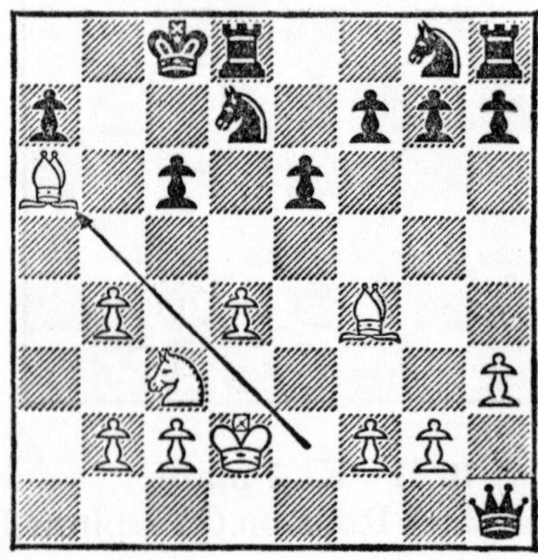

(202) 4. B—Q R 6 mate.

This demonstrates the great power of two Bishops working together.

Margate, 1937

KOBLENZ *v* JAMESON

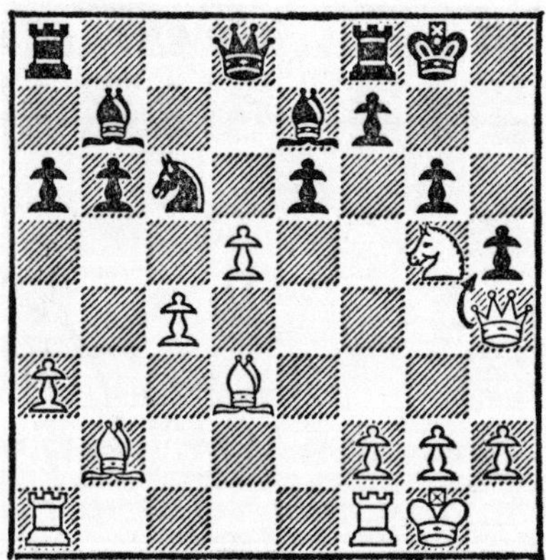

(203) White to play.
White's two Bishops bear down upon Black's King's position, and the White Queen is now offered up to remove the Pawn at Black's K Kt 3.

1. Q × P!!

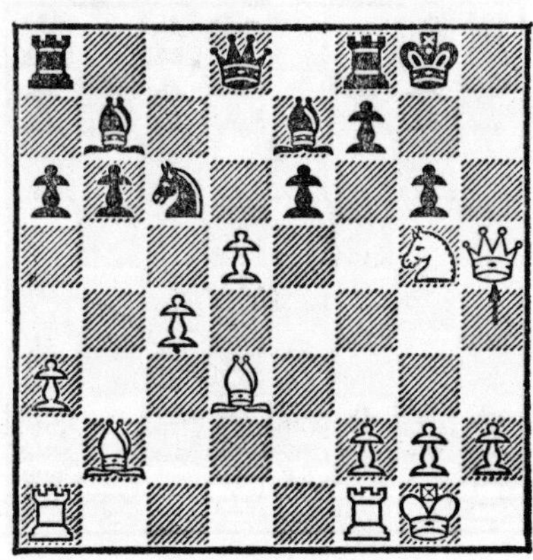

(204) 1. .... Resigns.
Because if now 1. .... P × Q; 2. B—R 7 mate! If Black plays 1. ....B × Kt; 2. Q—R 8 mate. If 1. .... B—B 3; 2. Q—R 7 mate.

Hastings, 1934

KOLTANOWSKI *v* CRADDOCK

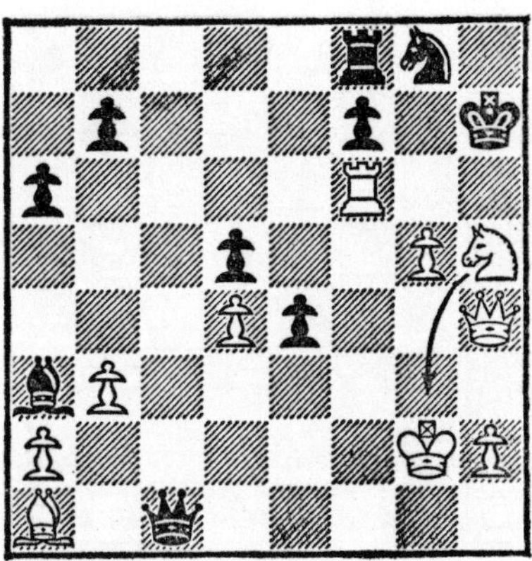

(205) White to play.
The conclusion of a neat combination.

1. Kt—Kt 3 disc ch K—Kt 2

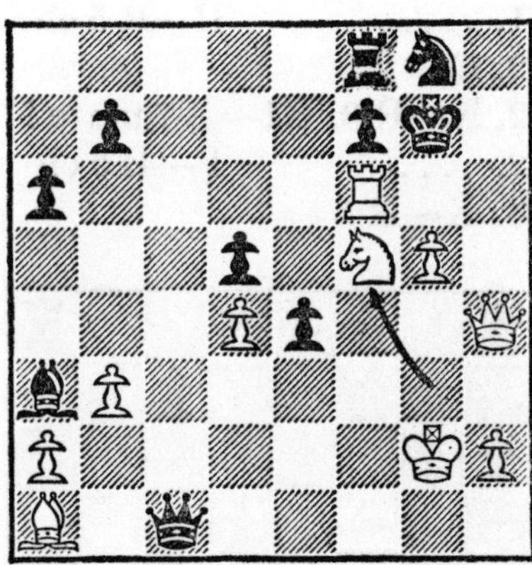

(206) 2. Kt—B 5 mate.
Black could have lasted a little longer by 1. ....Kt—R 3 when White replies 2. R × Kt ch etc.

Nuremberg, 1890

KURSCHNER *v* TARRASCH

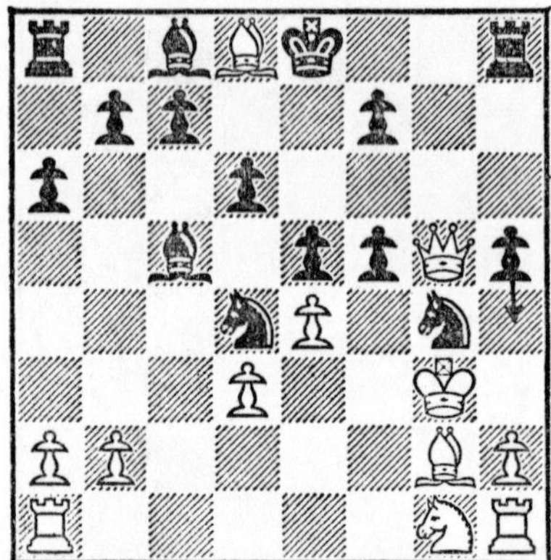

(207) Black to play.
Black is faced with a threat of mate in one move but his winning attack is already well under way.

1. .... P—R 5 ch
2. Q × P

If 2. K—R 3, Kt—B 7 mate ! !

2. .... P—B 5 ch
3. K—R 3

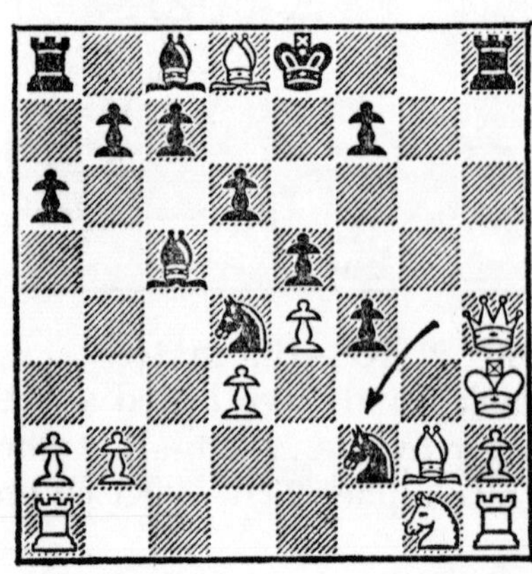

(208) 3. .... Kt—B 7 dble ch mate.

Moscow, 1927

RABINOWITSCH *v* LEVENFISH

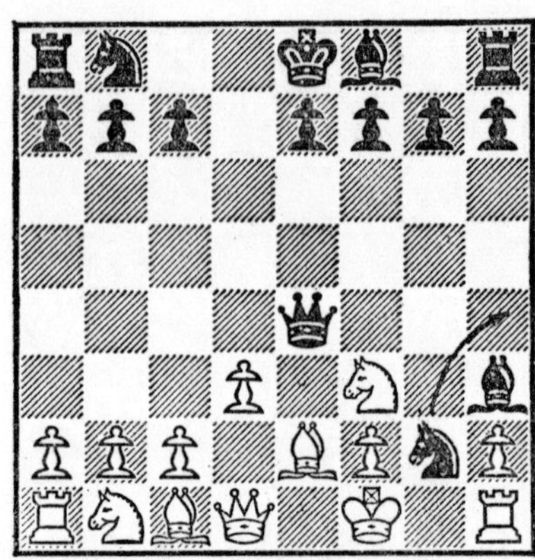

(209) Black to play.
The Black Queen, although *en prise* is quite secure !

1. .... Kt—R 5 disc ch
2. K—K 1

or if 2. K—Kt 1, Q—Kt 5 mate.

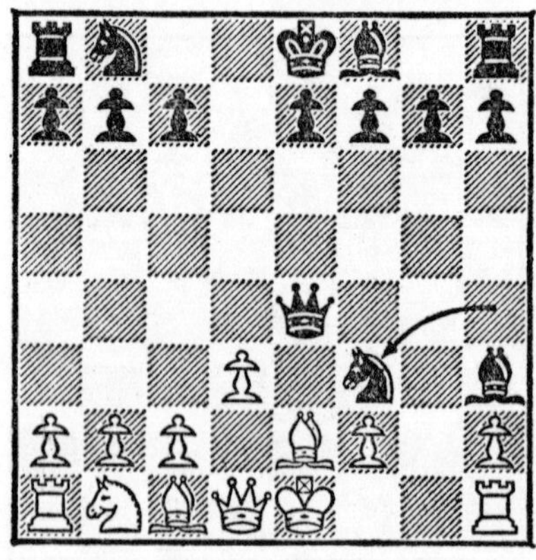

(210) 2. .... Kt × Kt mate !

In a simultaneous display
U.S.S.R., 1936
KASPARYAN *v* MANVELYAN

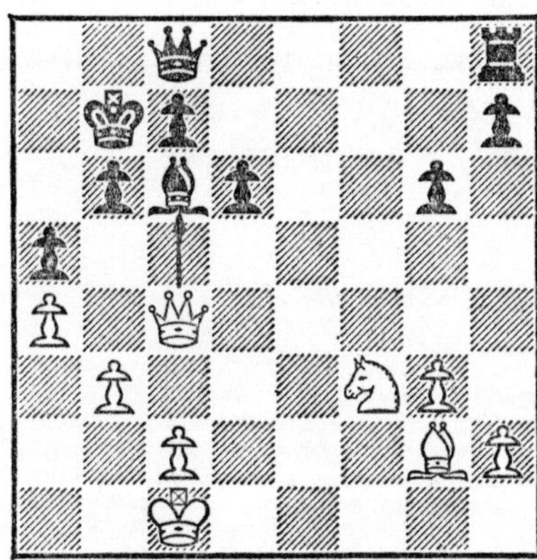

(211) White to play.

1. Q × B ch	K × Q
2. Kt—K 5 dble ch	

Note how White controls all the vital white squares.

2.	K—B 4 (fcd.)
3. Kt—Q 3 ch	K—Q 5
4. K—Q 2	Q—K 3

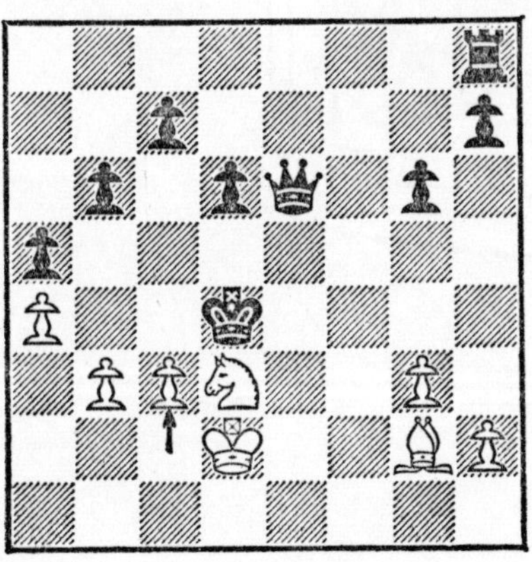

(212) 5. P—B 3 mate.
This is another example of the dangers the King has to face when forced out into the open.

London, 1834
LA BOURDONNAIS *v* MACDONNELL

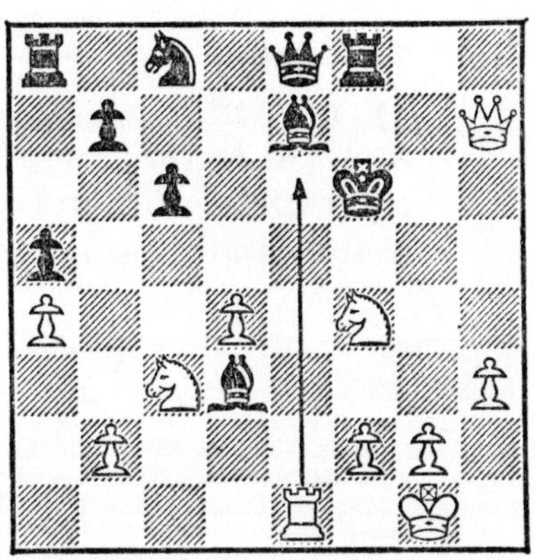

(213) White to play.

1. R—K 6 ch	K—Kt 4 (fcd.)
2. Q—R 6 ch	K—B 4 (fcd.)

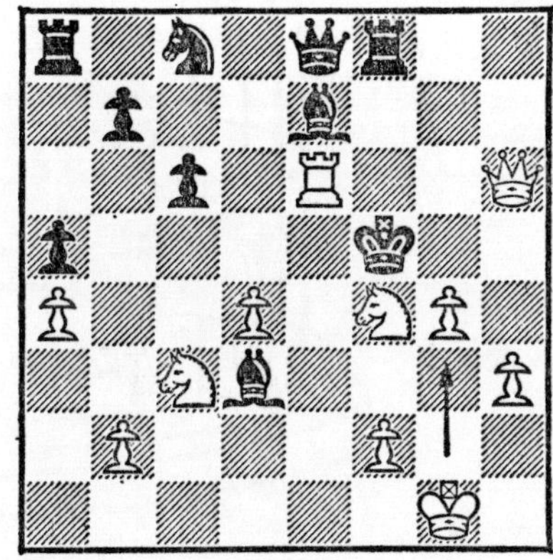

(214) 3. P—K Kt 4 mate.

The mates you have just seen were brought about by master chess players. We now give some mating finishes to games played by young players which are typical of many that we see every year in school matches and junior congresses.

London Primary Schools Individual Championships, 1958

D. MILLEN *v* T. SHADDICK

(11 *yrs.*) (11 *yrs.*)

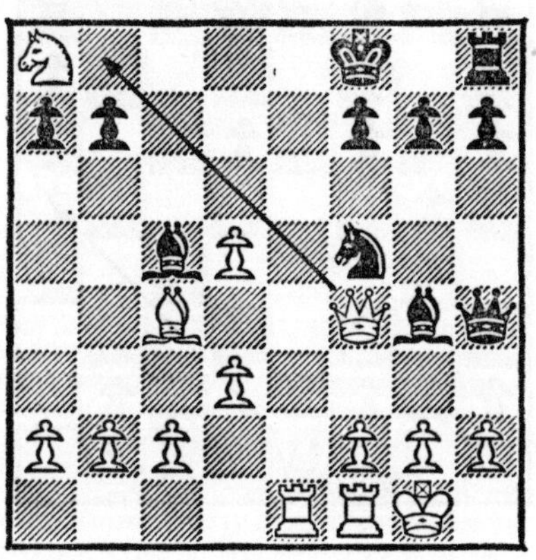

(215) White to play.
A back row mate is imminent.
1. Q—Kt 8 ch Q—Q 1 (fcd.)

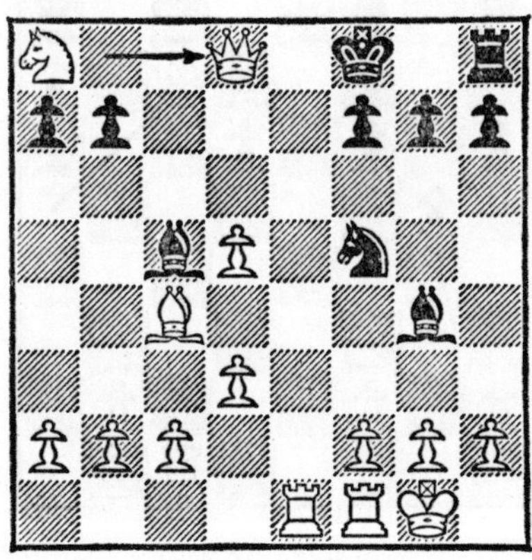

(216) 2. Q × Q mate.

School match, Bexley, Kent, 1957

R. TAYLOR *v* SHEILA FROST

(10 *yrs.*) (13 *yrs.*)

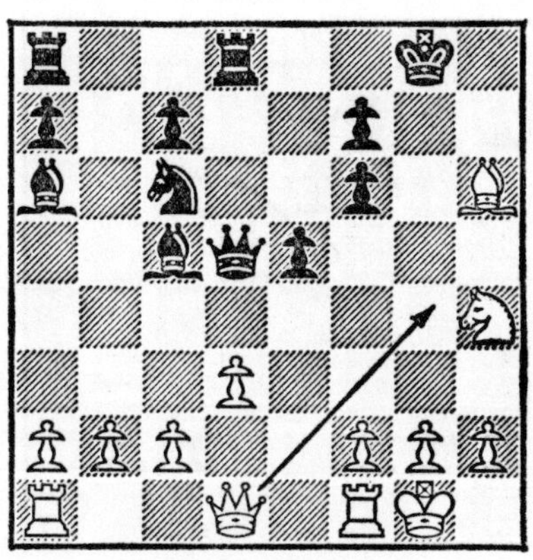

(217) White to play.
1. Q—Kt 4 ch K—R 2

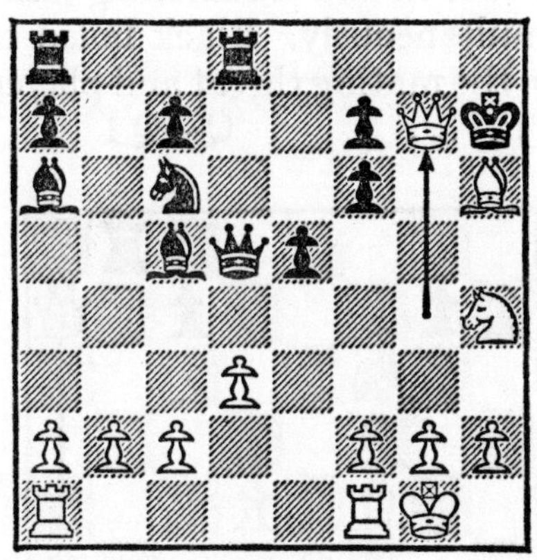

(218) 2. Q—Kt 7 mate.

School match, London, 1958

LYNDA BIGGS *v* J. HOWARD
(10 *yrs.*) (11 *yrs.*)

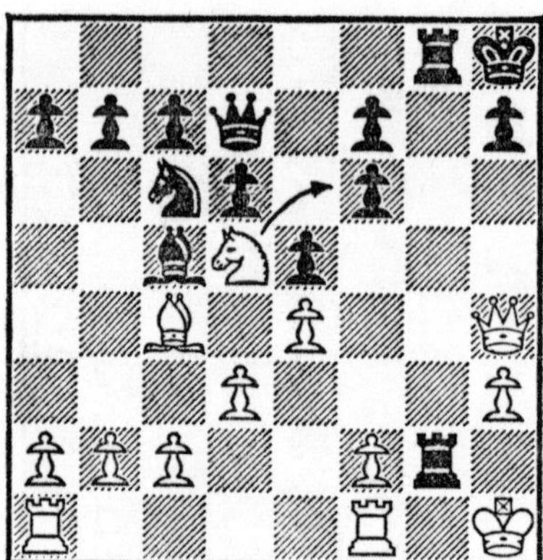

(219) White to play.

1. Kt × K B P forking Queen and Rook and threatening mate simultaneously. Black failed to see the mating threat and played

1. .... Q—Q 1

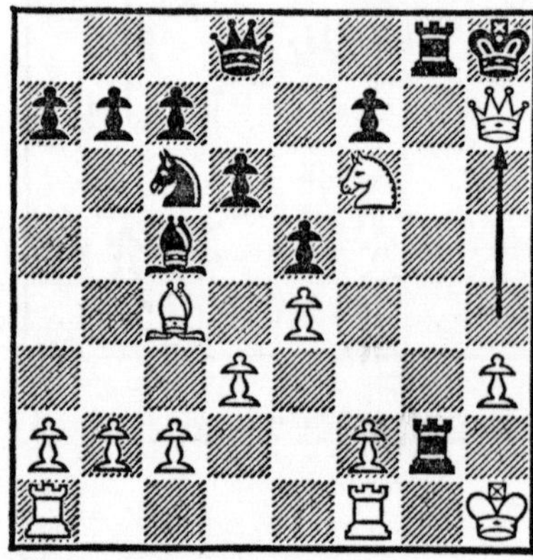

(220) 2. Q × P mate.
At best Black would have lost his Queen.

School match, London, 1958

L. BARNETT *v* P. HOWARD
(11 *yrs.*) (11 *yrs.*)

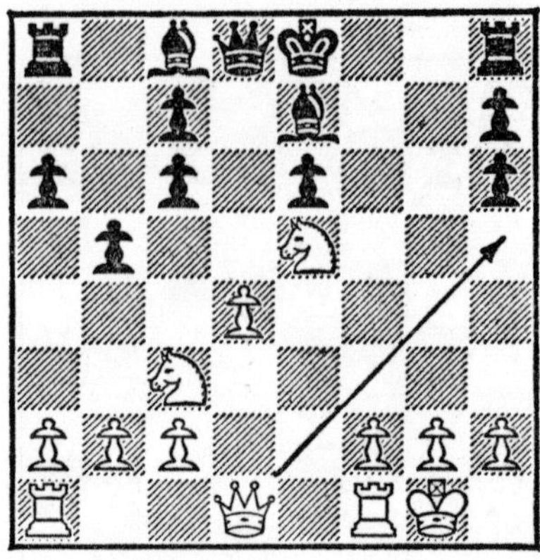

(221) White to play.
Black's King is defenceless.

1. Q—R 5 ch K—B 1 (fcd.)

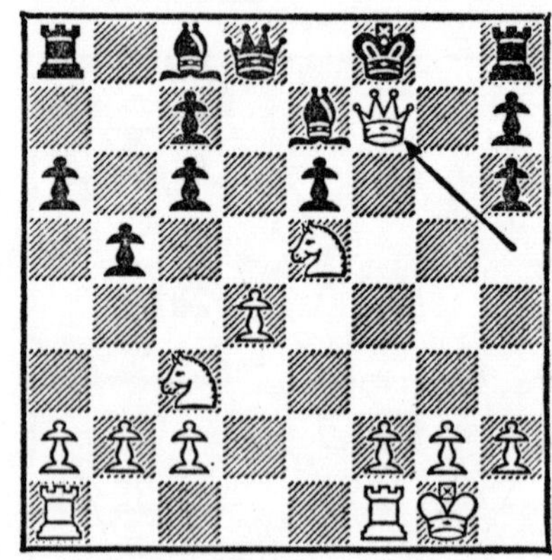

(222) 2. Q—B 7 mate.

Won by G. SHORTEN (10 *yrs.*) *in a match between a team of London Primary Schoolchildren and an adult club.*

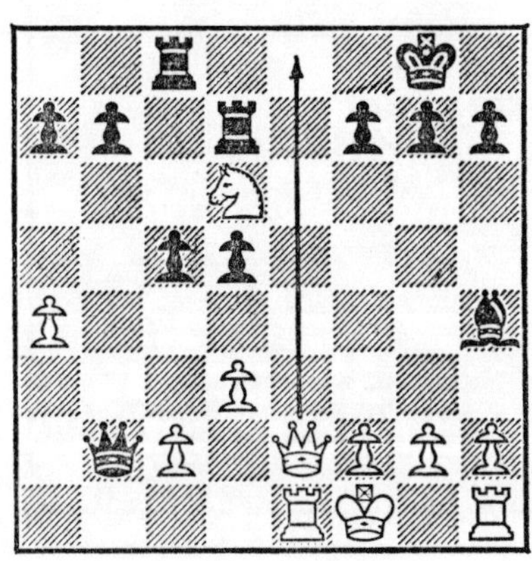

(223) White to play.
Typical back row mate.
1. Q—K 8 ch R × Q

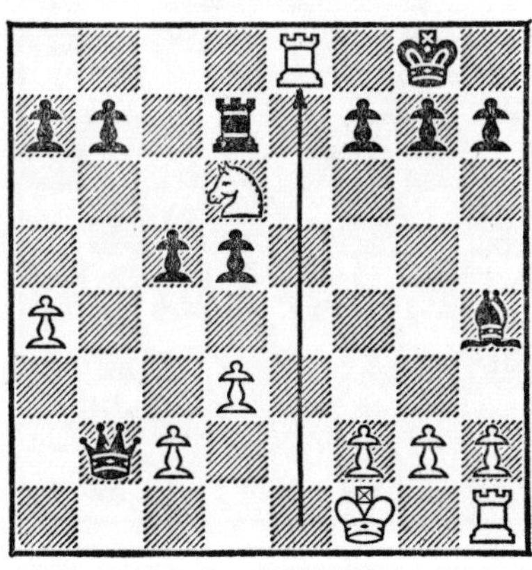

(224) 2. R × R mate.

School club match, London, 1959
B. TOMBLESON *v* J. NEWTON
(10 *yrs.*) (11*yrs.*)

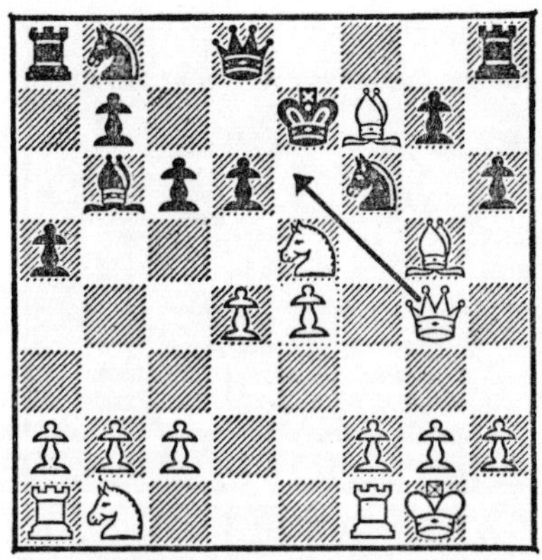

(225) White to play.
1. Q—K 6 ch K—B 1 (fcd.)

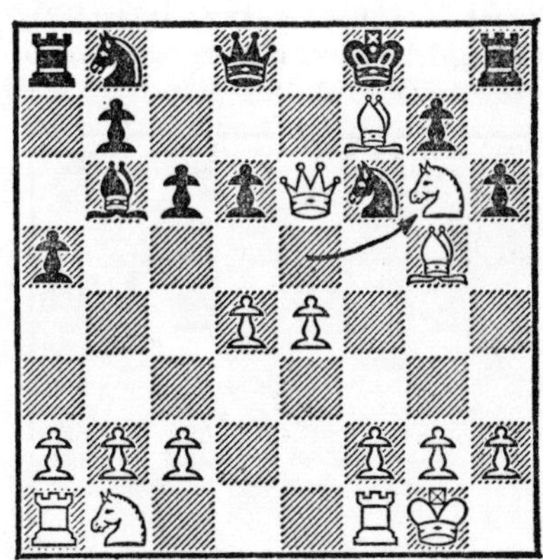

(226) 2. Kt—Kt 6 mate.

Schools match, London, 1959
H. WILLIAMS *v* R. JUNIPER
(11 *yrs.*) (11 *yrs.*)

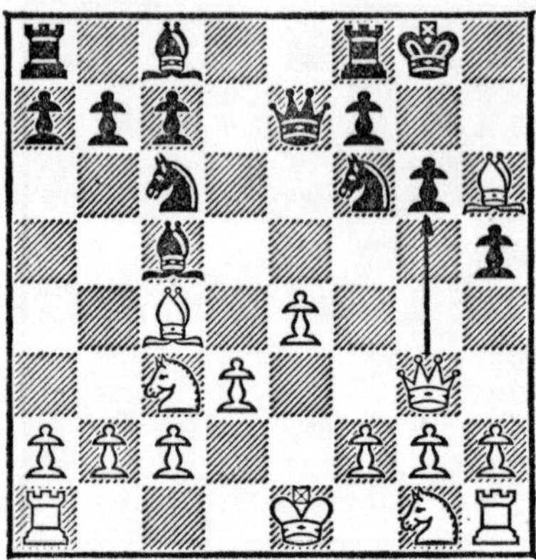

(227) White to play.
A weak pawn structure in front of Black's castled King.

1. Q × P ch! K—R 1 (fcd.)

for Black's K B Pawn is pinned.

(228) 2. Q—Kt 7 mate.

Schools match, London, 1957
MAUREEN SHARP *v* M. GOMAN
(9 *yrs.*) (10 *yrs*)

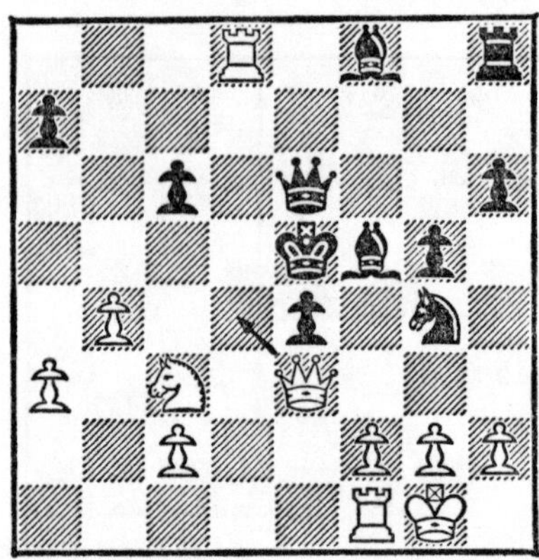

(229) White to play.
Black's King is exposed.

1. Q—Q 4 ch K—B 5 (fcd.)

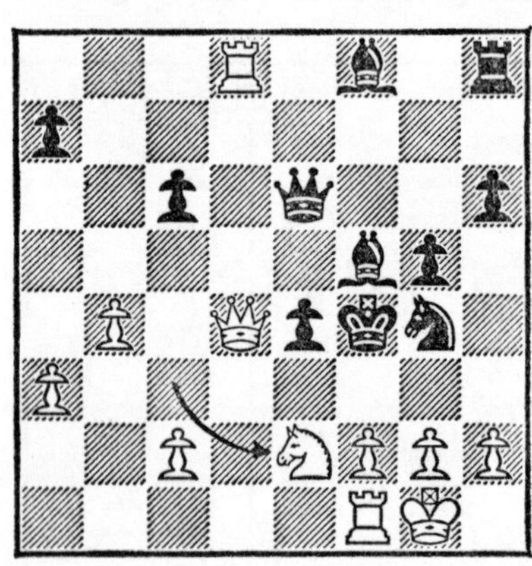

(230) 2. Kt—K 2 mate.

School match, Barnet, 1959
A. HORROCKS *v* P. R. BROOME (13 *yrs.*)

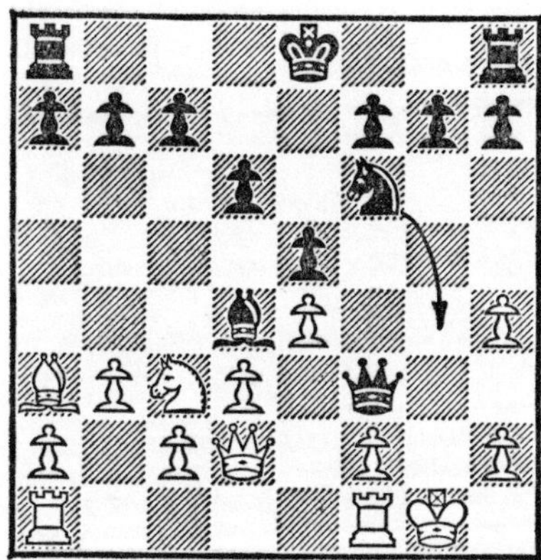

(231) The Pawn barrier in front of the White King has been broken.

1. . . .	Kt—Kt 5
2. Q—K 2	Q—R 6

threatening mate by Q × R P

3. K R—Q 1	Q × P ch
4. K—B 1	

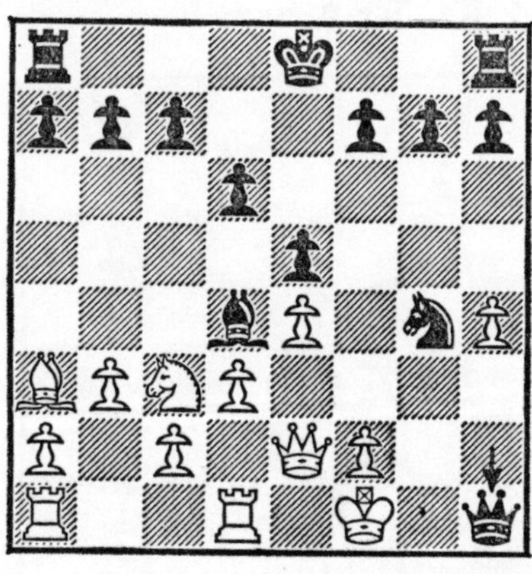

(232) 4. . . . . Q—R 8 mate.

London Boys Championships, London, 1957
P. WANN (15 *yrs.*) *v* M. BROIDO

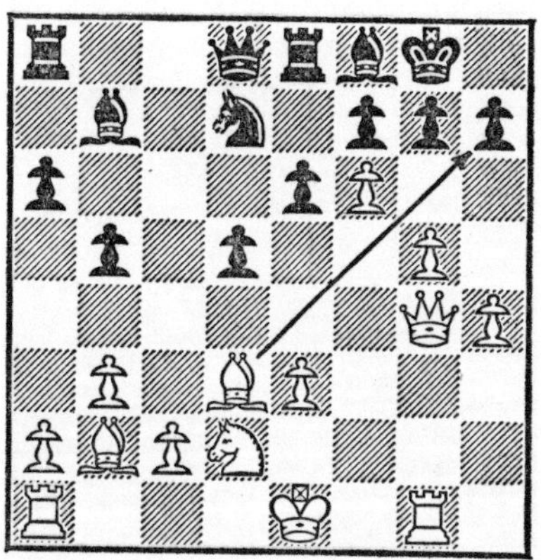

(233) A Pawn onslaught.

1. B × P ch	K × B
2. P—Kt 6 ch	K—Kt 1
3. P × P ch	K × P
4. Q—Kt 6 ch	K—Kt 1
5. P—B 7 ch	K—R 1

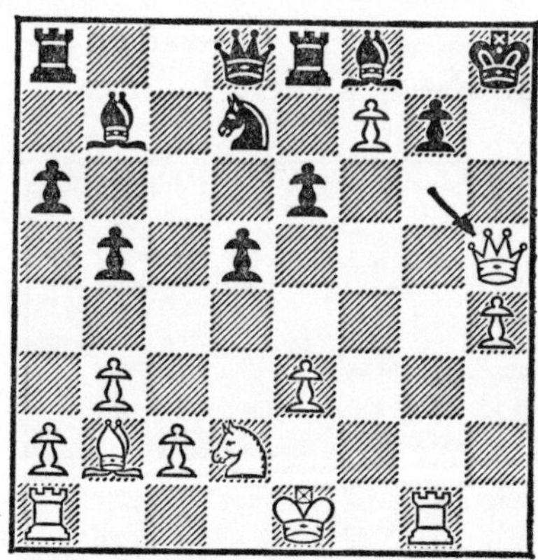

(234) 6. Q—R 5 mate.
6. Q—R 6 also mates for the Black K Kt Pawn is pinned by White's Bishop on Q Kt 2

Played by correspondence in Estonia, 1932

A. KARU *v* P. KERES (16 *yrs.*)

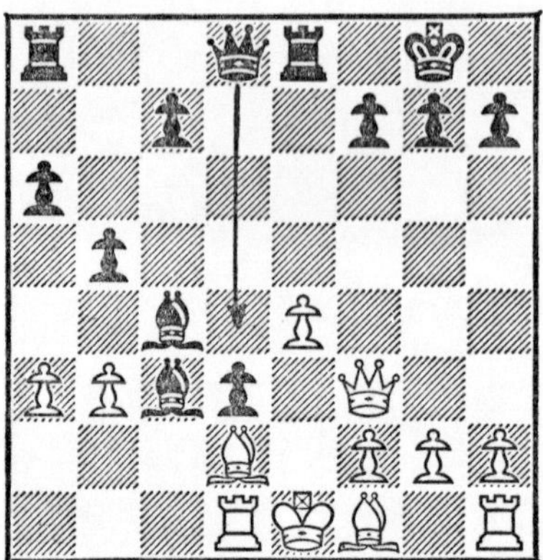

(235) A breakthrough in the centre.

1	Q—Q 5

threatening ....R × P ch etc.

2. B × B	Q × B ch
3. R—Q 2	R × P ch
4. Resigns	

for if 4. Q × R, Q—B 8 ch; 5. R—Q 1 there follows

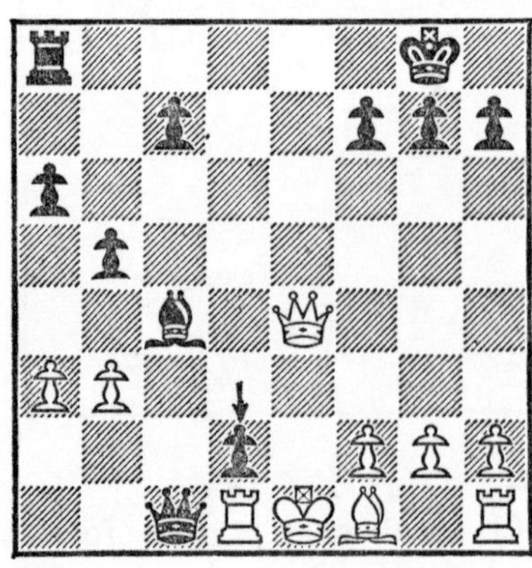

(236) 5. .... P—Q 7 mate.

Played in World Junior Championship, Birmingham, 1951

P. HARRIS *v* M. N. BARKER (17 *yrs.*)

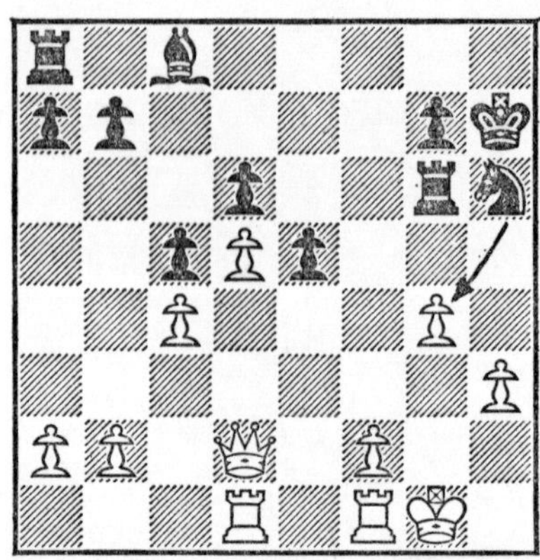

(237) Black has sacrificed his Queen and in return has a crushing attack against an exposed King.

1.	Kt × P
2. P × Kt	B × P
3. K—R 2	R—R 1
4. R—K Kt 1	K—Kt 1 disc ch
5. K—Kt 2	

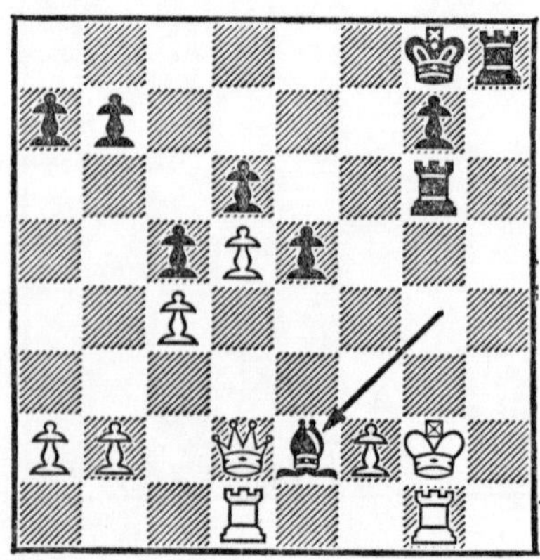

(238) 5. .... B—K 7 disc ch
6. Resigns

Played in London Boys Championships, London, 1957

D. R. PRESTON *v* R. J. COOTES (17 *yrs.*)

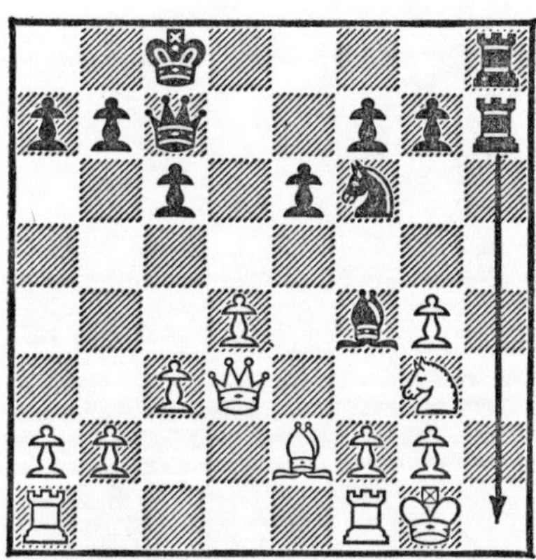

(239) Open file and a smothered King!

1.	R—R 8 ch
2. Kt × R	

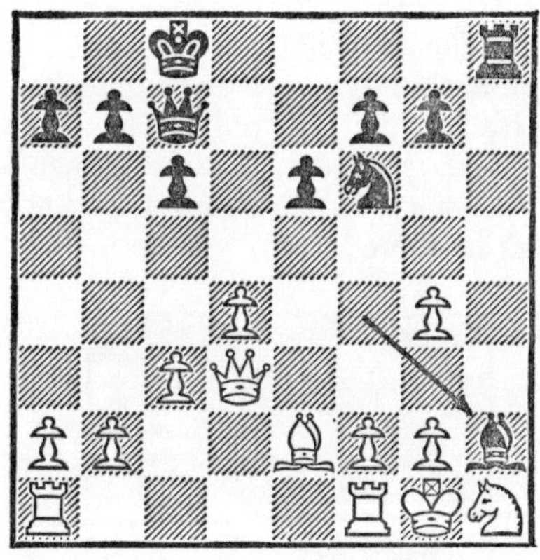

(240) 2. .... B—R 7 mate.

Played in World Junior Championship, Copenhagen, 1953

O. PANNO (18 *yrs.*) *v* J. SHERWIN

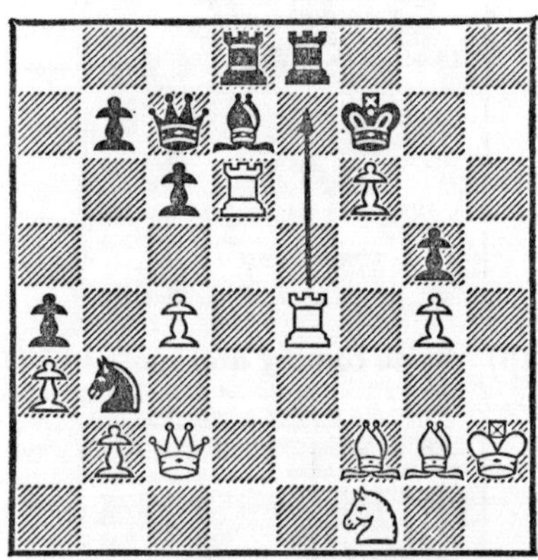

(241) Control of the 7th rank.

1. R—K 7 ch	R × R
2. Q—R 7 ch	Resigns

for if

2.	K—B 1
3. Q × R ch	K—Kt 1

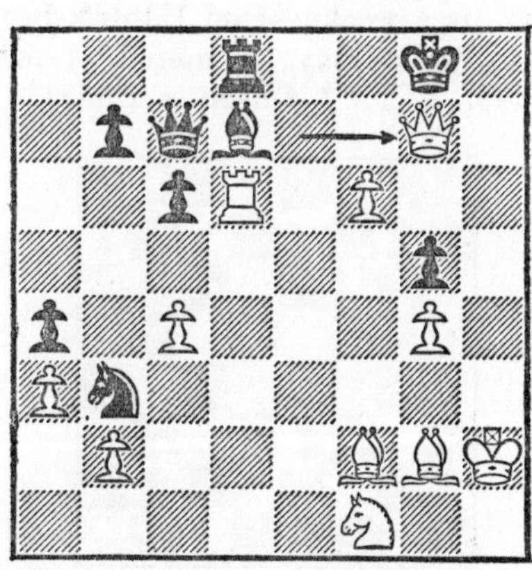

(242) 4. Q—Kt 7 mate.

QUIZ ON "CHECKMATE IN THE MIDDLE GAME"

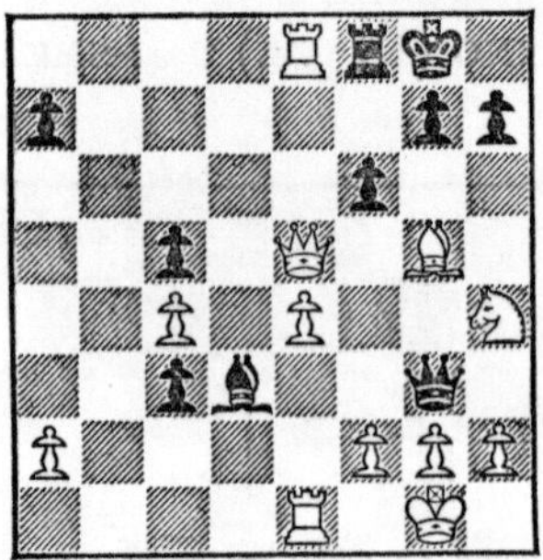

(Q.13) White to play and mate in two.

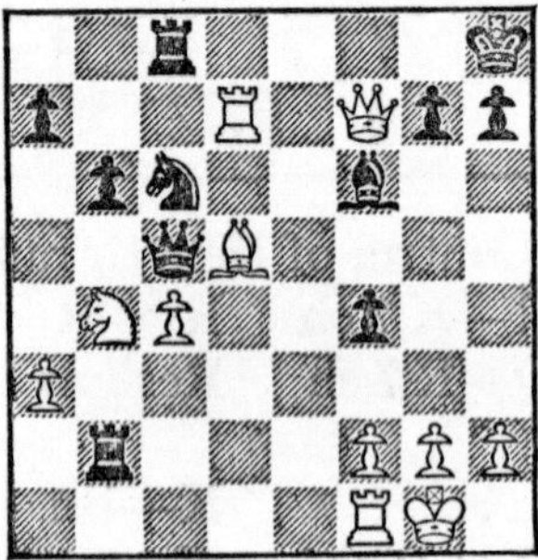

(Q.14) Black to play.
There is a weakness on White's back row. White may be mated in four moves. A clue? Queen sacrifice!

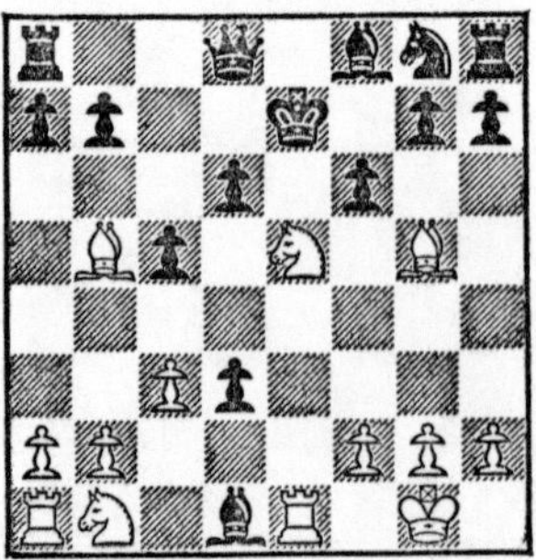

(Q.15) White to play and mate in two.

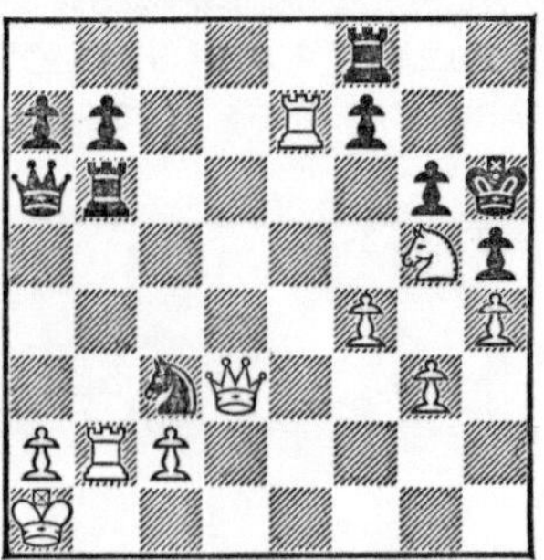

(Q.16) Black to play and mate in two.

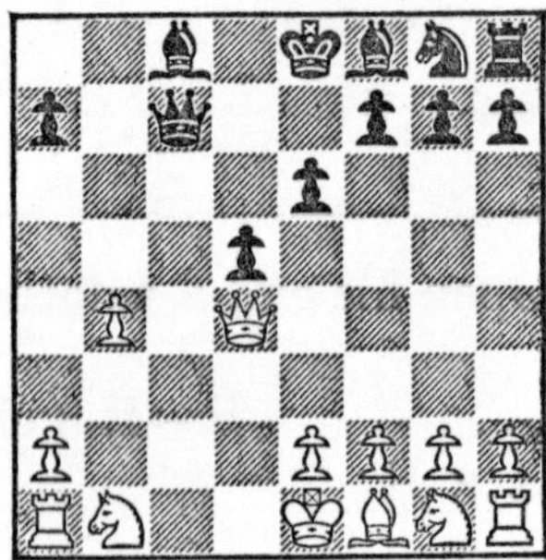

(Q.17) Black to play.
Black is already ahead in development despite the fact that only a few moves have been played. This advantage is quite enough, however, for Black now mates in three!

(Q.18) White to play and mate in three.

Answers to Quiz on " Checkmate in the Middle Game " on pages 193-4.

2. WINNING ADVANTAGES

We are going to look at some games at a stage just before one of the opponents resigned or was mated and discover what kind of winning advantages the eventual victor must have enjoyed.

In this chapter and later in the book we use simple symbol drawings, which are intended to help you to see rapidly the nature of the positions alongside which they appear. In this way control and direction of attack are pin-pointed.

Munich, 1958

FARRE *v* GUDMUNDSSON

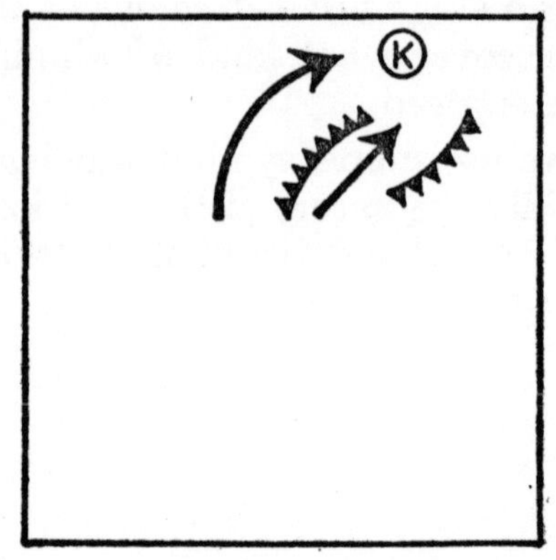

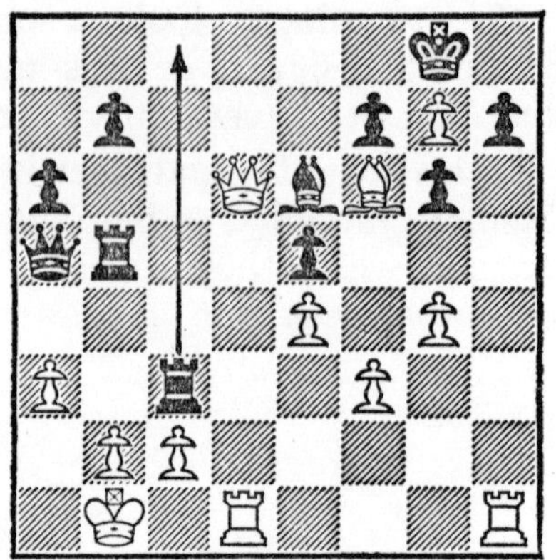

(243) White has advanced the K R Pawn until finally it reaches K Kt 7 by means of a capture and remains a permanent queening threat. Now White has broken through the Queen's file threatening mate by Q—B 8.

1.	R—B 1
2. Q—B 8 ch	R × Q (forced)
3. P × R = Q ch	K × Q

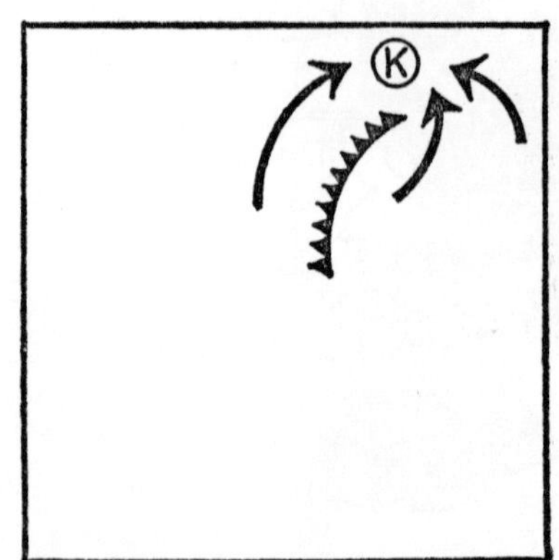

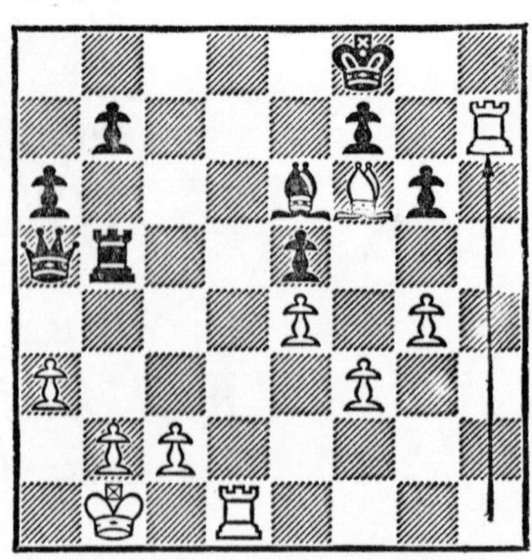

(244) 4. R × P and Black resigns. (R—R 8 mate cannot be prevented.)

Zagreb, 1958

GLIGORIC *v* KERES

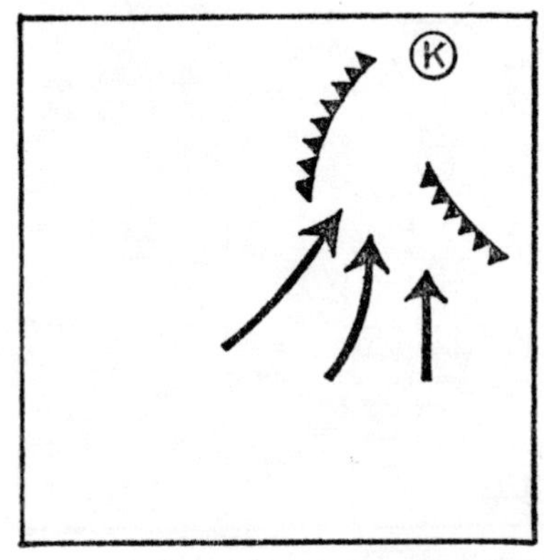

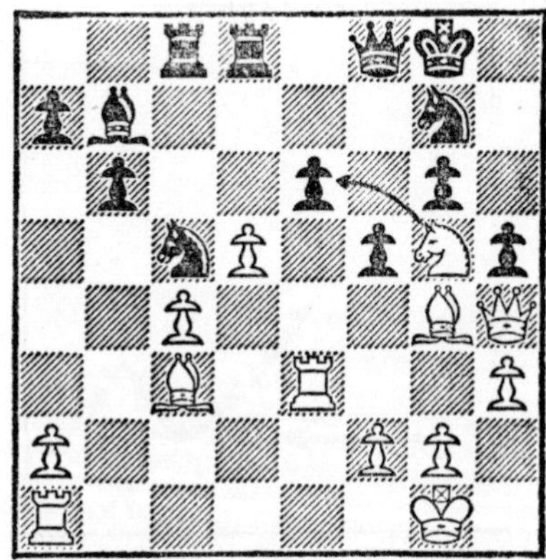

(245) King's side attack against a disorganised defence.

1. Kt × P	Kt (Kt 2) × Kt
2. P × Kt	R—K 1

White threatened P—K 7 forking Rook and Queen

3. B × R P

threatening 4. B × P followed by Q—R 7 or R 8 mate

3.	Q—R 3

If 3. ....P × B, then 4 R—Kt 3 ch and mate follows.

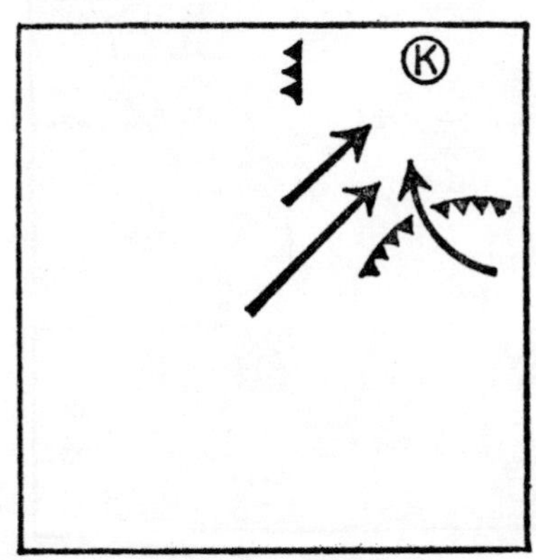

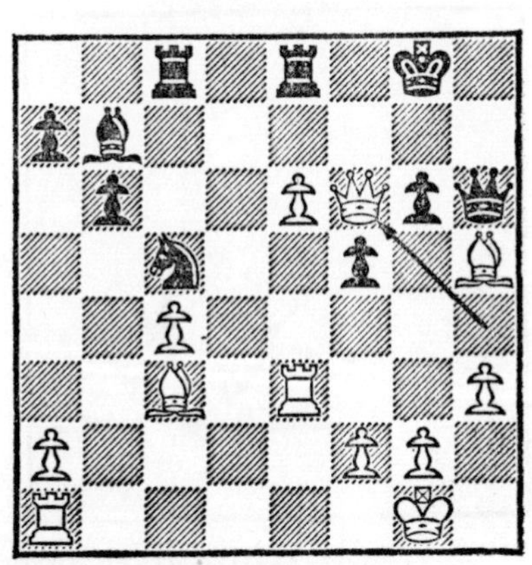

(246) 4. Q—B 6	P—B 5 ?

4. ....R—B 1 would have kept the game going just a little longer—5. Q × Kt P ch, Q × Q; 6. B × Q etc.

5. Q—B 7 mate

NIMZOWITSCH *v* CAPABLANCA

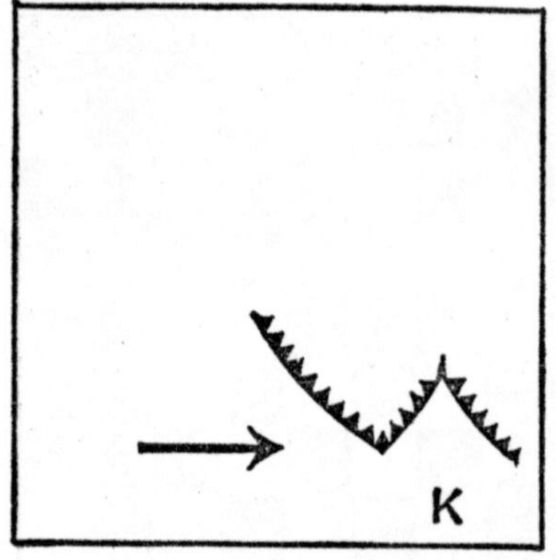

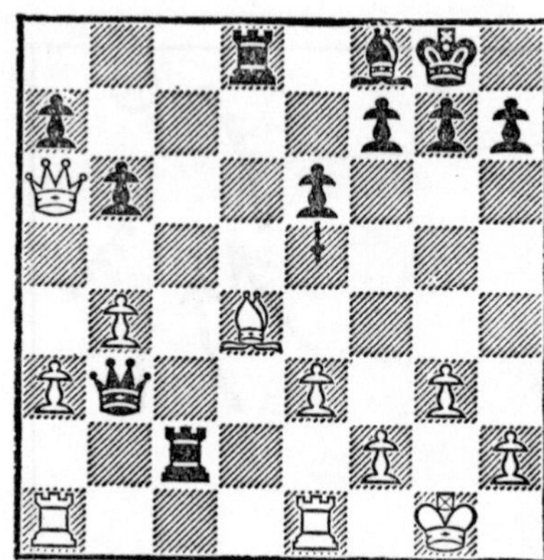

(247) Black has already established one Rook on the 7th rank and plays 1. .... P—K 4 attacking the Bishop in order to penetrate with the other Rook.

2. B × K P	R (Q 1)—Q 7
3. Q—Kt 7	R × P
4. P—Kt 4	

allowing the Bishop to protect the Pawn on K R 2

4.	Q—K 3
5. B—Kt 3	R × P !

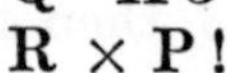

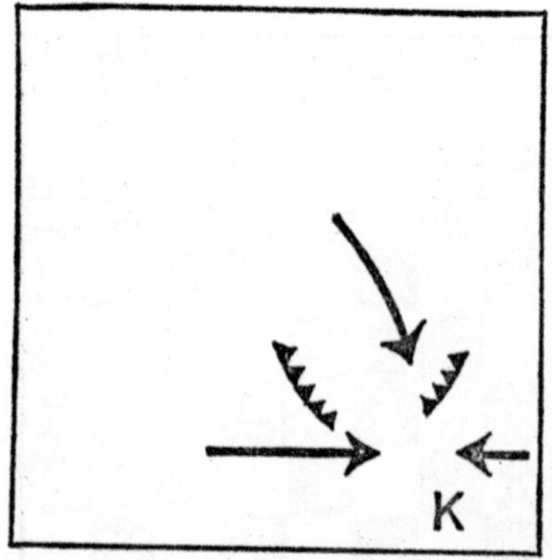

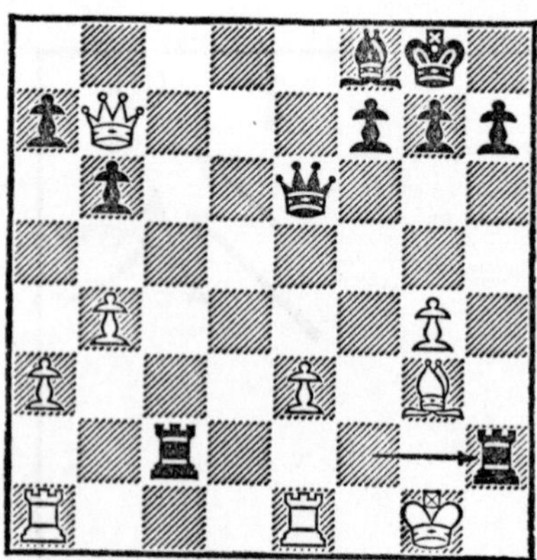

(248) White dare not play 6. B × R because of the threat of mate. 6. .... Q × Kt P ch; 7. K—R 1, Q—R 6; and mate cannot be avoided. In the end White had to give up Queen and Pawn for the two Black Rooks and lost the Pawn battle several moves later.

Moscow, 1935

CAPABLANCA *v* LEVENFISH

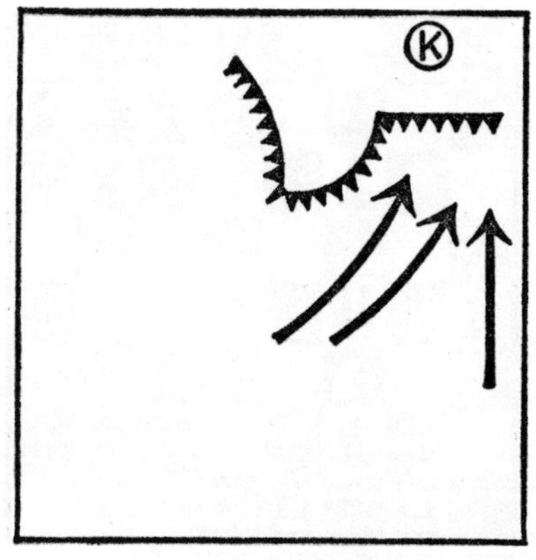

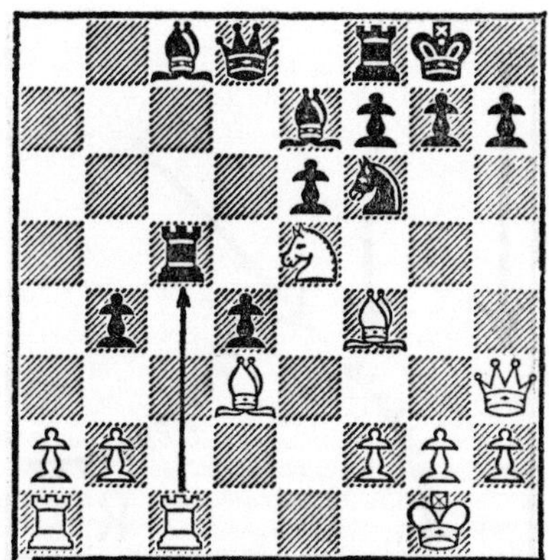

(249) White has engineered a strong King's side attack in which Queen, two Bishops and Knight co-operate.

1. R × R	B × R
2. B—K Kt 5	

threatening B × P ch

2.	P—R 3
3. Kt—Kt 4	B—K 2
4. B × Kt	P × B

If 4. ....B × B; 5. Kt × P ch, P × Kt; 6. Q × R P, R—K 1; 7. B—R 7 ch and mate follows.

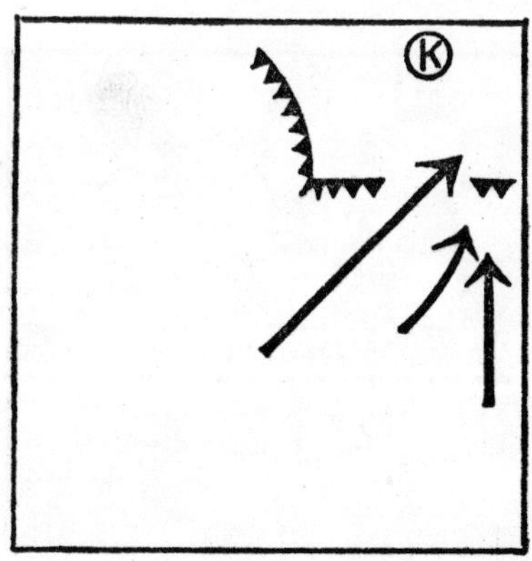

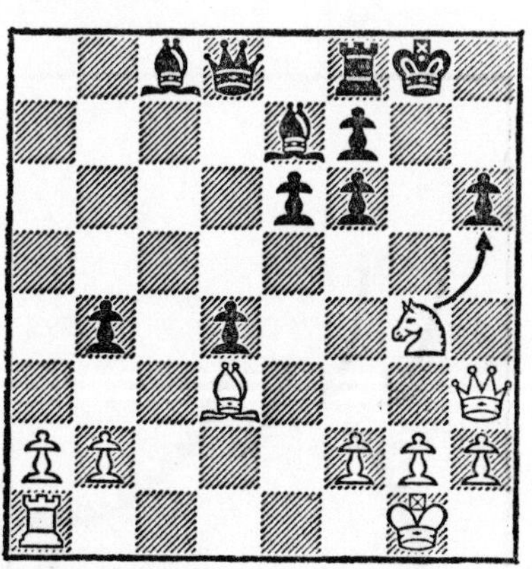

(250) The breakthrough! White now played

5. Kt × R P ch	K—Kt 2
6. Q—Kt 4 ch	K—R 1

7. Q—R 5 and Black resigned two moves later.

St. Petersburg (now Leningrad), 1914

NIMZOWITSCH *v* CAPABLANCA

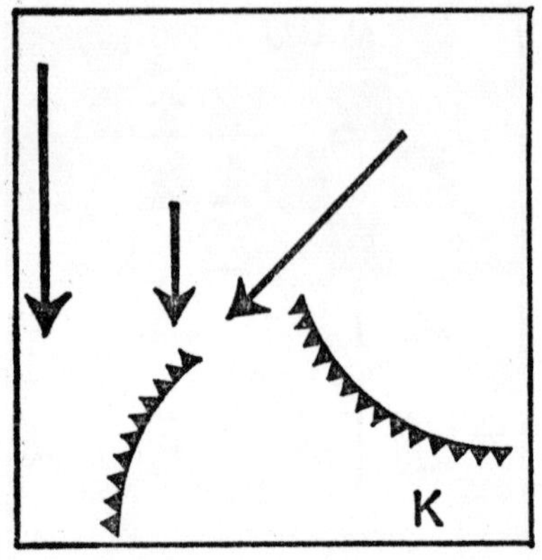

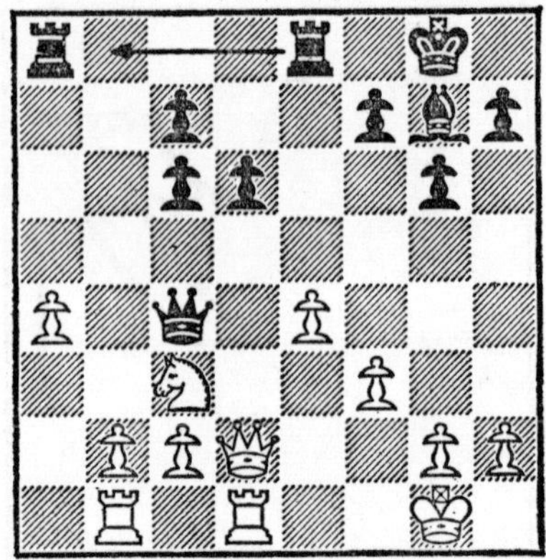

(251) Black's Queen is strongly placed in the centre and is assisted by the two Rooks exerting pressure on White's Pawns. Black's Bishop controls a long diagonal through the centre, while White's Knight can only move at the price of giving up a Pawn and letting a Black Rook through on an open file. Black played

1.	K R—Kt 1
2. Q—K 3	R—Kt 5

threatening to pin Queen against King by 3. ....B—Q 5

3. Q—Kt 5	B—Q 5 ch
4. K—R 1	R (R 1)—Kt 1

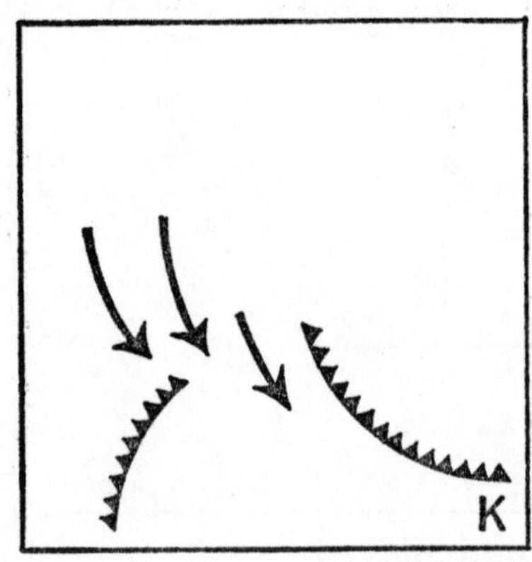

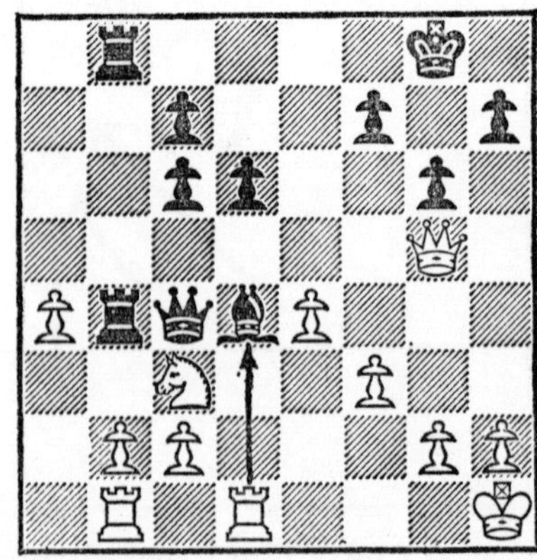

(252) Black now threatens to win the Knight by....B × Kt. White cannot reply 5. P × B because of 5. ....R × R, etc., so White is forced to play 5. R × B, Q × R. With extra material Black wins.

Vienna, 1898

TARRASCH *v* SHOWALTER

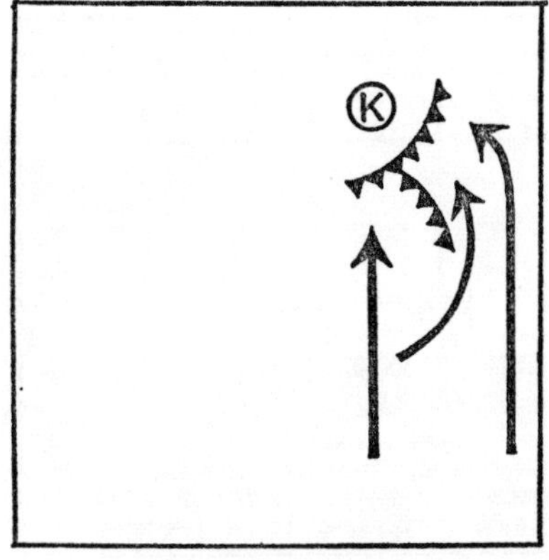

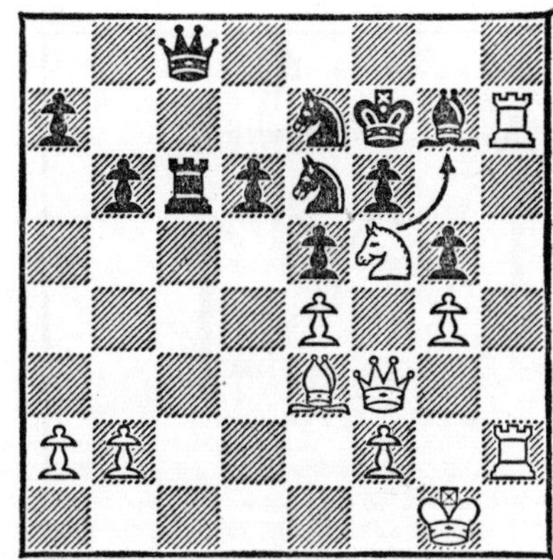

(253) Black's control of the Q B file serves him little advantage as White has already broken through with doubled Rooks on the K R file and aided by Queen, Bishop and Knight plays a decisive series of moves.

1. Kt × B	Kt × Kt
2. B × K Kt P	Q—K 3
	to protect the Bishop's Pawn

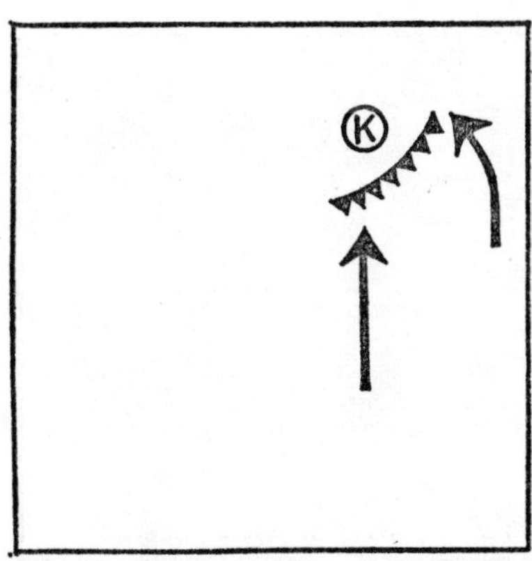

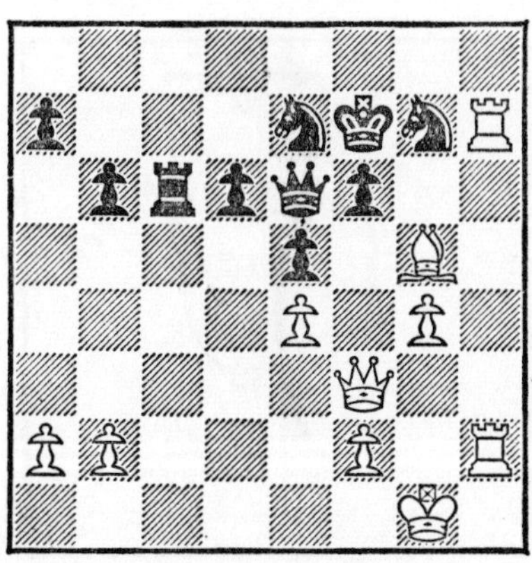

(254) In this position Black resigned without waiting for White to reply as there is no good defence against White's 3. B—R 6 ! The Black Knight at Kt 2 is pinned and would be doubly attacked—it cannot be saved.

MILNER-BARRY *v* NORMAN

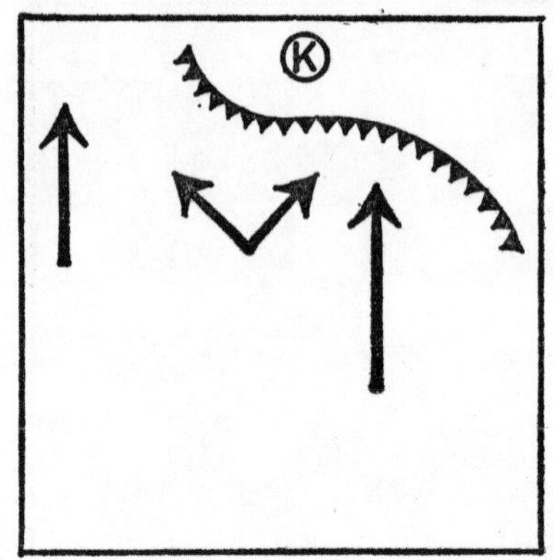

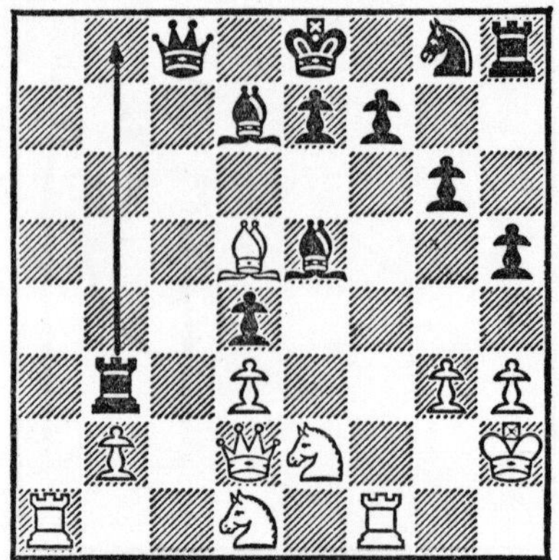

(255) White controls two open files and, with the co-operation of the Bishop at Q 5, attacks the squares Q R 8 and K B 7 simultaneously. Black has yet to bring his Knight and Rook into play.

1.	....	R—Kt 1	5.	Kt × P	B × B
2.	B × P ch	K—Q 1	6.	R × B	R—Kt 3
3.	R—B 1	Q—R 3	7.	R—KB8 ch	K—Q 2
4.	B—B 4	B—Kt 4			

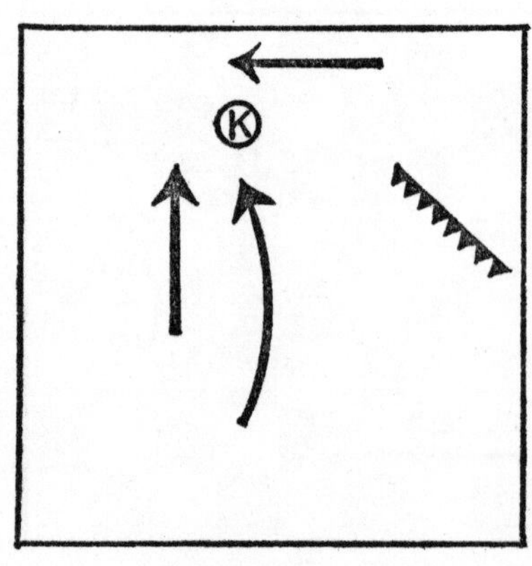

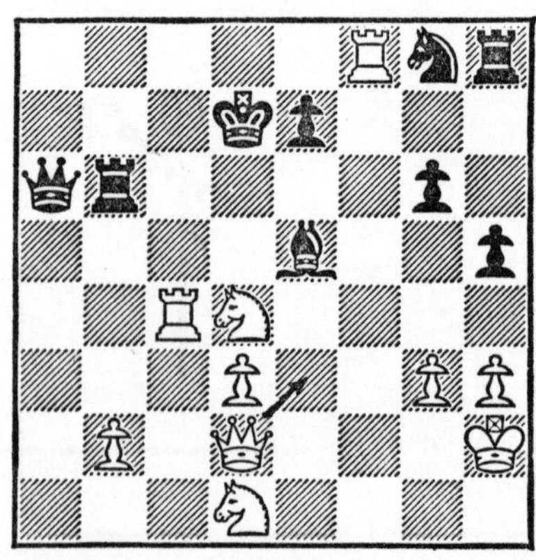

(256) White has now penetrated Black's defences.

8. Q—K 3 B—Kt 2 9. R (B 8)—B 8 Resigns

In the closing stages of this game you will notice how White's Rooks play a major part controlling open files and penetrating to the back ranks of Black's position.

Budapest, 1921

KOSTICH *v* E. STEINER

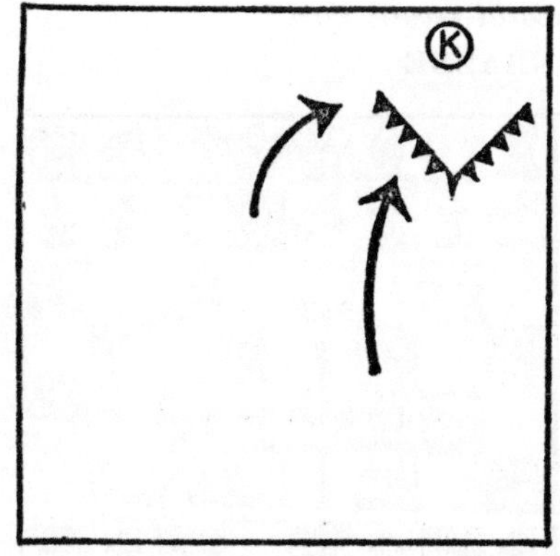

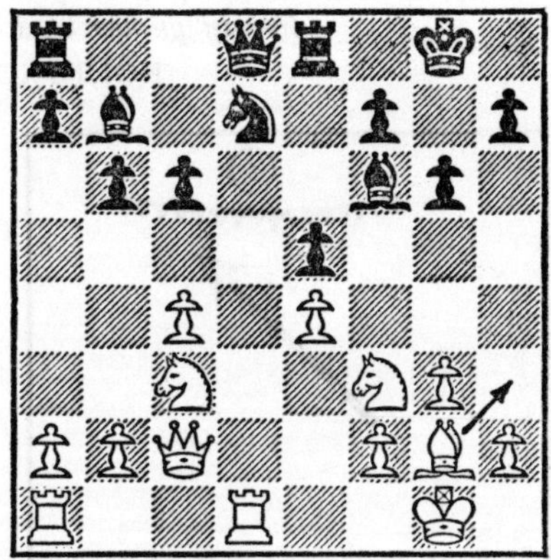

(257) White attacks strongly down the Queen's file and threatens B—R 3 attacking the pinned Black Knight on Q 2.

1. B—R 3	R—K 2
2. R—Q 6	Q—B 2
3. Q R—Q 1	R—Q 1
4. Q—Q 2	

Still more pressure

4.	B—B 1

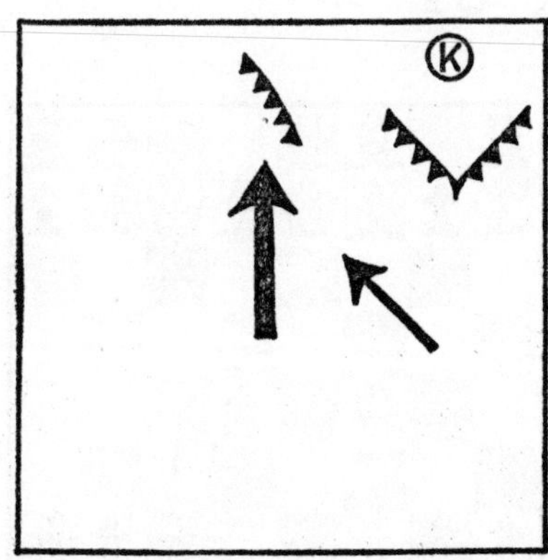

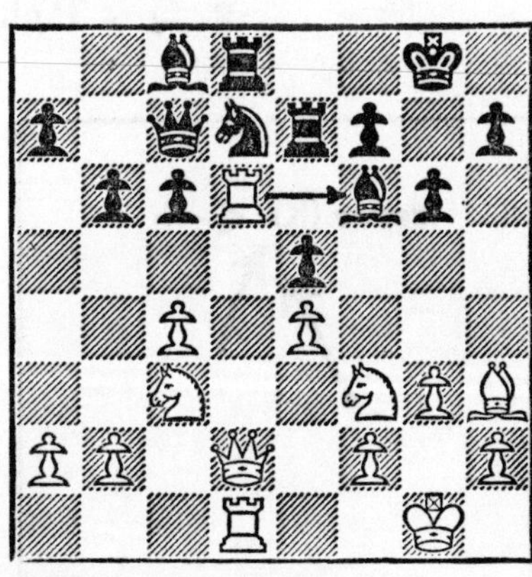

(258) White has increased the pressure down the Queen's file by doubling up the Rooks and Queen.

5. R × B and Black resigns

If 5. ....Kt × R; 6. Q × R ch, etc.

Antwerp, 1931

One of the games played by Koltanowski in the Antwerp Blindfold Exhibition, 1931, *where he won twenty games and drew ten—a world record then!*

KOLTANOWSKI *v* DENHAENE

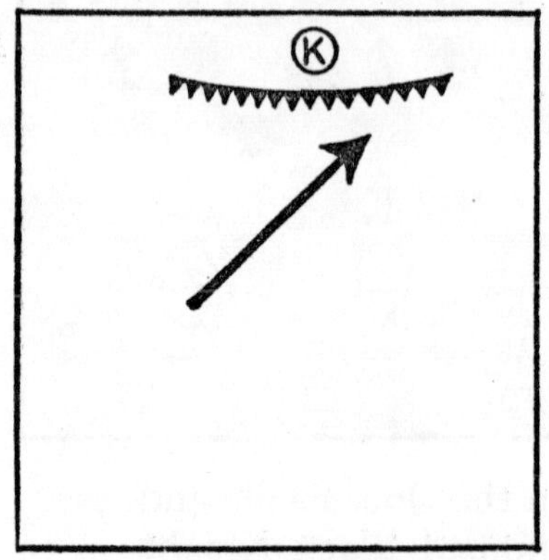

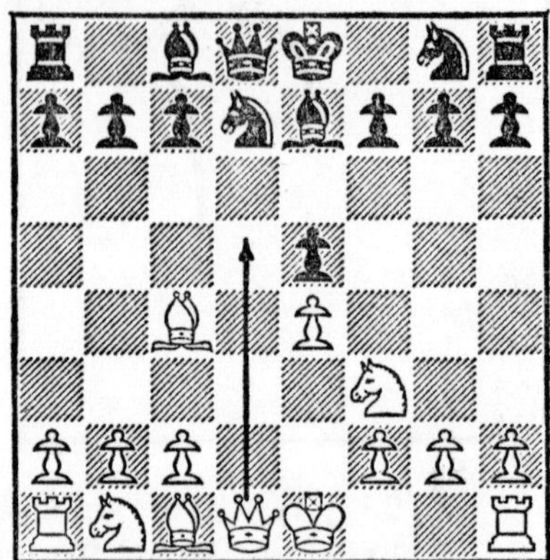

(259) Black has not developed his pieces well and White enjoys much space to manœuvre.

1. Q—Q 5

Central control and threatening mate by Q × B P. 1. . . . . Kt—R 3 will not do because of 2. B × Kt

1.	Q Kt—B 3
2. Q × P ch	K—Q 2

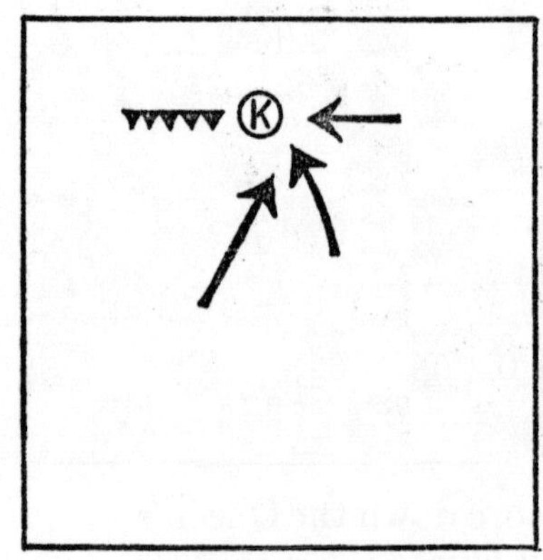

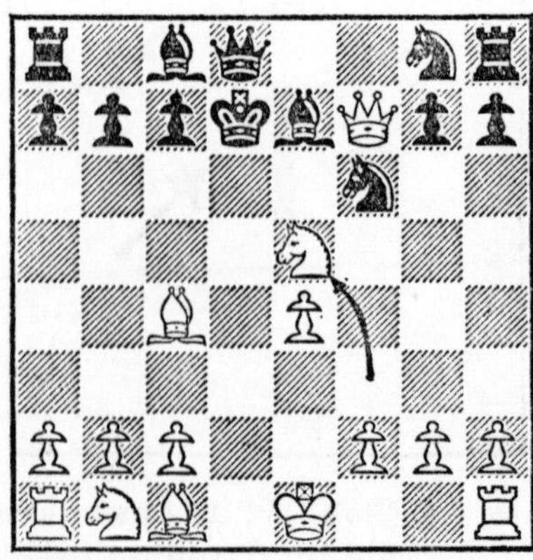

(260) 3. Kt × P ch and Black resigns. No hope now—the Black King is hopelessly exposed.

You have seen examples where players have been able to move pieces into positions where they enjoy more space than their opponents, are controlling vital squares, or have their forces grouped for an attack which their opponents are badly positioned to defend.

WINNING ADVANTAGES

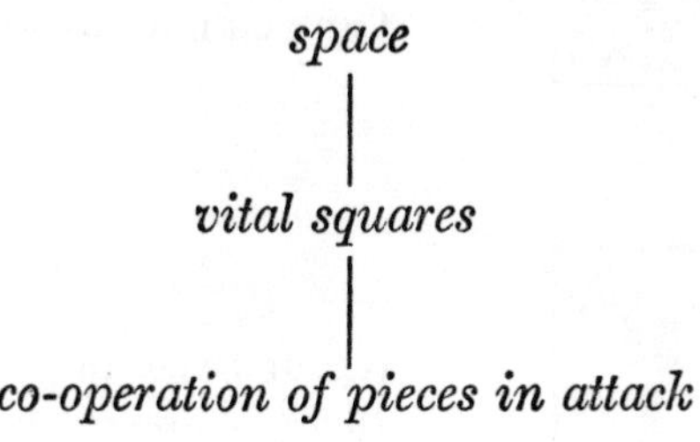

QUIZ ON "WINNING ADVANTAGES"

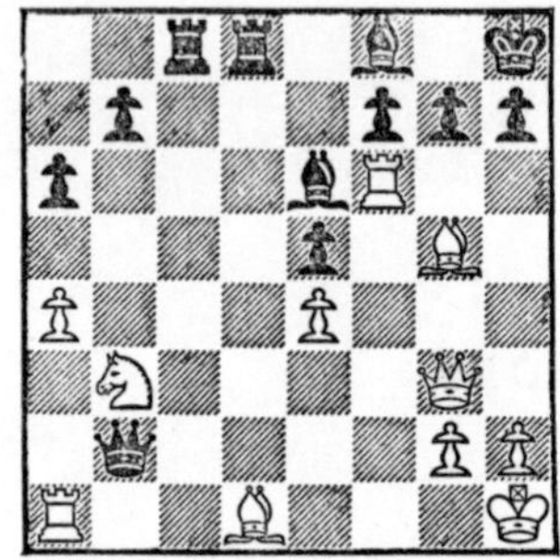

(Q.19) Black to play.
Black's two Rooks and Queen control important and open lines. This advantage is sufficient to win the game, for after Black made his next move, White resigned!
The game was won by Euwe, world champion 1935-1937.
Can you find his winning move?

(Q.20) Black to play.
Black is faced with the threat of Q × P ch. However, Black can prevent White from finding time to do this, by a series of checks ending in mate. What are the moves?

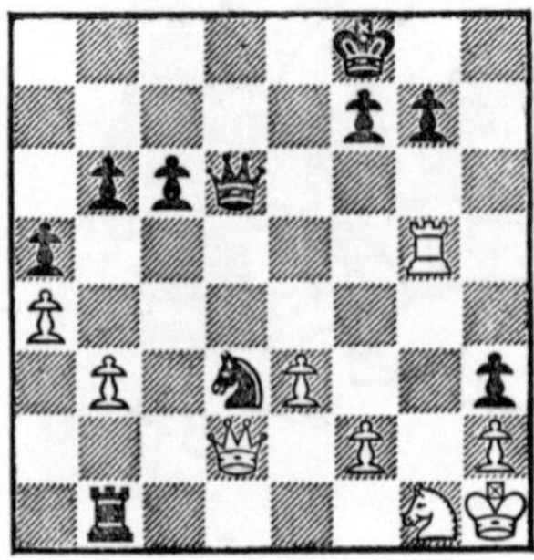

(Q.21) Black to play.
Were the White Queen not protecting the Bishop's Pawn, Black could play Kt × P mate! Suggest a move by which Black can take advantage of the situation.

Answers to Quiz on " Winning Advantages " on page 194.

3. ROOM TO MOVE

A successful army must be able to move and change direction rapidly. For these manœuvres it needs routes of various kinds to transport the troops.

The roads and railways of the chessboard are files, ranks and diagonals. A Knight can leap over obstructions from one point to another with little difficulty, but the Queen, Rooks and Bishops need open lines. Routes to them mean open lines—clear files, ranks and diagonals.

If you want your chess army to be able to manœuvre with rapidity, then you must give your pieces room. Fast moving Rooks first need clear files, leading into ranks in the heart of enemy territory. If you want your Bishops to be mobile, seize long clear diagonals.

There follow some typical examples of positions where one player enjoys greater mobility—more space in which to move and so more choice of moves. Such an advantage should eventually lead to victory.

The first two examples—diagrams 261-262 give you some idea of the kinds of situation we are going to discuss.

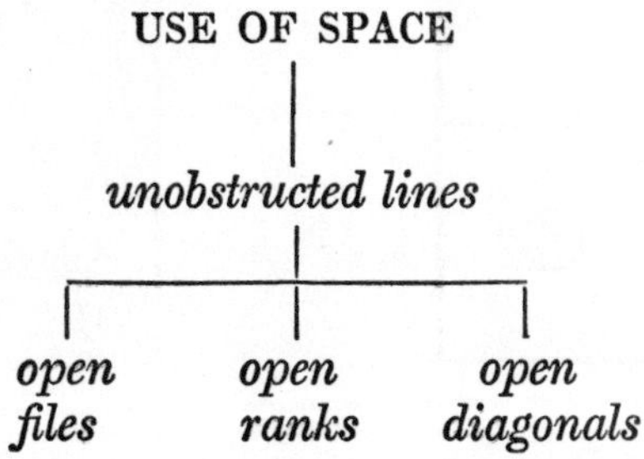

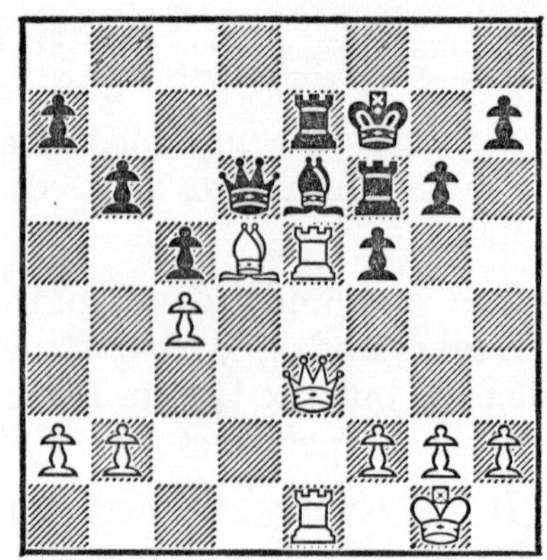

(261) White to play.

Black's pieces are held down by the threatened break-through in the centre. While Black's Rooks are passive and defensive, White's Rooks are in an aggressive position. The Black Queen is restricted but White's Queen has the choice of operating on either side, or in the centre. For example White can play **Q—R 6** with possibilities of a King's side attack.

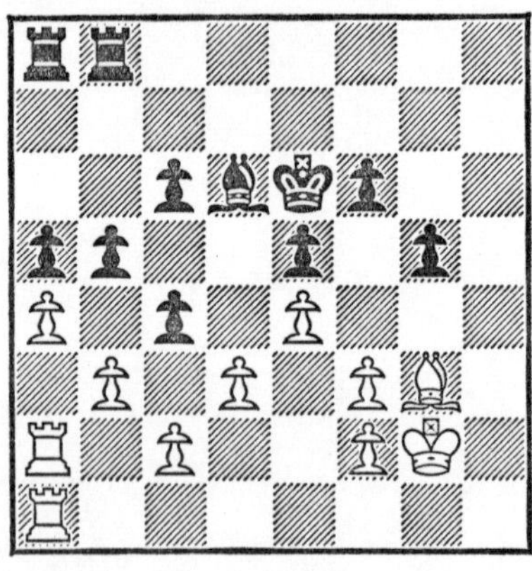

(262) Black to play.

White's Bishop is shut out of the game and so White is playing just as if he were a piece down. But Black's Bishop has much more freedom and consequently he should win with his Queen's side Pawn attack.

You will appreciate the points discussed in the previous two examples if you set them up on a board and try them out against your friends.

Now we are going to examine some actual games played where room to move was a vital factor in deciding the result.

Bled, 1931

ASZTALOS *v* STOLTZ

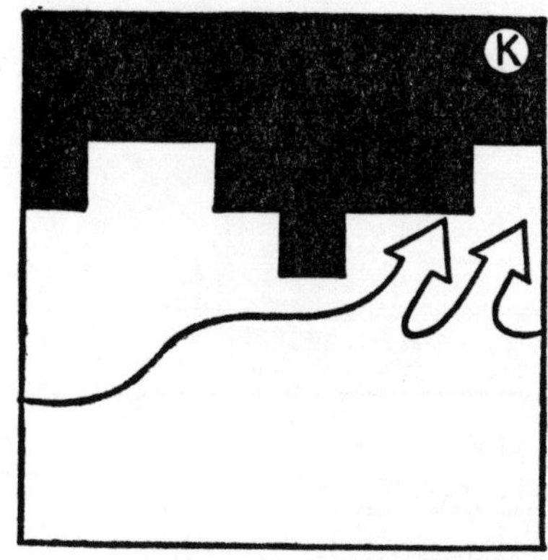

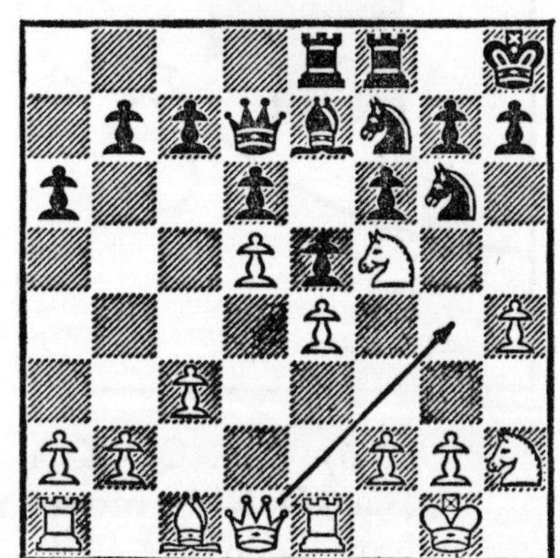

(263) It can clearly be seen that Black's position is very cramped. White plays

1. Q—Kt 4

threatening P—R 5 and Black's Knight would be lost as he cannot move it away because of the Q × P mate which would follow.

1. .... R—K Kt 1

freeing the Knight by guarding the Kt P.

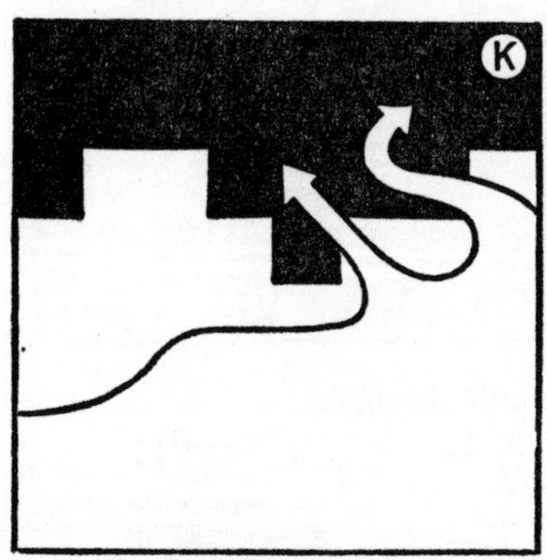

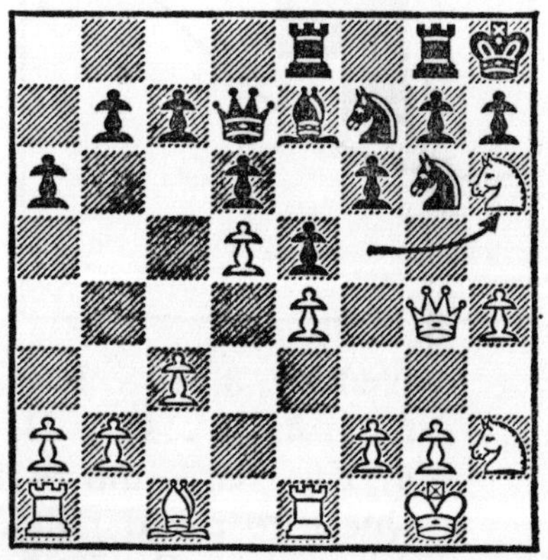

(264) 2. Kt—R 6 winning Queen.

If Black replies 2. ....Q × Q then 3. Kt × Kt mate!

Hamburg, 1930

YATES *v* MARIN

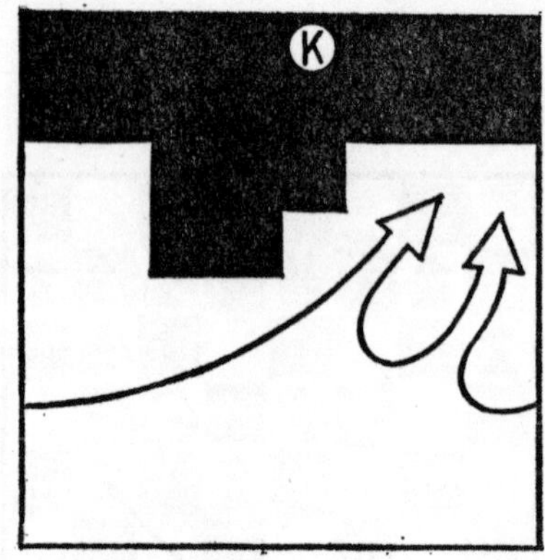

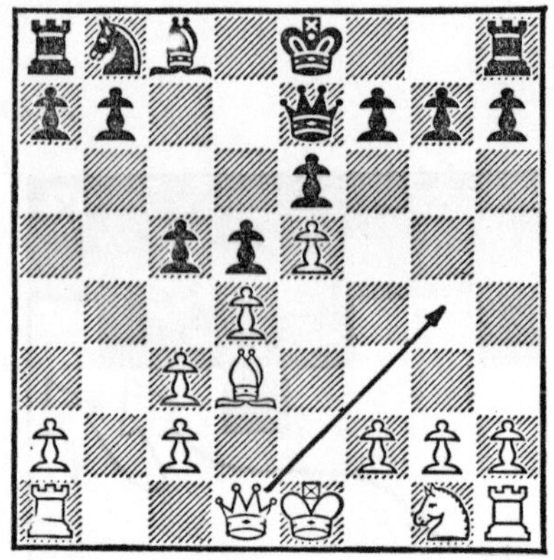

(265) 1. Q—Kt 4 O—O

Black's King moves right into trouble. Better would have been 1. ....P—K B 4 in an attempt to free his position. As it is, all the Queen side pieces remain undeveloped and no pieces are placed to resist the coming King side onslaught.

2. Kt—B 3 P—B 5

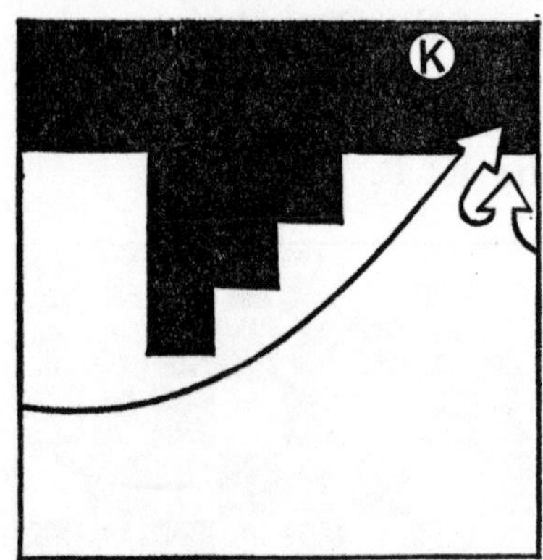

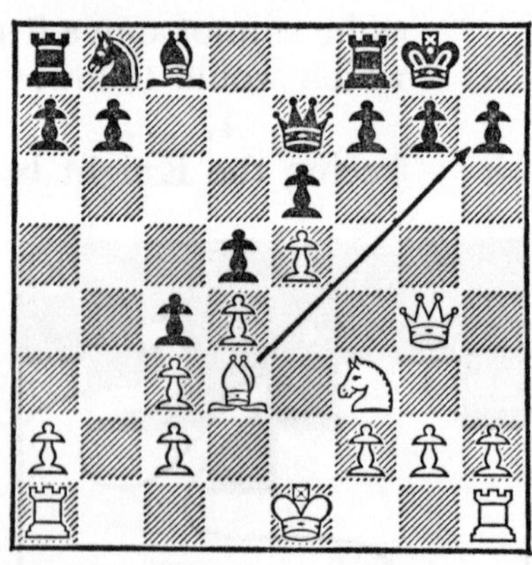

(266) 3. B × P ch Black resigns

for if 3. ....K × B; 4. Q—R5 ch, K—Kt 1 (forced); 5. Kt—Kt 5 and Black would have to give up the Queen to avoid mate. Or 3. ....K—R 1; 4. Q—R 5 followed by B—Kt 6 disc ch and Q—R 7 mate.

Moscow, 1899

THREE AMATEURS *v* EMMANUEL LASKER

(*Emmanuel Lasker was World Champion for 26 years*)

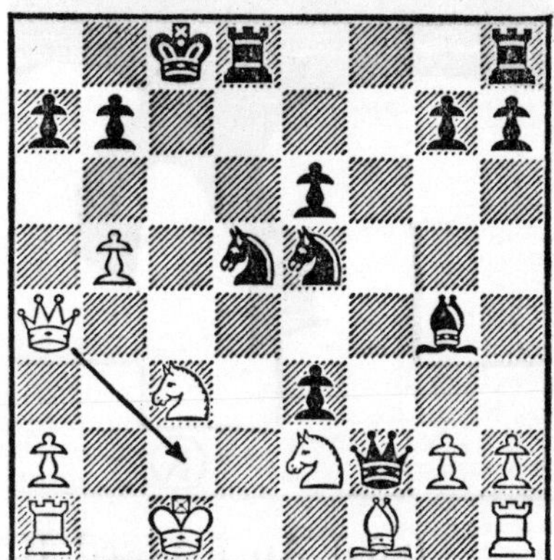

(267) Black enjoys two centrally placed Knights, Rook on the open file, active Bishop and an advanced Pawn on the 6th rank with Queen in attendance. White's King position is exposed and both White's Rooks and Bishop have yet to be brought into play.

1. Q—B 2	Kt—Kt 5
2. Kt—Q 1 disc ch	Kt × Q
3. Kt × Q	

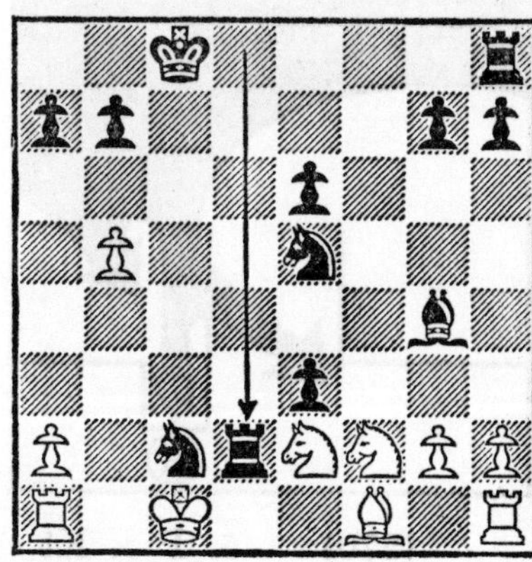

(268)

3.	R—Q 7
4. Resigns	

White's position is hopeless. Both White's Knights and Queen's Rook are attacked, and material must be lost.

Whitby, 1958

GOSLING *v* MURRAY

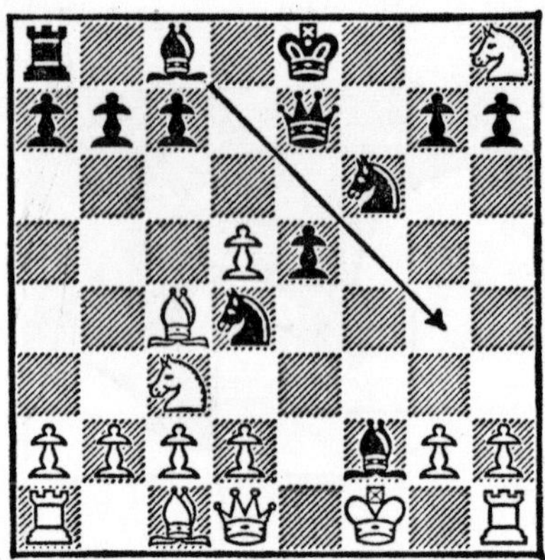

(269) An exposed King feels the draught as Black's extremely mobile attack bears down on him.

1.	B—Kt 5

attacking Queen and bringing yet another piece into the attack.

2. B—K 2	Kt × B
3. Kt × Kt	Kt—K 5

making way for the Queen at B 3

4. P—Q 3	Q—B 3

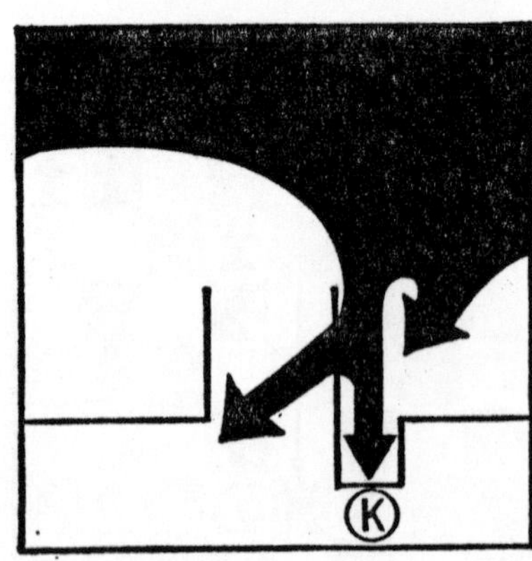

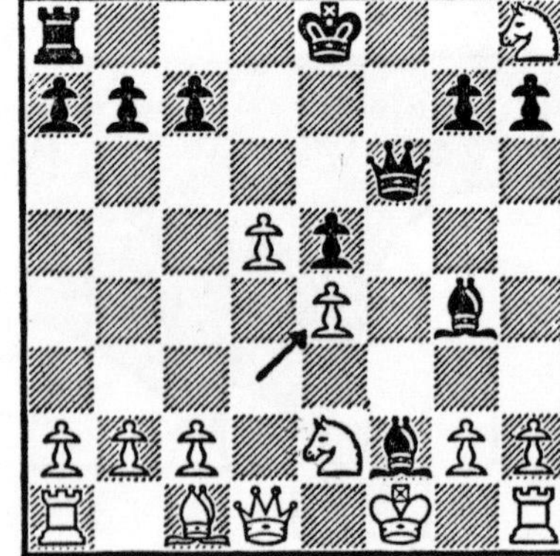

(270)	5. P × Kt	B—K 6 disc ch
	6. Resigns	

for if 6 K—K 1, Q—B 7 mate or 6 Kt—B 4, Q × Kt ch; and mate can only be delayed by giving up the White Queen with 7. Q—B 3.

Ostend, 1907

VAN VLIET *v* ZNOSKO-BOROVSKY

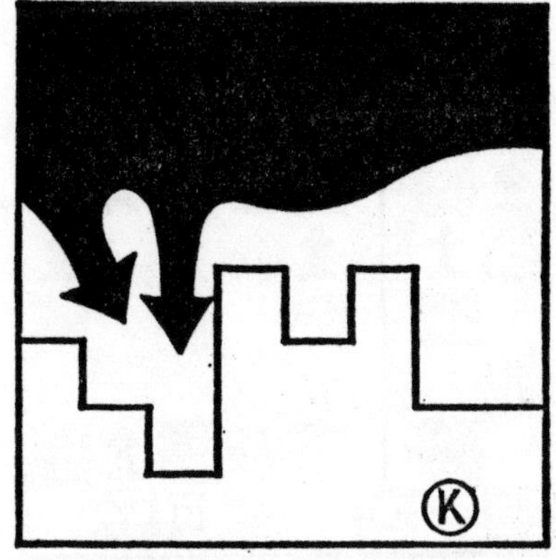

(271)

	White	Black
1.	....	Kt—B 7
2.	B × Kt	Q × B
3.	Q × Q	R × Q
4.	P—K R 3	B—Q 3
5.	Kt—Kt 1	Kt—K 5
6.	K Kt—Q 2	B—Q 6

Black's forces move up to the attack

	White	Black
7.	Kt × Kt	B × Kt

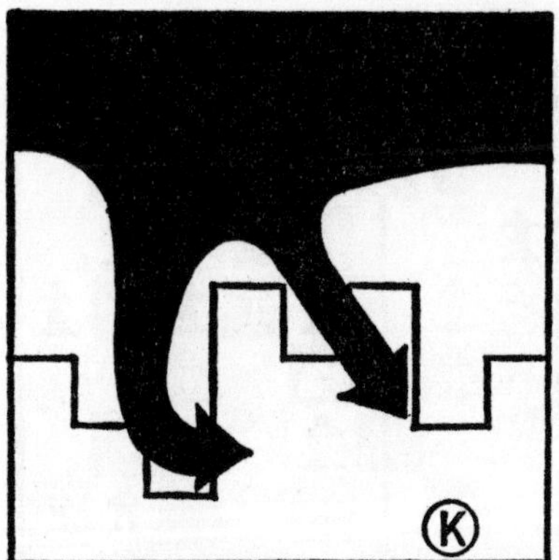

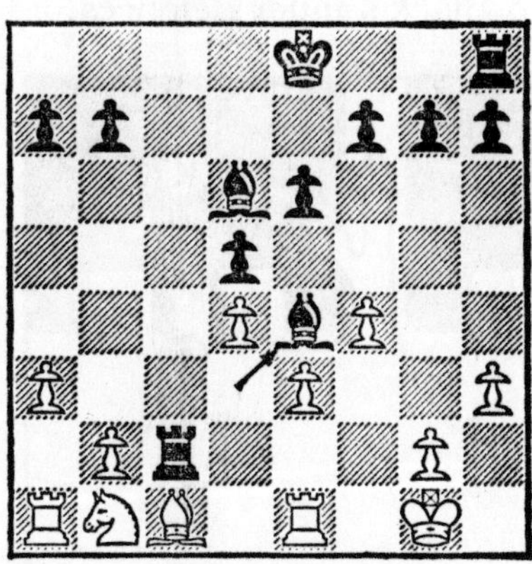

(272) Black enjoys a Rook established on the 7th rank and after K—Q 2 can double up Rooks on the Q B file.

White's backward Pawn at K 3 gives White difficult defensive problems. Several moves later Black's superior position forced White to resign.

STEINITZ *v* SELLMAN

(273) White gains a firm grip on the Q B file and has usefully posted Knights at Q R 5 and Q 4.

1. R × R	Q × R
2. R—B 1	Q—Q Kt 1
3. Q—Q B 2	B—Q 1
4. Kt (R 5)—B 6	Q—Kt 2
5. Kt × B ch	R × Kt

This exchange of minor pieces allows the entry of White's major pieces into Black's inner defences.

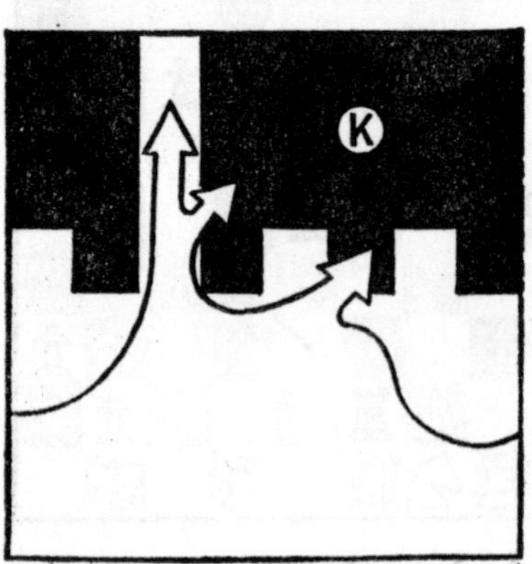

(274) 6. Q—B 7. White has now penetrated to the 7th rank. Black's Bishop is shut out of the game and the Black Knight pinned. By contrast White's Bishop is free to move. Later, White was able to establish this Bishop on Q 6 moving the Knight via K B 3 to K Kt 5.

QUIZ ON "ROOM TO MOVE"

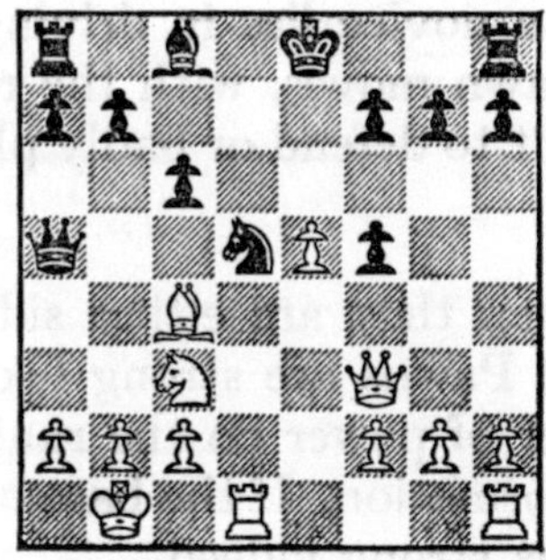

(Q.22) White to play.
How can White increase the scope of his Bishop and Queen's Rook?

(Q.23) It is Black to move.
Say whether you would rather be Black or White in this position and give your reasons.

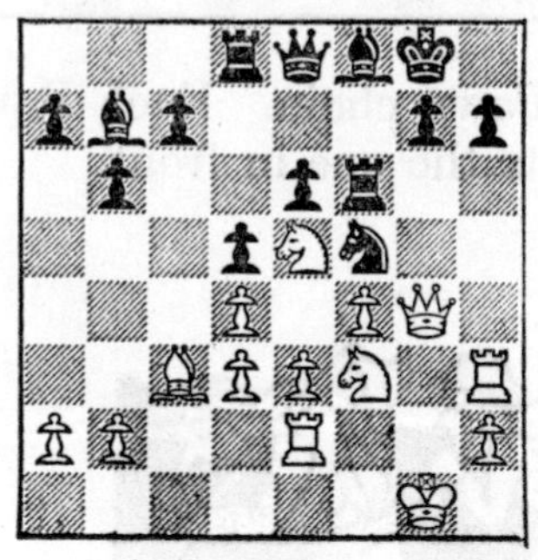

(Q.24) White to play.
Position after ....B—K B 1. Material is equal. Who is the stronger, Black or White ? Give reasons.

Answers to Quiz on " ***Room to Move*** *" on page* 194.

4. PAWN PLAY

Since Pawns may not be moved backwards, it is essential, before pushing a Pawn forward, to ensure that such a move will not be regretted later in the game. A typical weakness of the novice lies in driving his opponents' pieces away with ill-considered Pawn moves, with the result that the Pawns, losing contact, become difficult to defend or badly placed for the rest of the game.

Pawn groups are strongest and safest when they are either side by side or in chain. The side by side (adjacent) Pawns are strong because not only do they create a considerable barrier of power on the ranks in front but are able to be converted to a chain formation. If the base of the Pawn chain is securely protected, the chain is strong indeed.

(275) Adjacent Pawns.

(276) Pawn chain. Each Pawn protects the one in front.

277

(277) This diagram shows a position with everything removed except the Pawns. The structure we see is called a *Pawn skeleton.* White has a good opening Pawn formation illustrating an example of a Pawn chain linked with advanced adjacent Pawns. This was the Pawn skeleton during a game between Capablanca (White) and Jaffe played in New York in 1910.

Here is the full position

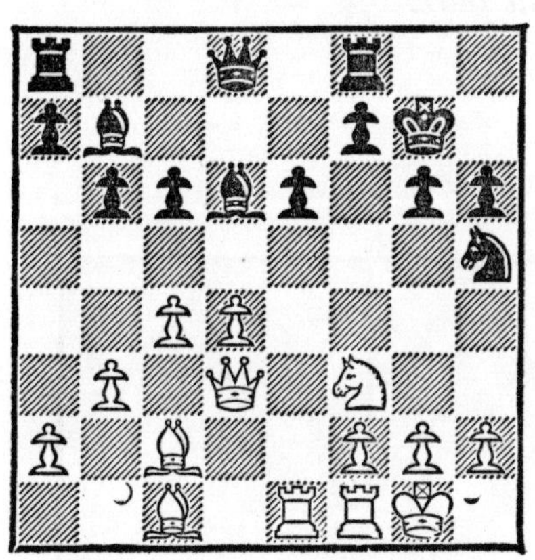

(278) Notice how the strong Pawn formation is fully backed up by well-placed pieces. The final moves were as follows :

CAPABLANCA	JAFFE
1. R × P	Kt—B 3
2. Kt—K 5	P—B 4
3. B × P ch	K × B
4. Kt × P ch	

and Black resigned as he cannot avoid mate.

PAWN MAJORITIES

In the following position you see that Black and White each have four Pawns yet clearly White has an easy win by playing P—Kt 5 forcing a passed Pawn which cannot be stopped. White's advantage is due to the fact that, although both sides may force a passed Pawn, White's passed Pawn is on the Queen's side, remote from the interference of the opposing King.

(279) When both players have castled on the King's side, a Pawn majority on the Queen's side is a clear advantage.

We now show three stages in a game between the American grand-master Reuben Fine (Black) and Collet played in Stockholm in 1937, *in which the Queen's side Pawn majority plays an important part.*

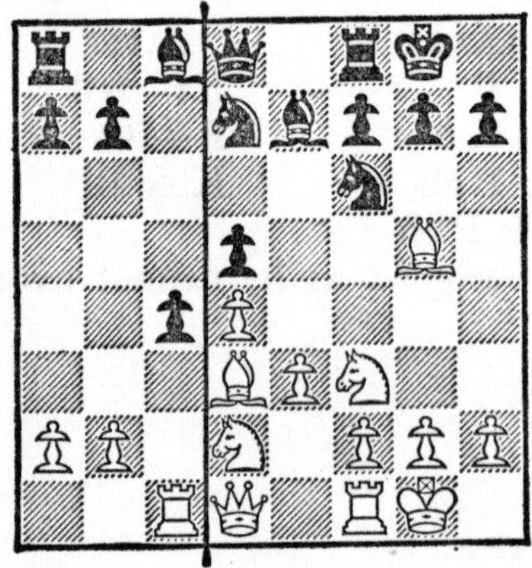

First stage

(280) Black, by his last move, has created his Queen's side Pawn majority. On the left of the line we see Black has three Pawns to White's two.

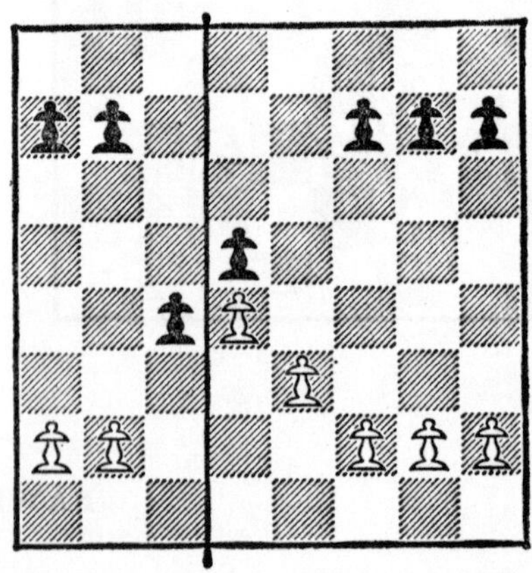

(281) Here the Pawn formation is shown without the supporting pieces.

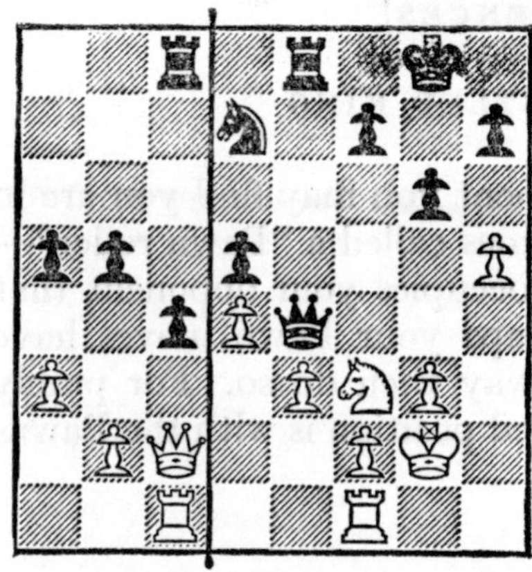

Second stage

(282) Most of the minor pieces have been exchanged. Exchanges favour the holder of the Pawn majority for Pawns gain in strength as the number of pieces on the board diminish.

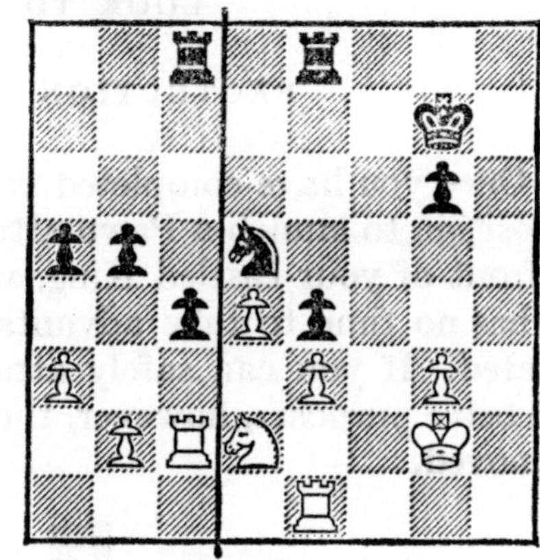

Third stage

(283) The game is now well advanced. The Queens have been exchanged; the Pawn majority is secure and the White King has not been given an opportunity to leave the King's side of the board.

Final stage

(284) Further exchanges have been made and each side is now left with Rook and two Pawns. The 3—2 Pawn majority on the Queen's side has now been converted to 1—0! It will be seen that although both sides have two passed Pawns, it is Black's Pawn on the Queen's side which decides the issue. White resigned in a few more moves, for he could only prevent Black's Rook's Pawn from queening by giving up his Rook.

PROTECTION OF THE CASTLED KING

Once you have completed your development you may find you are in a position to launch a Pawn attack—sometimes called a "Pawn roller"—in front of your castled King, which so preoccupies your opponent that he has no time to take advantage of the gaps your Pawn moves have created. If you can safely attack in this way then do so. For purely defensive purposes, however, the safest castled position is with the Pawns unmoved.

(285) Best!

Although we do not say the following positions are *always* secure, they are generally found to be safe during normal development.

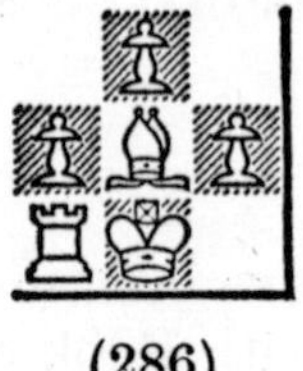

(286)

(287)

(288)

(289)

THESE POSITIONS ARE CONSIDERED WEAK

See game on page 123, diagram 327

(290) Where the Bishop on Kt 2 has been captured or exchanged. Very weak indeed if your opponent's White square Bishop is still in play.

See page 113, (Q. 27)

(291) The square Kt 3 is known as a "hole" since an opponent's piece placed on it is safe from Pawn attack.

Especially weak are the Pawn positions shown in diagrams (292) and (293), if your opponent has a White square Bishop still on the board.

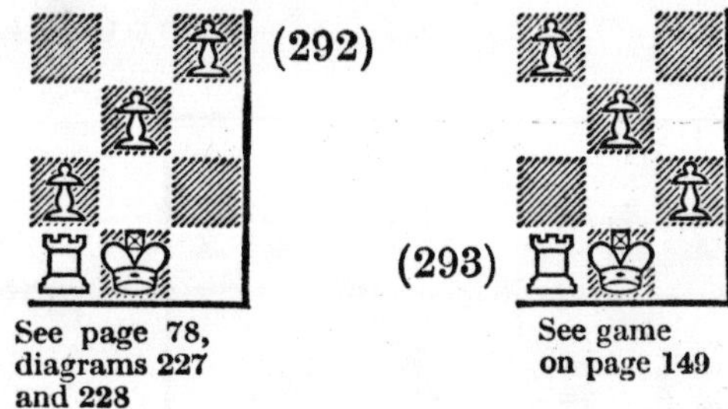

(292) See page 78, diagrams 227 and 228

(293) See game on page 149

Avoid early defensive Pawn moves in front of the castled King—such Pawn weaknesses create easy targets.

BASIC PATTERNS OF PAWN WEAKNESSES

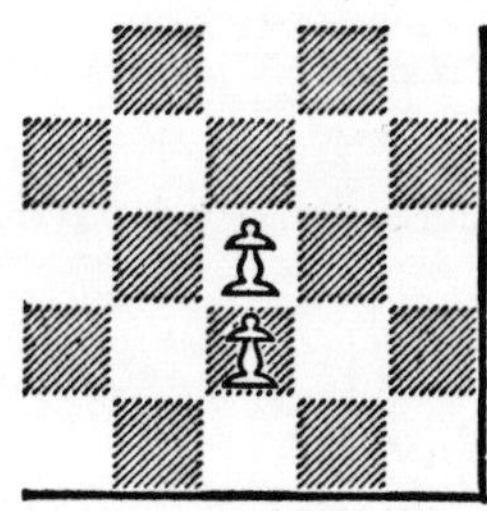

(294) *Doubled Pawns*

The backward Pawn of the two is limited in its movement and where either or both Pawns are isolated, becomes a target for attack by enemy pieces.

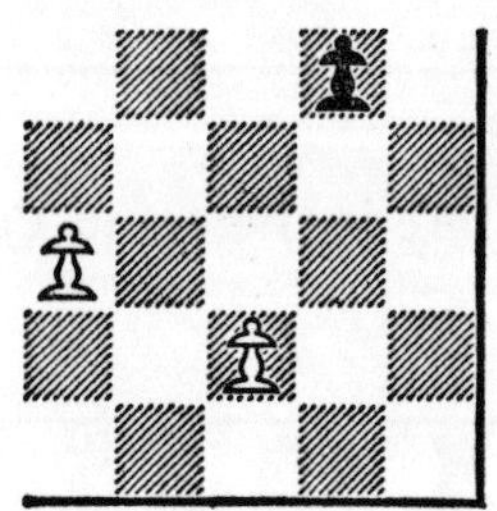

(295) *Isolated Pawns*

An isolated Pawn becomes a target for enemy pieces. It cannot be defended by other Pawns and so its defence must be by pieces which would otherwise be usefully employed in attack.

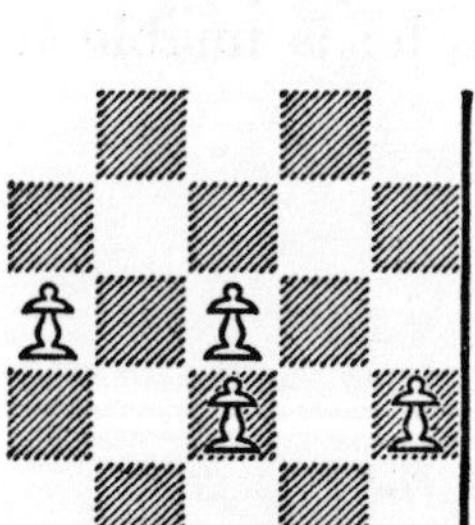

(296) *Doubled and Isolated Pawns*

A common and serious weakness.

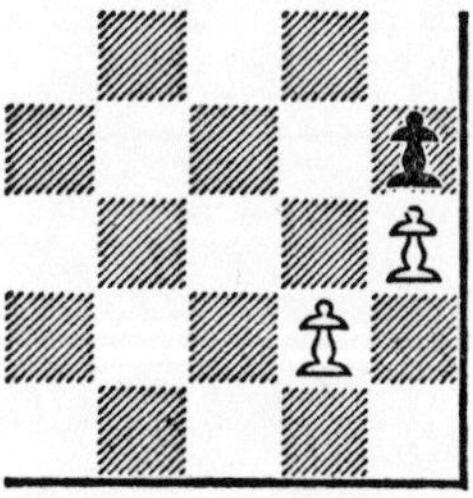

(297) *Backward Pawns*

Enjoying no partner to support it, a backward Pawn can only advance with almost certain risk of capture.

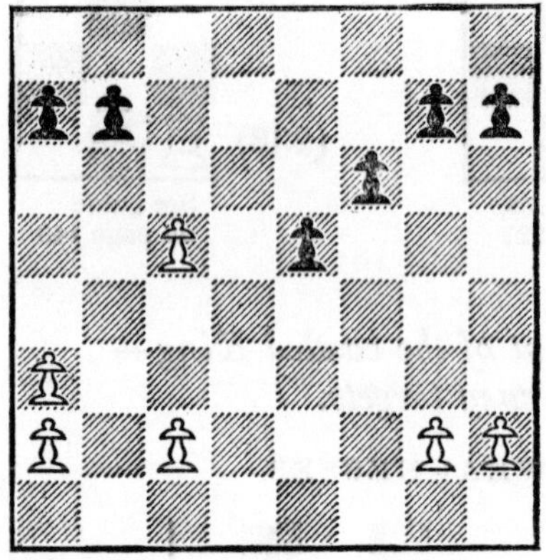

(298) Look at this Pawn skeleton. Black and White each have six Pawns but four of White's Pawns are doubled.

Here is the same Pawn structure with pieces on the board.

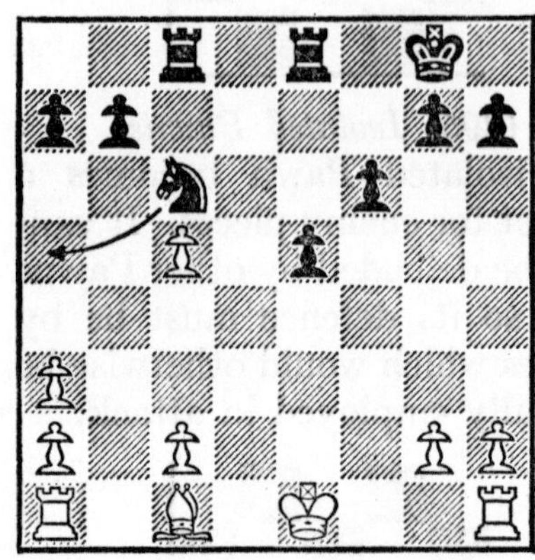

(299) Black to play.
1. . . . . Kt—R 4 uncovering an attack by the Rook on White's Pawn on B 5. This attacked Pawn cannot be defended by another Pawn so if it is to be defended, a piece must be called to its protection, e.g. **2. B—K 3** and Black now attacks another Pawn and the Bishop by **2. . . . . Kt—B 5** and White finds he is unable to defend both Pawns.

Avoid doubled Pawns. They become easy targets.

Pawn skeleton

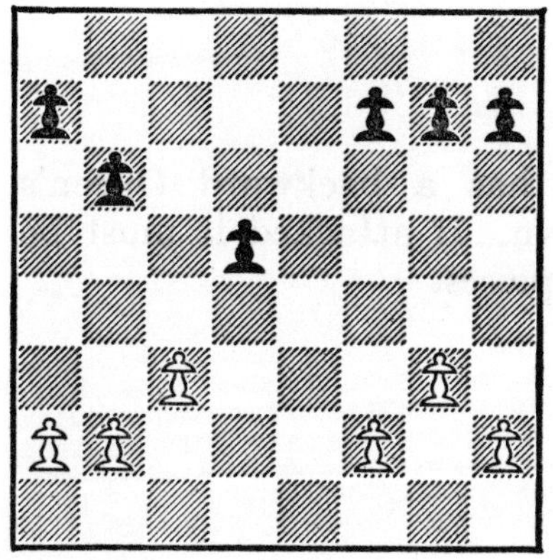

(300) Black's Queen's Pawn, if attacked, must be protected by pieces, as it is isolated from its companions.

The full position

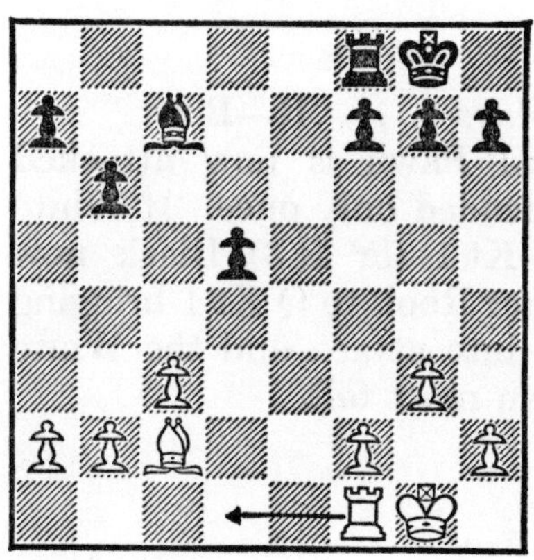

(301) White to play.
1. R—Q 1 attacking the isolated Pawn. The only defence of the Pawn would be by 1. . . . . R—Q 1 but White would follow up with 2. B—Kt 3 and the Pawn must now fall.

Attack the isolated Pawn

Pawn skeleton

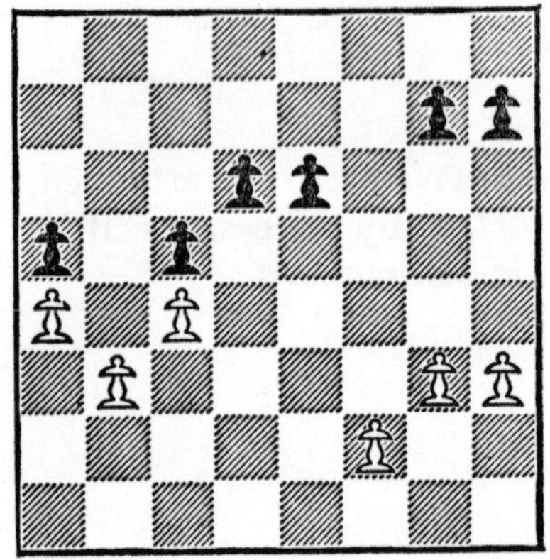

(302) White has a backward Queen's Knight's Pawn. If attacked it must be defended by pieces.

The full position

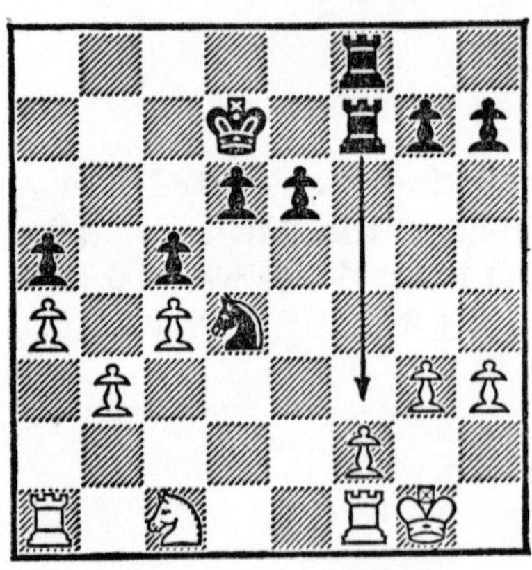

(303) Black plays 1. . . . .R—B 6.
The backward Pawn is now attacked twice and defended only once. If White plays 2. R—Kt 1 (or R 3) Black now moves his other Rook to Q Kt 1 bringing a third piece into attack and the White Knight's Pawn must fall.

QUIZ ON "PAWN PLAY"

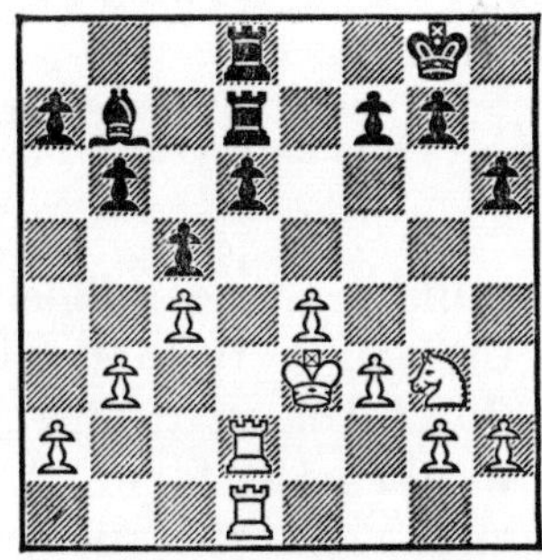

(Q.25) White to play.
How would you go about winning a Pawn?

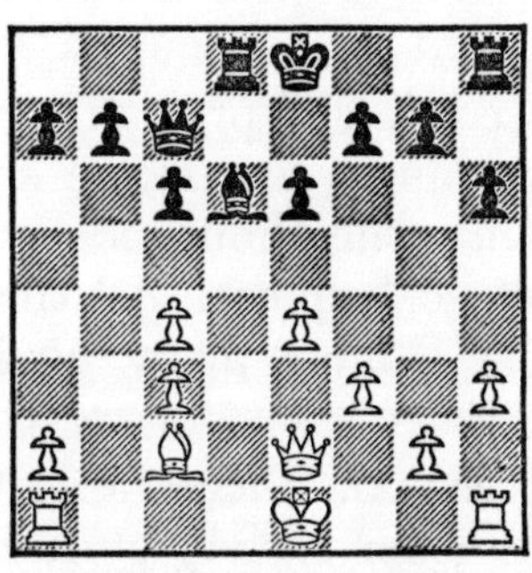

(Q.26) Black to play.
White's doubled and isolated Pawns are an easy target. Suggest a way of winning one of them.

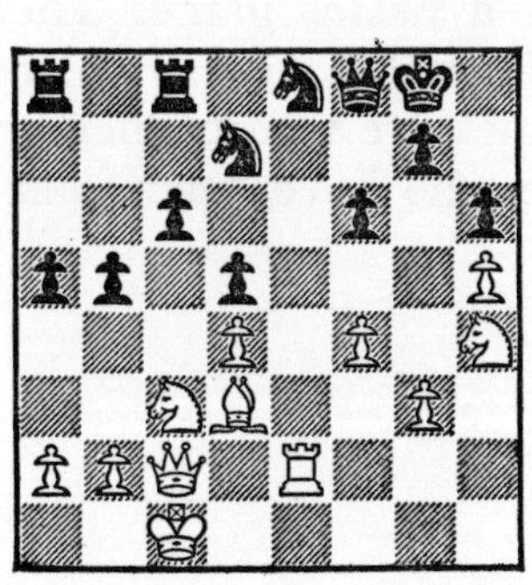

(Q.27) White to play and win.
Black's castled position is riddled with weaknesses.

Answers to Quiz on "Pawn Play" on page 194.

The Forces Move into Position

1. WINNING WITH CONTROL OF THE CENTRE

In the year 216 B.C. the Carthaginian army, under the generalship of Hannibal, met the Romans in battle near Cannæ, a Roman village. Hannibal anticipated that the Romans would attack the centre first, and, as his weaker soldiers retreated, the Romans would press forward. But he had a plan to meet this, for, when the Romans charged and pushed the Carthaginian centre well back, the wings closed in and attacked the Roman central flanks. The Carthaginian centre was greatly encouraged by this support, and charged their enemy's front with renewed vigour.

Gradually the Roman infantry was forced back, pressed so close together that they were hardly able to move, much less strike a blow. Those on the outside were killed at once, while the thousands crushed together in the centre were compelled to look on helpless. All that day the massacre never ceased, and by dusk the Roman army no longer existed.

The centre is important to the chess player too. Pieces able to use the centre are more mobile and can move in a wider variety of directions either for defence or attack, and it is generally found that the player who is able to command the centre enjoys a better game. There are exceptions to this rule due to successful attacks on the wing or to blunders by the opponent; nevertheless, far more games are won by players who have had control of the centre than by those who have been denied this control.

Examine these positions :

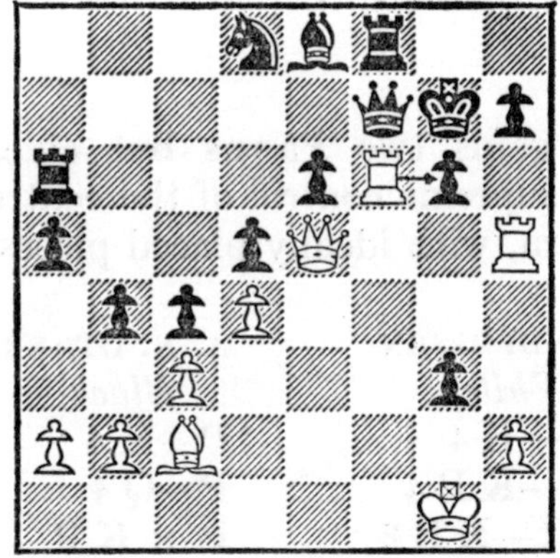
(304) R × Kt P double checkmate

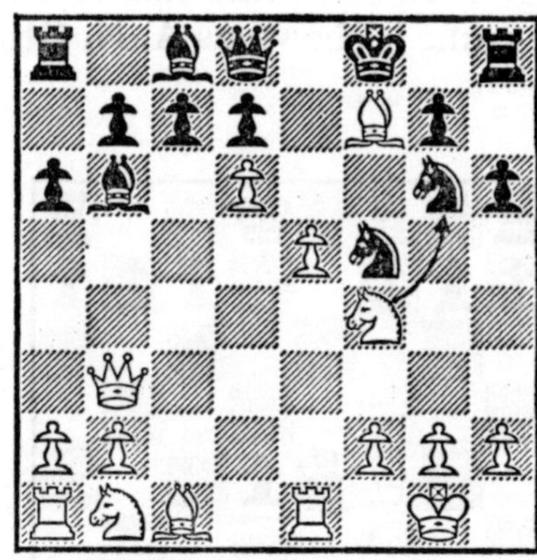
(305) Kt × Kt mate

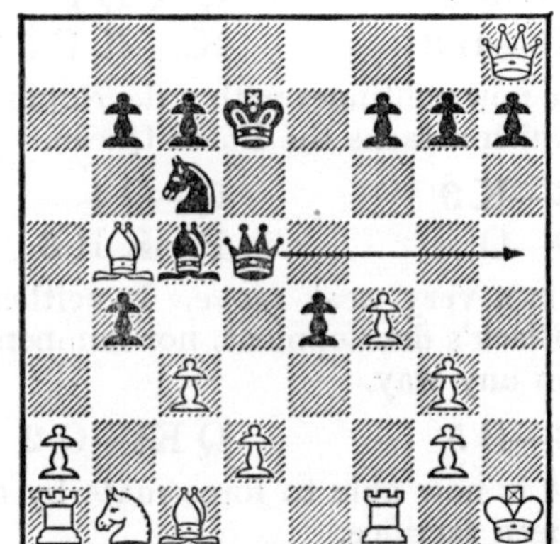
(306) . . . . Q—R 4 mate

(307) B × P mate

In each case the victor has enjoyed control of the centre. That this domination of the centre and mate should go together need not surprise us for the latter is usually the logical result of the other.

This game was won by A. Anderssen against "A. N. Other." Sometimes it is desirable not to give the name of the loser. After all every chess player has at one time or another played a game he would rather forget. In cases like this or where the name of the player is not known, the name is shown as A. N. Other.

(308) Position after 9. . . . . Kt—K B 3

Black gains two Pawns but gives White supreme control of the centre in return, with ideally placed pieces.

A. ANDERSSEN *White*	A. N. OTHER *Black*
1. P—K 4	P—K 4
2. P—K B 4	P—Q 4
3. Kt—K B 3	P × K P
4. Kt × P	B—Q 3
5. B—B 4	B × Kt
6. P × B	Q—Q 5
7. Q—K 2	Q × K P
8. P—Q 4	Q × Q P
9. Kt—B 3	Kt—K B 3

White now continues with a developing move which attacks the Black Queen.

10. B—K 3	Q—Q 1
11. O—O	P—K R 3

This is a very weak move. It neither assists Black's development, nor hampers White in any way.

12. B—B 5	Q Kt—Q 2

White is now able to force mate by a neat Queen sacrifice.

13. Q × P ch!	Kt × Q
14. B × P mate!	

Although Black could have avoided this mate by castling on move 11, instead of the weak move he played, defeat was inevitable as a result of neglecting sound development.

(309) Position after 12. . . . . Q Kt—Q 2

The previous example was of a game which was over almost before the middle game was reached. Here again control of the centre wins for White, but this time it takes a little longer.

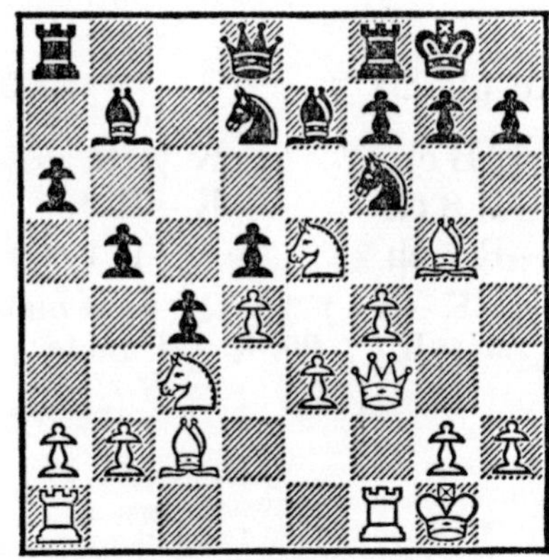

(310) Position after 13. . . . . P—Kt 4

PILLSBURY *White*	MARCO *Black*
1. P—Q 4	P—Q 4
2. P—Q B 4	P—K 3
3. Kt—Q B 3	Kt—K B 3
4. B—Kt 5	B—K 2
5. P—K 3	O—O
6. Kt—B 3	P—Q Kt 3
7. B—Q 3	B—Kt 2
8. P × P	P × P
9. Kt—K 5	Q Kt—Q 2
10. P—B 4	P—B 4
11. O—O	P—B 5
12. B—B 2	P—Q R 3
13. Q—B 3	P—Kt 4

Black has concentrated upon a Queen side Pawn advance and has, in fact, a Queen side Pawn majority. In the meantime White has a powerful Knight at K 5 supported by two forward Pawns and his other pieces sweep across the centre.

14. Q—R 3	P—Kt 3
15. P—B 5	P—Kt 5
16. P × P	R P × P
17. Q—R 4	P × Kt
18. Kt × Kt	Q × Kt
19. R × Kt	

If now 19. . . . . B × R; 20. B × B and White mates by Q—R 8.

19.	P—R 4
20. Q R—K B 1	

And now the last of White's pieces has come into play.

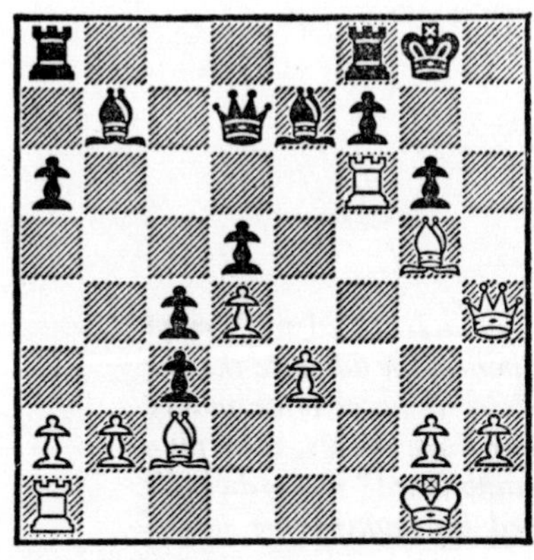

(311) Position after 19. R × Kt

20.	R—R 3
21. B × P	P × B
22. R × R ch	B × R

White now "announced" mate in six moves

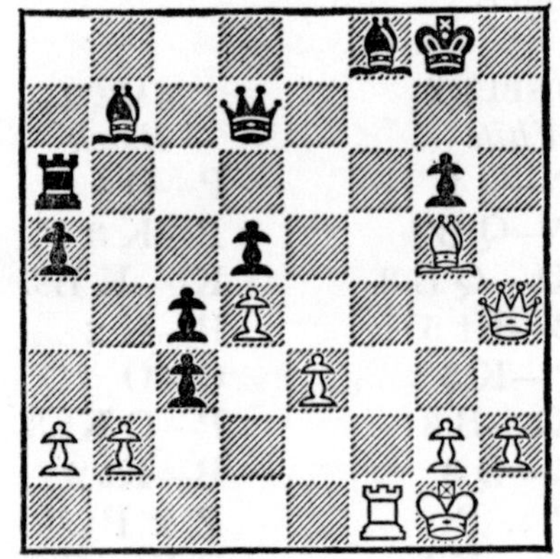

(312) Position after
22. ....B × R

White to play.

23. R × B ch	K × R
24. Q—R 8 ch	K—B 2
25. Q—R 7 ch	K—B 1

If 25.....K—K 1; 26. Q—Kt 8 mate
or 25. ....K—K 3; 26. Q × P mate.

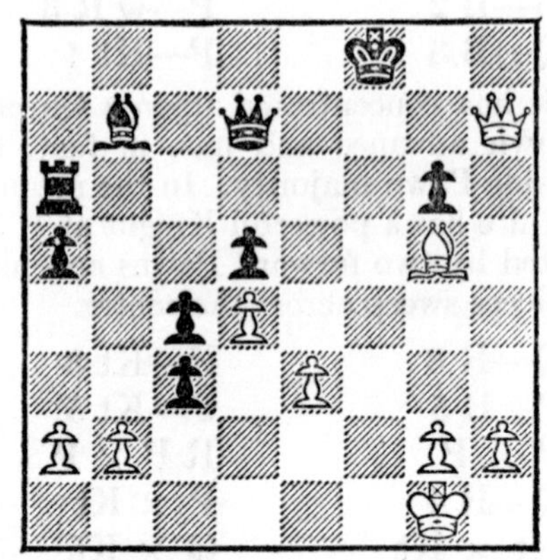

(313) Position after
25. ....K—B 1

26. Q × Q

And whatever move Black may play there follows:

27. B—R 6
28. Q—Kt 7 mate

NOTE: *When a player "announces" mate in a specified number of moves it means that he tells his opponent in advance that he is going to checkmate him. Our advice is never to announce mate! If you have a mate in two or three moves, then play it out. It is surprising how many "announced" mates dwindle into muttered apologies when tested by making the actual moves!*

2. PIECES AND THE CENTRE

Most of the pieces increase their possible range of movement, i.e. mobility, when placed near or at the centre. For example a Knight placed on the edge of the board commands fewer squares than when centrally placed. Similarly with the Bishop and Queen.

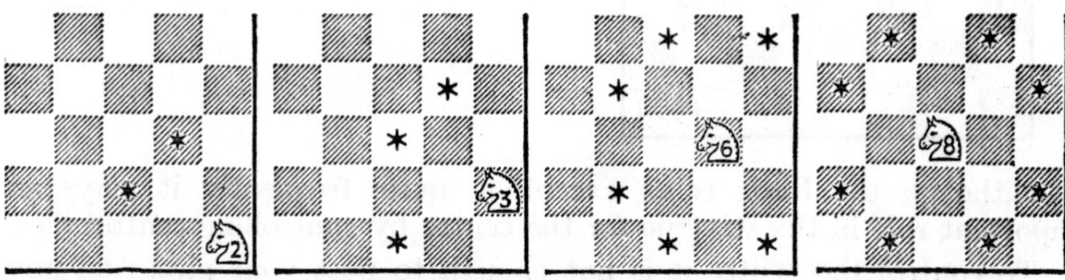

(314) A Knight in the corner commands 2 squares.

(315) In this position 3 squares.

(316) In this position 6 squares.

(317) A Knight placed near the centre commands 8 squares.

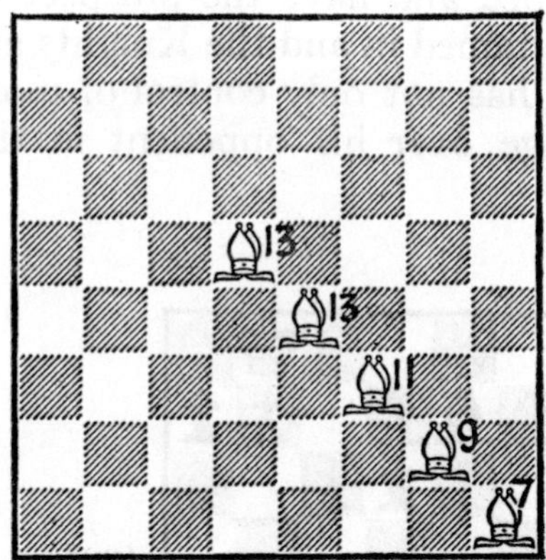

(318) Here you see a Bishop placed on five different squares. Next to each appears a number showing how many squares it commands.

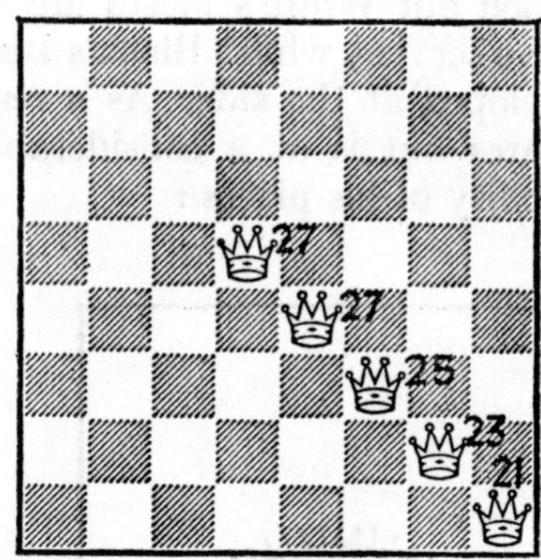

(319) Here a Queen is shown on five different squares showing the number of squares it commands from each position.

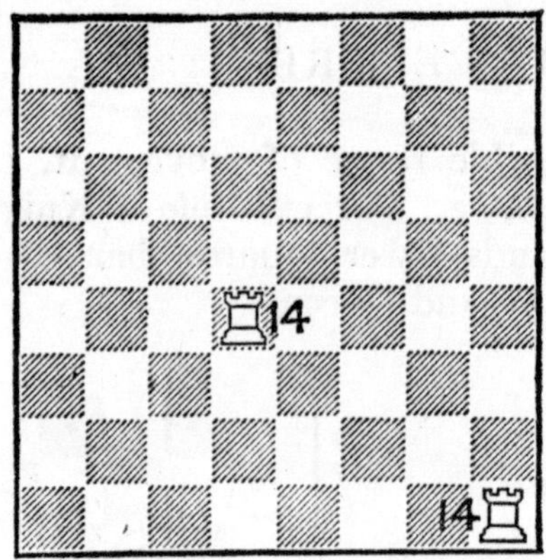

(320) Here you see a Rook in the corner and another in the centre. Each controls 14 squares. This is the case *wherever* a Rook is placed.

Although the Rook is an exception, quite frequently it plays an important role in the struggle for the centre by controlling central files.

To control the centre it is not enough to post your pieces on any squares in the middle of the chessboard which happen to be free from attack. A Bishop is helpless in or near the centre if it is destined to be hemmed in by Pawns for most of the game. Similarly a Knight has little prospect if advanced to a forward square from which it can be driven at once by sound enemy development or attack.

In the following position both sides have developed their pieces and castled but White's pieces are well developed and have the prospect of active service, whilst Black's Bishops are hemmed in and the Knights are developed at the side. As a result, White has not only control of more squares but is at a considerable advantage over his opponent in the mobility of his pieces :

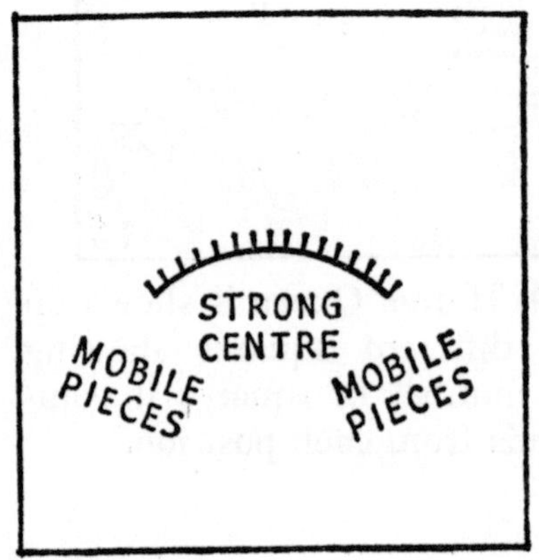

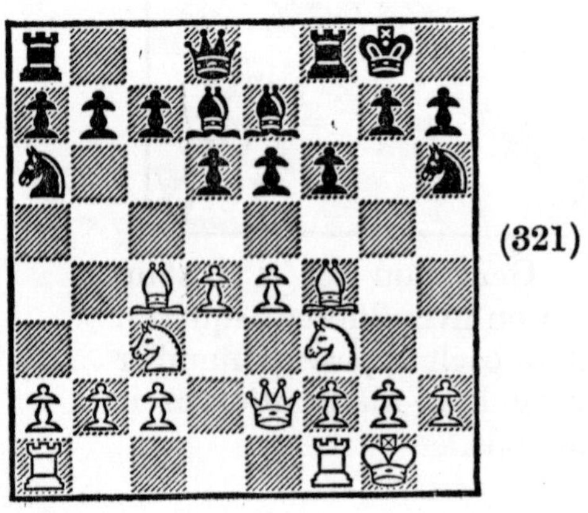

(321)

In this game won by Sir George Thomas in 1933, we see how a strong centre is built up from which a successful King's side attack emerges. The game is an object lesson in sound development and shows the maximum use of pieces which are given scope for free movement, as opposed to the restriction which arises from a cramped defence.

SIR GEORGE THOMAS *White*	MONTICELLI *Black*
1. P—K 4	P—K 4
2. Kt—K B 3	Kt—Q B 3
3. B—Kt 5	P—Q R 3
4. B—R 4	P—Q 3
5. B × Kt ch	P × B
6. P—Q 4	P—B 3
7. B—K 3	Kt—K 2
8. Q—Q 2	Kt—Kt 3
9. Kt—B 3	B—K 2
10. P—K R 4	

White in ten moves has secured the centre and launched his attack.

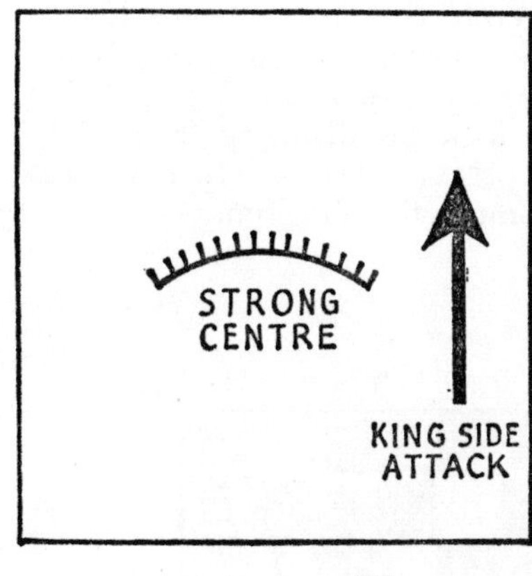

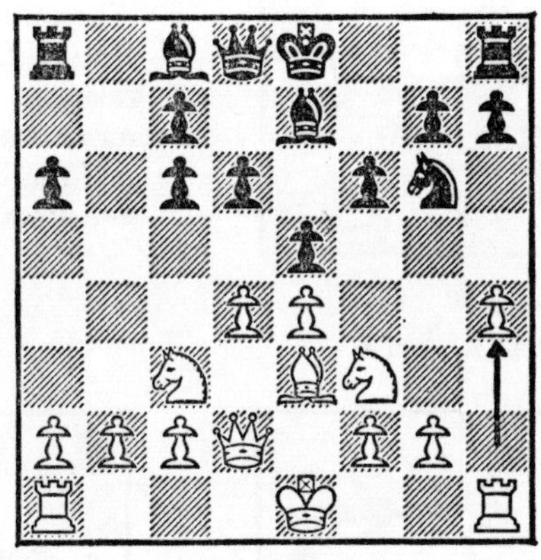

(322) Position after 10. P—KR4

10.	O—O
11. P—R 5	Kt—R 1
12. O—O—O	Kt—B 2
13. Q R—Kt 1	B—Q 2

Let us look again at the centre, at White's expansion against Black's poor development. Contrast the role of White's Rooks supporting advancing Pawns, with Black's Rooks which have been allowed very little part in the game.

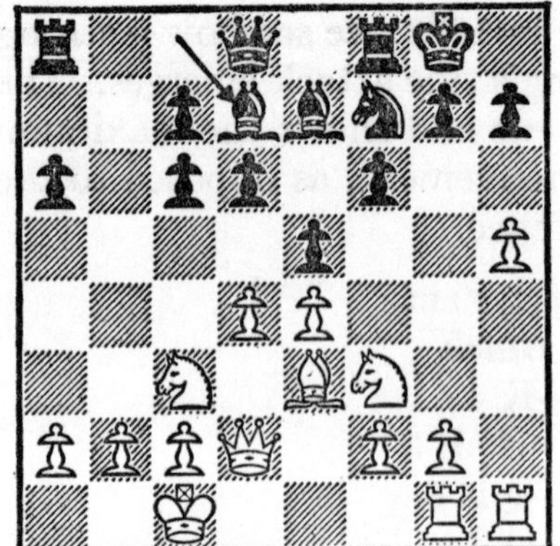
(323) Position after 13. . . . .B—Q 2

The attack proceeds.

14.	P—K Kt 4	P × P
15.	Kt × P	Kt—K 4
16.	Q—K 2	Q—B 1
17.	Kt—B 5	R—K 1
18.	P—B 4	Kt—B 2
19.	P—R 6	Kt × P

White has such advantage in position that he can afford to sacrifice a piece.

20.	Kt × Kt P !	K × Kt
21.	Q—R 2	Kt—B 2
22.	Q × P ch	K—B 1
23.	P—B 5	B—Q 1
24.	Q—Kt 6	K—K 2
25.	R—R 7	R—B 1
26.	B—R 6	B—K 1

And now the last move in the game!

27. Q—Kt 7

Supported by the White Bishop which enjoyed the freedom of a long open diagonal, White threatens Black's King's Rook. As it cannot be protected, Black resigns. Black's two Bishops can do no more than look on dismally from their self-made prison. See position in 325 and its accompanying diagram.

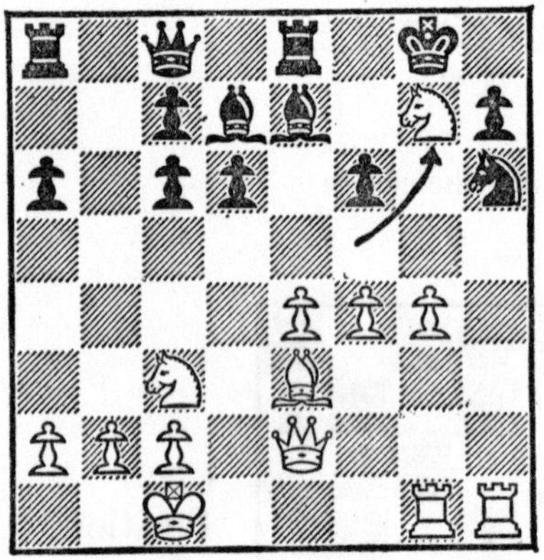
(324) Position after 20. Kt × Kt P

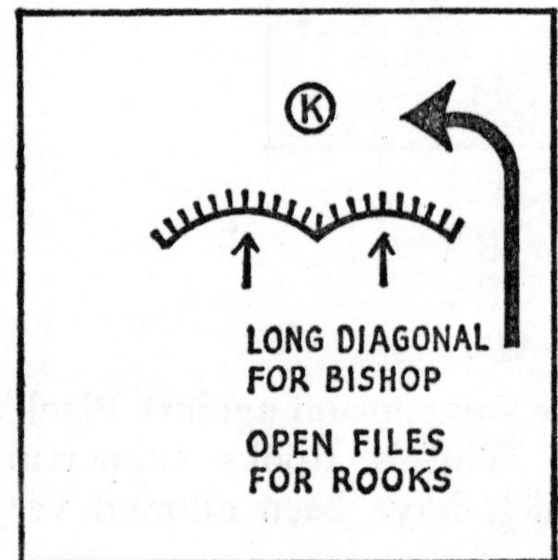

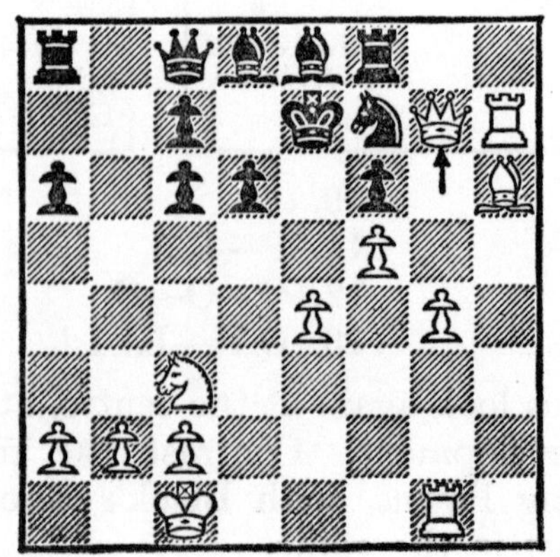
(325)

In this game Black severely restricts White's development and is so rich in position as a result that he is able to sacrifice his Queen and Knight and still have plenty of material left with which to win!

Warsaw, 1917

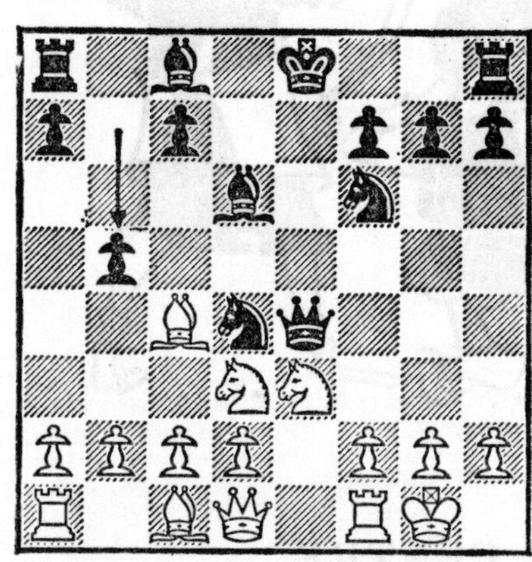

(326) Position after 10. . . . .P—Q Kt 4

BELSITZMANN *White*	RUBINSTEIN *Black*
1. P—K 4	P—K 4
2. Kt—K B 3	Kt—Q B 3
3. Kt—B 3	Kt—B 3
4. B—Kt 5	Kt—Q 5
5. B—B 4	B—B 4
6. Kt × P	Q—K 2
7. Kt—Q 3	P—Q 4
8. Kt × P	Q × P ch
9. Kt—K 3	B—Q 3
10. O—O	P—Q Kt 4
11. B—Kt 3	B—Kt 2

In exchange for a Pawn, Black has both Bishops on open diagonals in support of an attacking Queen. A Pawn is a cheap price to pay for such development!

12. Kt—K 1	Q—R 5
13. P—Kt 3	Q—R 6
14. P—Q B 3	

Attacking the Knight. As White has several pieces completely out of play, Black considers that even if he gives up the Knight, he still has enough pieces in action to win.

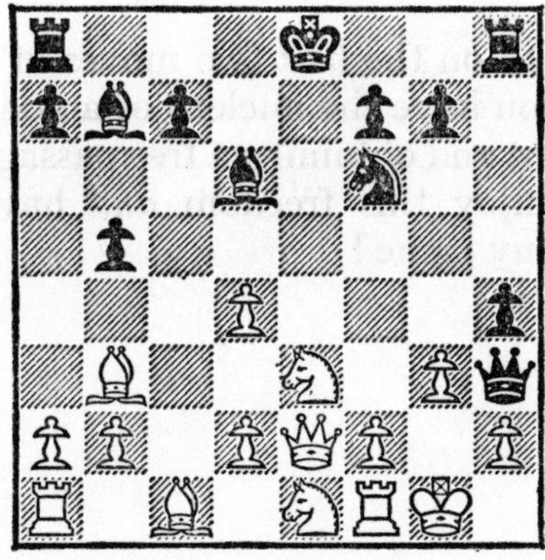

(327) Position after 16. Q—K 2

14.	P—K R 4
15. P × Kt	P—R 5
16. Q—K 2	

Black now gives up his Queen!

16.	Q × R P ch
17. K × Q	P × P dble ch
18. K—Kt 1	R—R 8 mate

Look again at White's piece development. Neither King's Rook nor Queen's Bishop can move, even after 18 moves!

Long diagonals for Bishops—open files for Rooks!
Open lines win the day for Black!

3. PAWNS AND THE CENTRE

Pawns are an ideal "spearhead" of an early thrust in the centre. When a Pawn occupies the centre it attacks two important squares and prevents their occupation by enemy pieces.

If you are able to play P—K 4 and P—Q 4 on the first two moves of a game without incurring any disadvantage you have the nucleus of a good centre hindering your opponent's development and obtaining a free passage for your Queen and both Bishops. To enjoy this freedom *and* have adjacent centre Pawns is a happy start to any game!

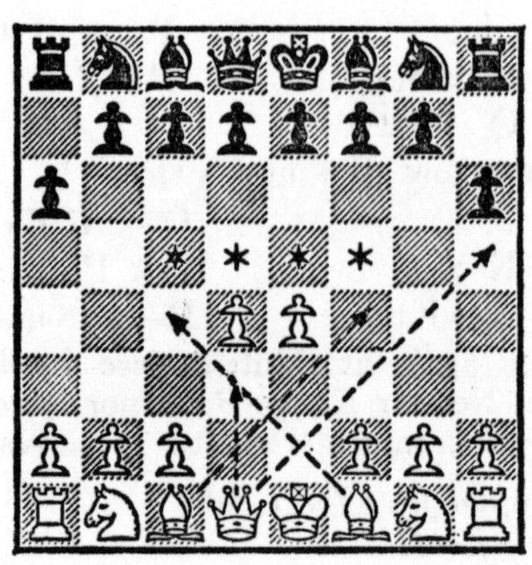

(328) White has a strong central Pawn barrier controlling the four squares marked *.

What can happen if you delay moving your centre pawns too long is shown in this short game. White obtains clear command of the centre following incorrect opening moves by Black.

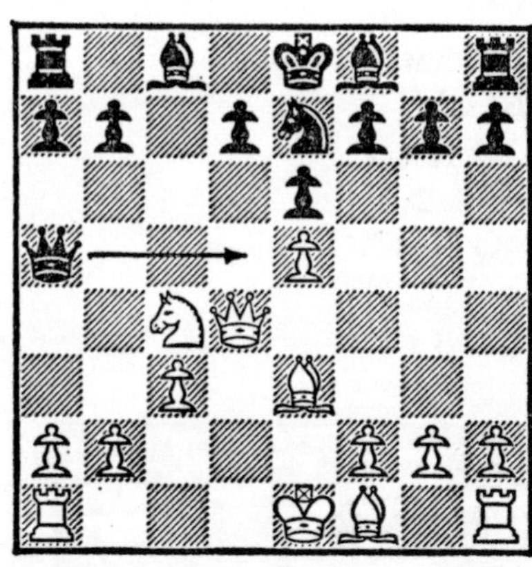

(329) Position before 10. ....Q—Q 4

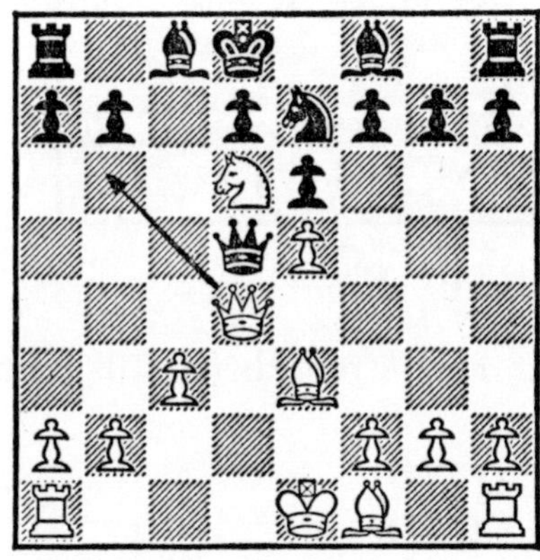

(330) Position before 12. Q—Kt 6 ch

Bristol, 1940

	WELCH *White*	A. N. OTHER *Black*
1.	P—K 4	P—Q B 4
2.	Kt—K B 3	Kt—Q B 3
3.	P—Q 4	P × P
4.	Kt × P	Kt × Kt
5.	Q × Kt	Kt—B 3

This is an oversight that begins Black's troubles. The Knight will soon be pushed back home again causing serious loss of time in completing Black's development.

6.	P—K 5	Q—R 4 ch
7.	P—B 3	Kt—Kt 1
8.	B—K 3	P—K 3
9.	Kt—Q 2	Kt—K 2
10.	Kt—B 4	

Black's position is severely cramped, and he now attempts to exchange Queens.

10. .... Q—Q 4

Hoping for 11. Q × Q, Kt × Q in which case his poor position is slightly improved. White, however, has no intention of assisting Black's development and replies :

11. Kt—Q 6 ch K—Q 1

A Queen sacrifice is called for !

12. Q—Kt 6 ch P × Q
13. B × P mate

Even if Black were given the opportunity of having his last three moves back, his early moves, giving up the centre without a struggle, still seal his ultimate doom.

Here Dr. Euwe is able to play P—Q 4 and P—K 4 on his first two moves whilst his opponent does not contest the centre with his Pawns at all.

Bournemouth, 1939

DR. EUWE *White*	ABRAHAMS *Black*
1. P—Q 4	P—Q Kt 4
2. P—K 4	B—Kt 2
3. P—K B 3	P—Q R 3
4. P—Q B 4	P × P
5. B × P	P—K 3

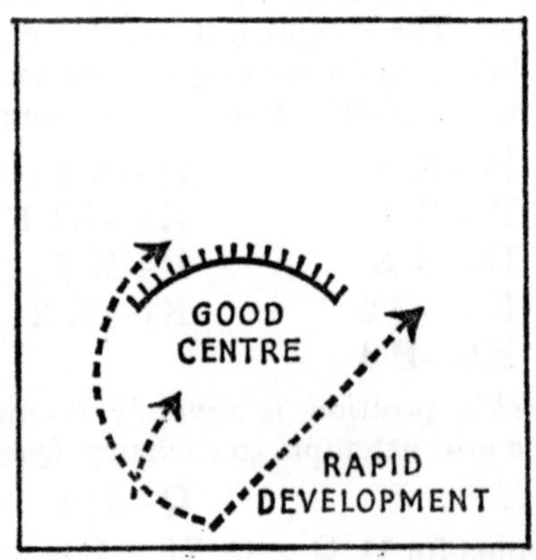

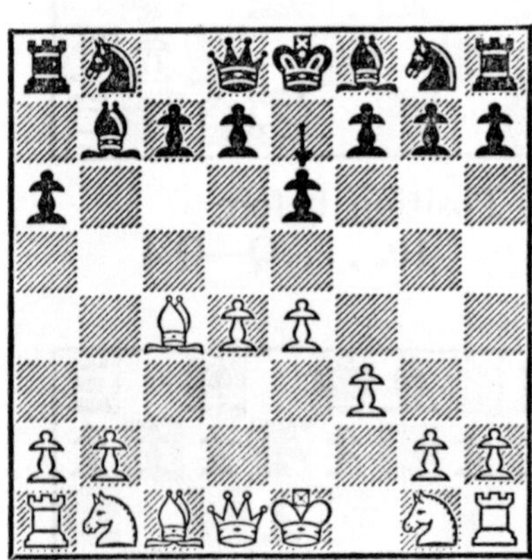

(331) Position after 5. . . . . P—K 3

White continues his sound development and strengthens still more his firm grip on the centre.

6. Kt—B 3	P—Q 4
7. Q—Kt 3	Kt—Q B 3
8. P × P	Kt × P

This attacks Queen and also threatens a Knight Fork . . . . Kt—B 7 ch.

9. Q × B	R—Kt 1
10. Q × R P	R—R 1

Black hopes that after chasing the White Queen away he will be able to play . . . . Kt—B 7 ch. White, however, allows the Queen to remain attacked.

11. B—Kt 5 ch K—K 2
12. P—Q 6 ch

and Black resigns. Why ? Because if he replies 12. ....P × P, White will continue 13. B—Kt 5 ch, P—B 3; 14. Q—Kt 7 ch, Q—B 2; 15. Q × Q mate. Or if 12. ....K—B 3; 13 P × P and Black is unable to reply 13. .... Q × P without losing the Queen by 14. Kt—Q 5 ch. Not only has Black an exposed King, but has to face an enemy Pawn on the 7th rank.

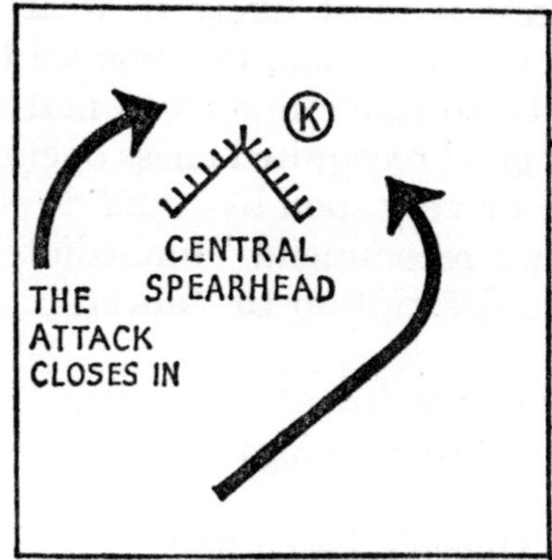

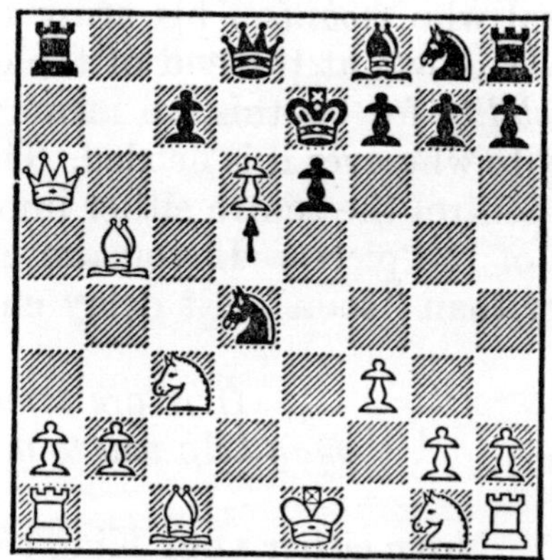

(332) Position after **12. P—Q 6 ch**

4. OPENING PLAY

MOBILISING YOUR FORCES

In chess, White has the first move. In fact he starts the game before his opponent! In a hundred yards sprint race between athletes of equal ability, for one to start before the other would ensure certain victory for him. In chess the advantage is not quite so decisive. White tries to keep the initiative for as long as he can and Black to seize the first opportunity to wrest it from him.

Chess is not so much a race, as a battle between two armies. The general who *mobilises* his army the quickest is most likely to wear the victor's crown at the end of the day. No wonder, then, in chess we talk of *mobility* for by this we mean the ability to move our chess material freely to wherever it is needed. The aim of good recognised chess openings is to control the centre either immediately or very soon by *rapid development* of the pieces. If you are a novice we recommend "immediately" rather than "soon" lest delay changes the description to "never."

Here are some useful hints which may help you to make sound chess openings

1. Move either your King's Pawn or Queen's Pawn first.
   If you are White 1. P—K 4 or 1. P—Q 4. 1. P—K 4 unlocks Queen and Bishop, whilst 1. P—Q 4 releases the Queen's Bishop. If you are able to play both Pawns out in the first two moves of the game, then you have freed Queen and both Bishops.

2. Develop your Knights before the Bishops.
   The best square for the Knight is generally (although not always) B 3, whilst the Bishop has a wider choice of squares, depending upon the play of your opponent. Reserve the development of your Bishops, therefore, until you have brought out your Knights, for this gives you a little more time to consider.

3. Unless you have a special reason, do not move a piece twice before you have completed your development, which will not be until all your pieces have moved off the back rank except King and Rooks.

For example, time wasted by moving a Knight several times in the beginning of a game means delay in mobilisation. This may prove disastrous. Develop *all* your pieces rapidly.

4. Do not bring out your Queen early, so that your opponent is able to harass it and develop his forces at the same time. An early Queen excursion has been the cause of many lost games.

5. Castle *early* and generally on the King's side, unless there is a special purpose for not doing so, e.g. see diagram 265 on page 98. Castling not only provides a haven for the King but also helps to bring the Rooks into play in co-operation with each other.

A Pawn is often sacrificed in the opening in order to gain some advantage in development or to apply pressure and force your opponent on to the defensive. Such pressure (or tempo) is of vital importance in the game for it is *aggressive* (but not reckless) chess which achieves the best results. Sometimes more than one Pawn is given up in this way and very occasionally a piece. The idea behind such *opening gambits* as they are called, is to gain a lead in development whilst your opponent is spending time capturing the gambit Pawn, and trying to hold on to the pawn advantage.

Although inspired attack generally brings greater rewards in chess than passive defence, always ensure that you get full value for your gambit sacrifice, lest when counting up the Pawns in the end game you find your gambit has proved to be your undoing!

In the standard openings which follow we have selected only a few from hundreds of variations which exist and even these we have chosen are not treated exhaustively. Our examples are given as a brief guide to some of the recognised and popular opening lines and for a more thorough examination of opening play we recommend reference to the numerous books which specialise in this aspect of the game. Do not, however, make the mistake of assuming that to become a proficient player it is enough to learn some of the early moves off by heart; it is more important, by far, to understand the motives behind the opening strategy recommended, and to see how this is linked with the principles of development which we have been discussing.

GIUOCO PIANO

(This is Italian and means " Quiet Game ")

	White	*Black*
1.	P—K 4	P—K 4
2.	Kt—K B 3	Kt—Q B 3
3.	B—B 4	B—B 4

These moves constitute the Giuoco Piano opening. In most variations White attempts to establish a Pawn at Q 4. If he plays 4. P—Q 4, Black will simply capture it. White prepares the way, therefore, with

4. P—B 3 Kt—B 3

Not 4. ....Q—B 3 ? which some novices prefer. This move is bad because the Queen will soon become a target. 5. P—Q 3 followed by B—Kt 5, and the Queen is chased away by White's good developing moves.

5. P—Q 4 P × P
6. P × P

And now the Pawn is established at Q 4.

6. .... B—Kt 5 ch

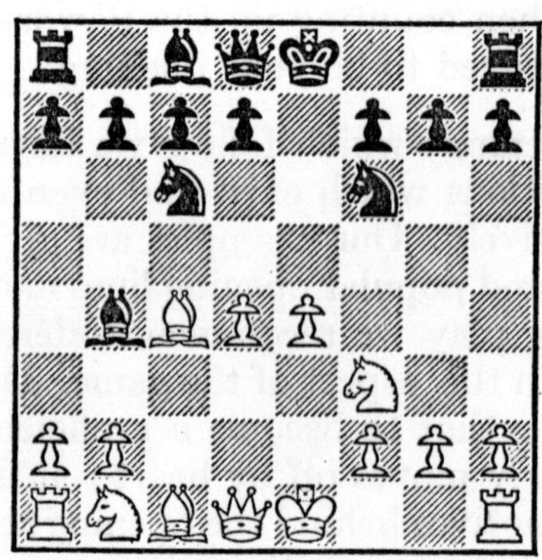

(333) Position after 6. ....B—Kt 5 ch

	White	*Black*
1.	P—K 4	P—K 4
2.	Kt—K B 3	Kt—Q B 3
3.	B—B 4	B—B 4
4.	P—B 3	Kt—B 3
5.	P—Q 4	P × P
6.	P × P	B—Kt 5 ch

Variation A

7.	Kt—B 3	Kt × K P
8.	O—O	Kt × Kt
9.	P × Kt	P—Q 4

Thus Black keeps pace with White in development.

Variation B

7.	Kt—B 3	Kt × K P
8.	O—O	B × Kt
9.	P—Q 5	B—B 3
10.	R—K 1	Kt—K 2
11.	R × Kt	P—Q 3

Variation A

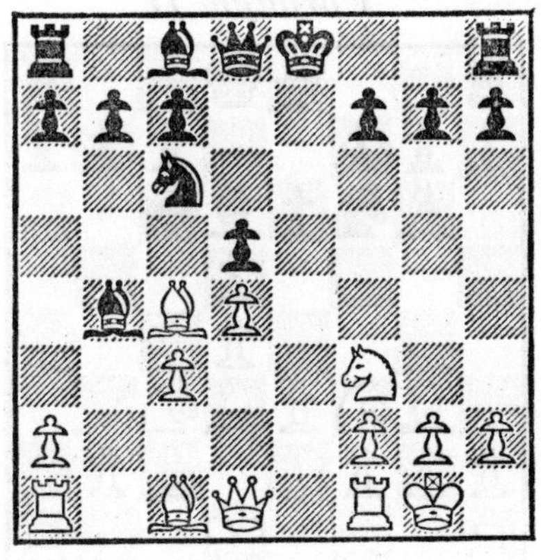

(334) Position after 9. . . . .P—Q 4

Variation B

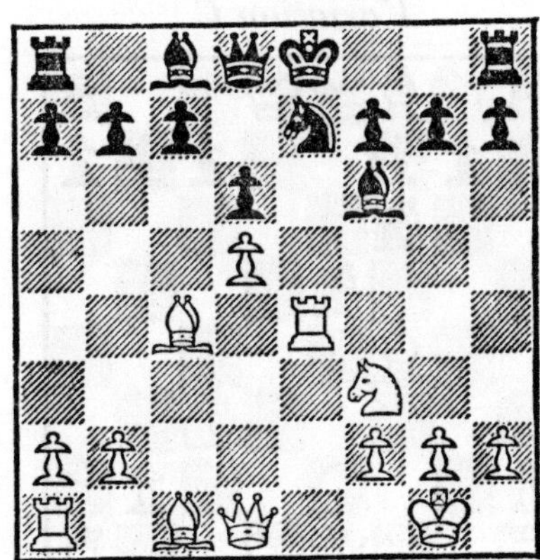

(335) Position after 11. . . . .P—Q 3

In both variations White gives up a Pawn for the sake of swifter development.

	White	*Black*
1.	P—K 4	P—K 4
2.	Kt—K B 3	Kt—Q B 3
3.	B—B 4	B—B 4

Variation C

4. P—B 3 Kt—B 3
5. P—Q 4 P × P
6. P × P B—Kt 5 ch
7. B—Q 2

instead of 7. Kt—B 3.

7. .... B × B ch
8. Q Kt × B

This defends the King's Pawn given up in variations A and B.

8. .... P—Q 4
9. P × P K Kt × P

Variation D

4. P—Q 3

Not as aggressive as 4. P—B 3.

4. .... Kt—B 3
5. Kt—B 3 P—Q 3
6. B—K 3 B—Kt 3

Not 6. ....B × B as after White has recaptured with the Pawn he has an open file for his Rook after O—O.

7. Q—Q 2 B—K 3
8. B—Kt 3

Variation C

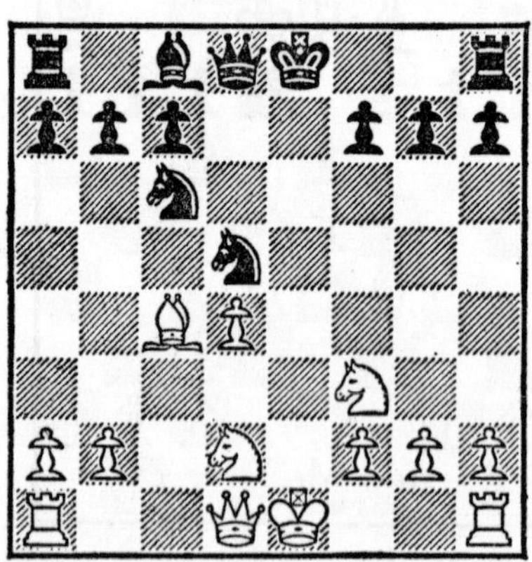

(336) Position after 9. ....K Kt × P

Although White does not give up a Pawn, Black reaches a strong position. White has an isolated Pawn.

Variation D

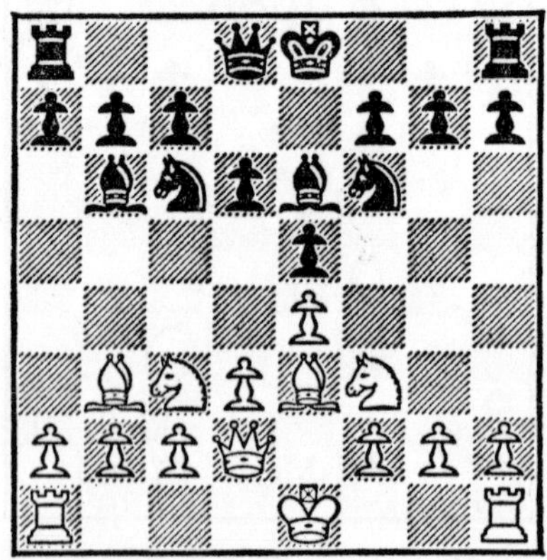

(337) Position after 8. B—Kt 3

A passive opening by White which sets Black no serious problems.

GIUOCO PIANO (*cont.*)

Illustrative Game played in Parana, in 1946.

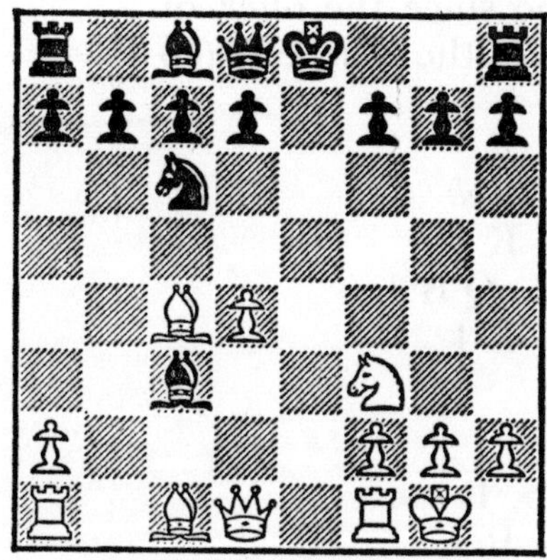

(338) Position after 9. . . . .B × P ?

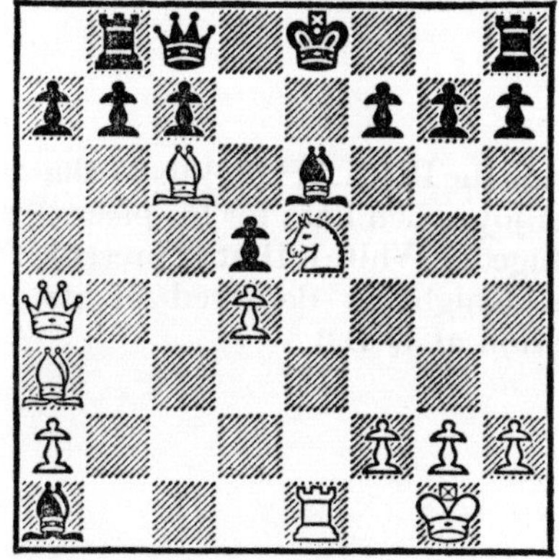

(339) Position after 15. B × Kt ch

Black delayed the completion of his development in order to win material, and paid the penalty. Whilst Black's King's Bishop was busy plundering, White was bringing *all* his pieces rapidly into play.

CORTE *White*	BOLBOCHAN *Black*
1. P—K 4	P—K 4
2. Kt—K B 3	Kt—Q B 3
3. B—B 4	B—B 4
4. P—B 3	Kt—B 3
5. P—Q 4	P × P
6. P × P	B—Kt 5 ch
7. Kt—B 3	Kt × K P
8. O—O	Kt × Kt
9. P × Kt	

Thus far we follow Variation A but Black's next move does not!

9.	B × P ?
10. B—R 3 !	

stopping 10. . . . .O—O.

10.	P—Q 4
11. B—Kt 5	B × R ?
12. R—K 1 ch	B—K 3
13. Q—R 4	

threatening 14. B × Kt ch, P × Kt; 15. Q × P ch winning Rook.

13.	R—Q Kt 1
14. Kt—K 5	

threatening 15. Kt × Kt, P × Kt; 16. B × P ch and the Black Queen is lost.

14.	Q—B 1

giving the King a flight square.

15. B × Kt ch	Resigns

for if 15. . . . .P × B; 16. Q × P ch, Q—Q 2; 17. Kt × Q! or 15. . . . .P × B; 16. Q × P ch, B—Q 2; 17. Kt—Kt 6 disc ch, K—Q 1; 18. B—K 7 ch, K—K 1; 19. B—B 6 mate. If 15. . . . .P × B; 16. Q × P ch, K—Q 1; 17. Kt × P ch, B × Kt; 18. B—K 7 mate.

EVANS GAMBIT

Named after its inventor, Capt. Evans.

This is related to the Giuoco Piano since the offer of the gambit Pawn follows the moves of the Giuoco Piano opening.

	White	*Black*
1.	P—K 4	P—K 4
2.	Kt—K B 3	Kt—Q B 3
3.	B—B 4	B—B 4
4.	P—Q Kt 4	

The gambit Pawn.

4.	....	B × P
5.	P—B 3	B—R 4
6.	P—Q 4	

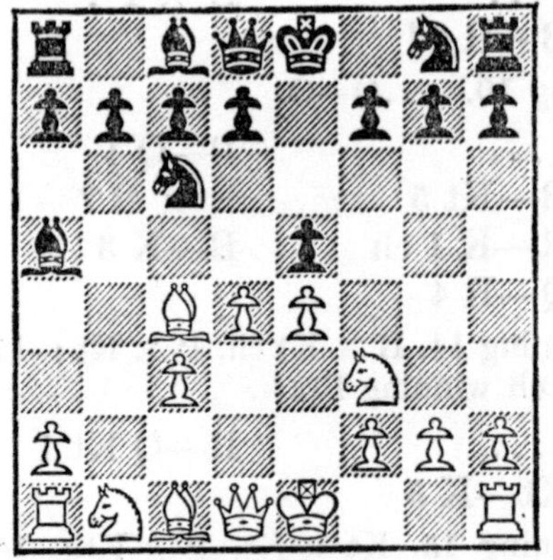

(340) Position after 6. P—Q 4

In return for the Pawn, White hits at the centre and enjoys open lines for his pieces. A disadvantage for White is that at present his Queen's Knight is deprived of its natural position at Q B 3.

This spirited gambit opening must be treated with respect by Black, for it produces games of considerable action. The most famous Evans Gambit game on record is that known as the 'Evergreen,' played between Anderssen and Dufresne, which we showed you in *Chess for Children* (p. 108).

EVANS GAMBIT (*cont.*)

	White	*Black*
1.	P—K 4	P—K 4
2.	Kt—K B 3	Kt—Q B 3
3.	B—B 4	B—B 4
4.	P—Q Kt 4	B × P
5.	P—B 3	B—R 4

Variation A

6.	P—Q 4	P × P
7.	O—O	B—Kt 3
8.	P × P	P—Q 3
9.	Kt—B 3	B—Kt 5

Variation B

6.	O—O	Kt—B 3
7.	P—Q 4	O—O

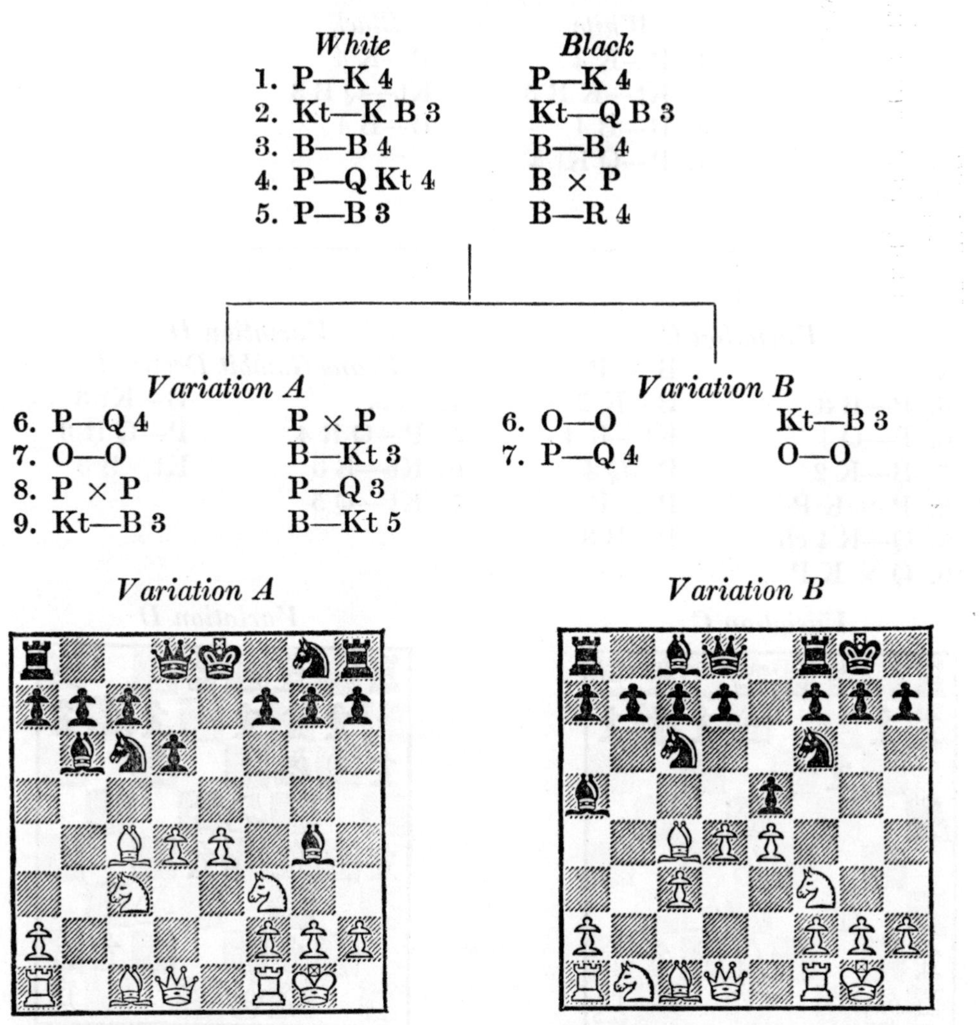

Variation A

(341) Position after 9. . . . .B—Kt 5

Variation B

(342) Position after 7. . . . .O—O

In both these variations White's attacking chances are considered worth the Pawn which has been given up.

EVANS GAMBIT (*cont.*)

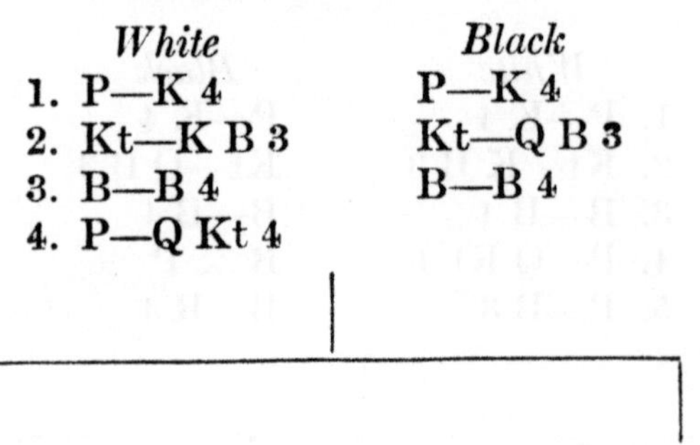

	White	*Black*
1.	P—K 4	P—K 4
2.	Kt—K B 3	Kt—Q B 3
3.	B—B 4	B—B 4
4.	P—Q Kt 4	

Variation C

4.	....	B × P
5.	P—B 3	B—K 2
6.	P—Q 4	Kt—R 4
7.	B—K 2	P—Q 4
8.	P × K P	P × P
9.	Q—R 4 ch	P—B 3
10.	Q × K P	

Variation D
Evans Gambit Declined

4.	....	B—Kt 3
5.	P—Q R 4	P—Q R 3
6.	Kt—B 3	Kt—B 3
7.	Kt—Q 5	

Variation C

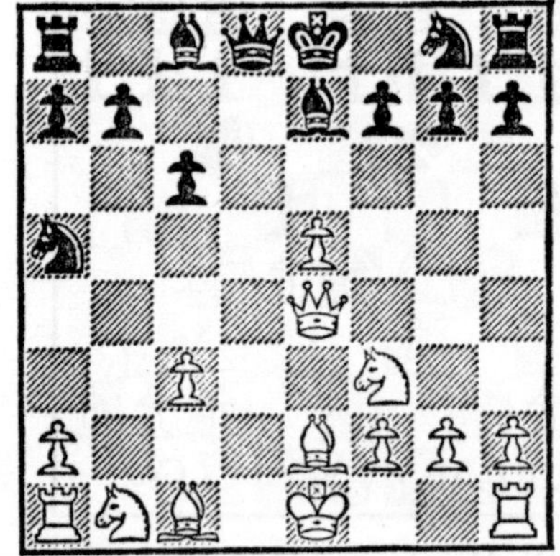

(343) Position after 10. Q × K P

White has the disadvantage of isolated Pawns on the Queen's Rook's and Queen's Bishop's files but enjoys more freedom of movement.

Variation D

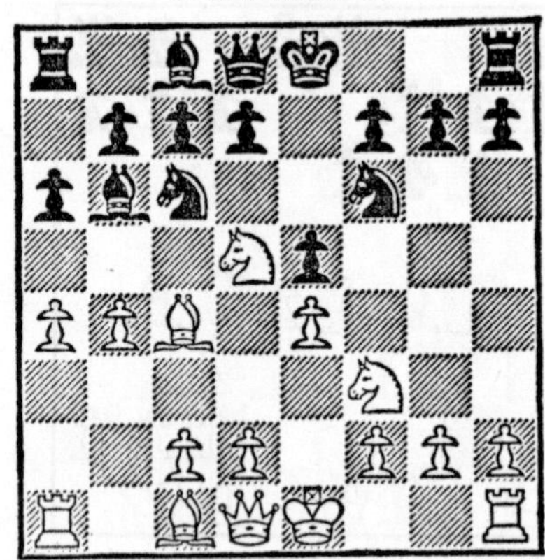

(344) Position after 7. Kt—Q 5

Black is slightly cramped, but with careful play has equal chances.

Illustrative Game, Vienna, 1862

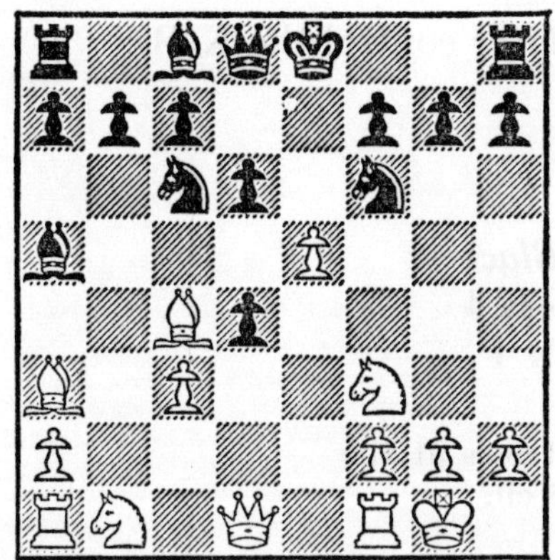

(345) Position after 9. P—K 5

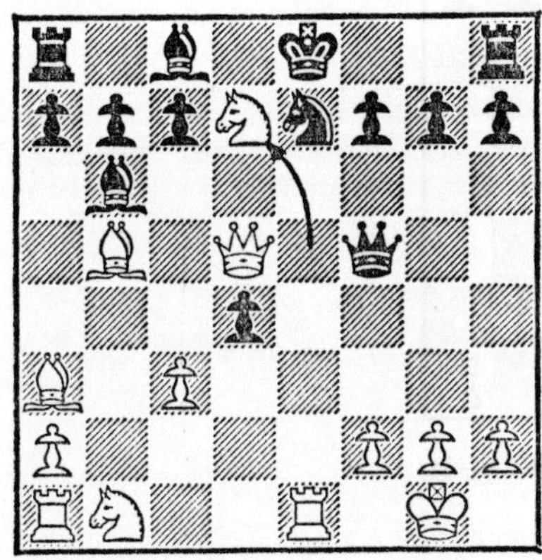

(346) Position after 15. Kt × Kt

STEINITZ *White*	PILHAL *Black*
1. P—K 4	P—K 4
2. Kt—K B 3	Kt—Q B 3
3. B—B 4	B—B 4
4. P—Q Kt 4	B × P
5. P—B 3	B—R 4
6. O—O	Kt—B 3
7. P—Q 4	P × P ?

This permits 8. B—R 3 and Black will find it difficult to castle. 7. . . . . O—O was correct.

8. B—R 3	P—Q 3
9. P—K 5	P × K P
10. Q—Kt 3	Q—Q 2
11. R—K 1	Q—B 4
12. B—Kt 5	

This is stronger than 12. B × P ch, for now White is threatening Kt × K P followed by Kt × Kt disc ch.

12. . . . . Kt—Q 2

Unpinning the Queen's Knight.

13. Q—Q 5	B—Kt 3
14. Kt × K P	Kt—K 2
15. Kt × Kt	

And having already given up two Pawns White now gives up his Queen.

15.	Q × Q
16. Kt—B 6 dble ch	K—Q 1
17. B × Kt mate	

Note that if 16. . . . . K—B 1, White still mates as shown.

KING'S GAMBIT

In this opening White offers up a Pawn for two reasons :

(*a*) to draw a Pawn away from Black's centre ;

(*b*) to attempt to open up and later control the K B file with Rook after O—O.

	White	*Black*
1.	P—K 4	P—K 4
2.	P—K B 4	P × P
3.	Kt—K B 3	

A sound early move. It strikes at the centre and stops ....Q—R 5 ch.

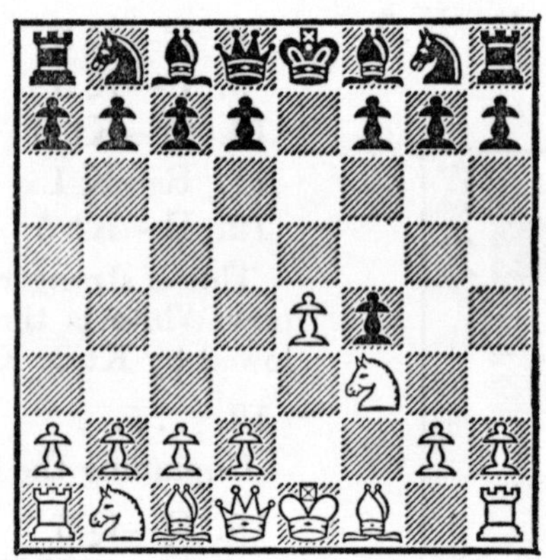

(347) Position after 3. Kt—K B 3

In giving up a Pawn, White strives at once to control the centre, having drawn Black's King's Pawn aside.

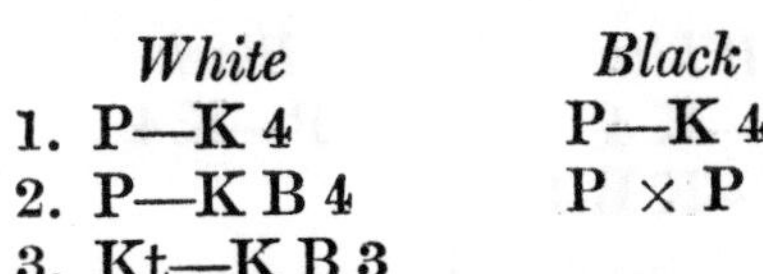

	White	*Black*
1.	P—K 4	P—K 4
2.	P—K B 4	P × P
3.	Kt—K B 3	

Variation A

3.	....	Kt—K B 3
4.	P—K 5	Kt—R 4
5.	P—Q 4	P—Q 4

Variation B

3.	....	P—Q 4
4.	P × P	Kt—K B 3
5.	Kt—B 3	Kt × P
6.	Kt × Kt	Q × Kt
7.	P—Q 4	

Variation A

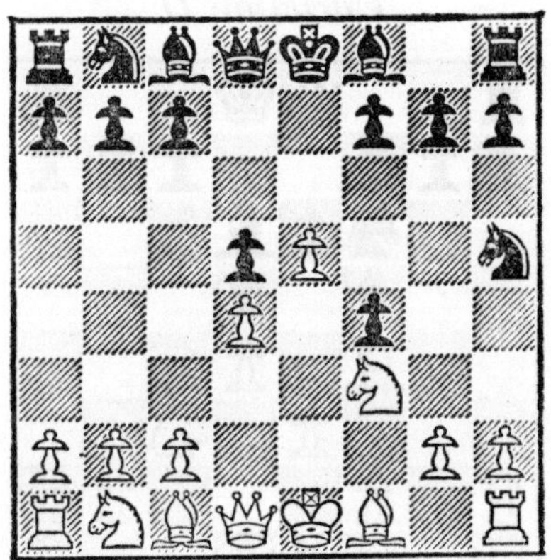

(348) Position after 5. . . . P—Q 4

Black has achieved a satisfactory position, and now gives protection to the Pawn on B 5 with the Knight at K R 4.

Variation B

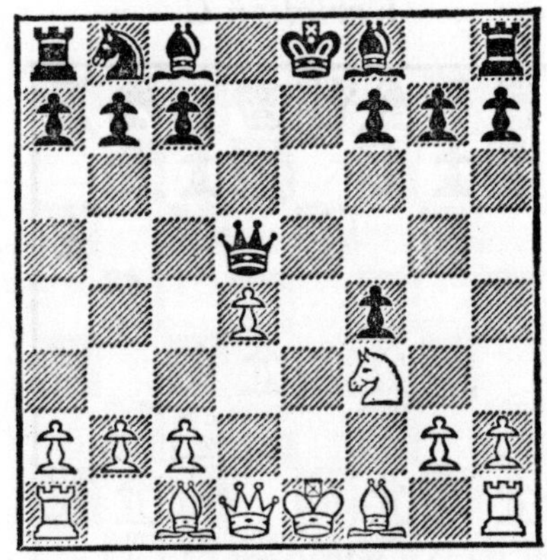

(349) Position after 7. P—Q 4

An example of the early emergence of the Queen. Although the position at this stage is equal, Black should ensure that the Queen is not used by White as a target when White's remaining undeveloped pieces are brought out, with a consequent gain in speed of development.

KING'S GAMBIT (*cont.*)

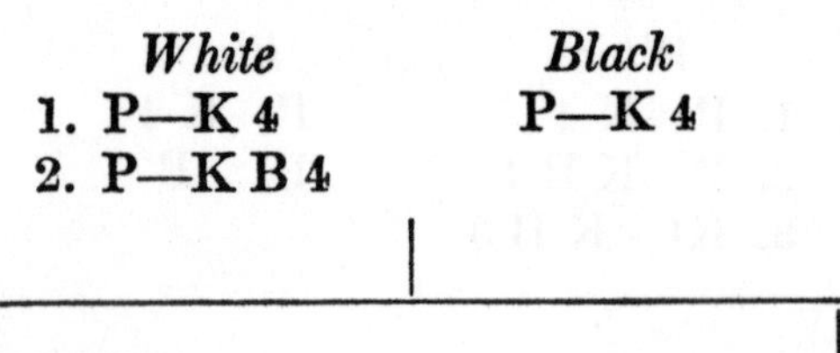

	White	*Black*
1.	P—K 4	P—K 4
2.	P—K B 4	

Variation C

2.		P × P
3.	Kt—K B 3	P—K Kt 4

And Black attempts to keep his Pawn advantage.

4.	B—B 4	B—Kt 2
5.	O—O	P—Q 3
6.	P—Q 4	P—K R 3

Variation D

King's Gambit Declined

2.		B—B 4
3.	Kt—K B 3	P—Q 3
4.	Kt—B 3	Kt—K B 3
5.	B—B 4	Kt—B 3
6.	P—Q 3	B—K 3

Variation C

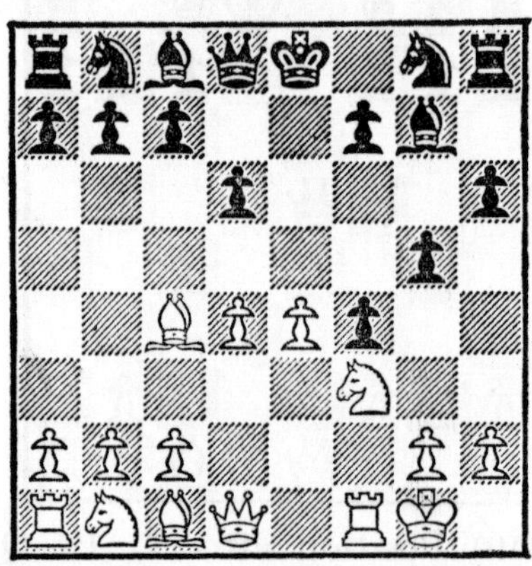

(350) Position after
6. . . . . P—K R 3

Black's King's side Pawn formation is obviously risky for him. White should seek to take advantage of the weakened Pawn formation, for Black's prospects become good once these Pawns take on the role of an attacking Pawn "roller."

Variation D

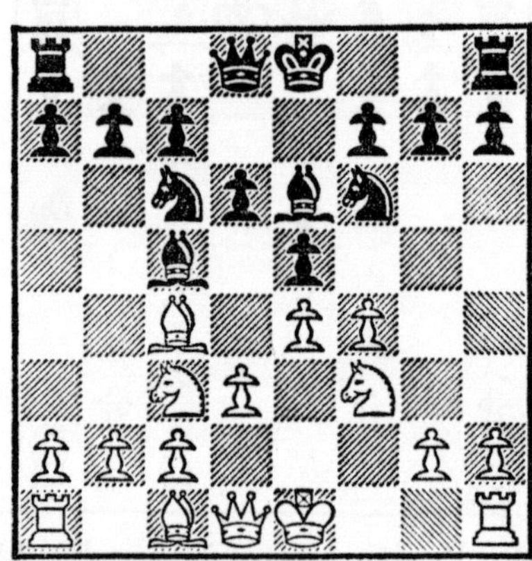

(351) Position after
6. . . . . B—K 3

White's two Pawns abreast at K 4 and K B 4 give White a very slight advantage.

Illustrative Game played by correspondence in 1949

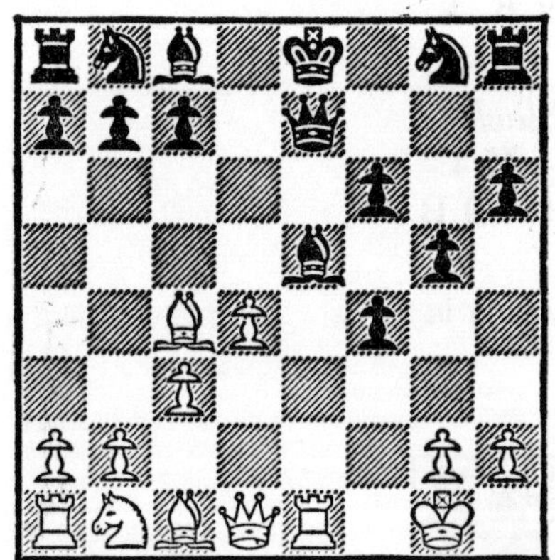

(352) Position after 10. . . . . P—K B 3

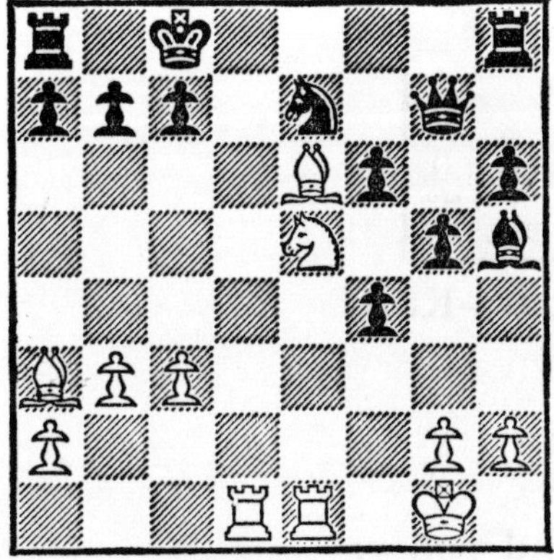

(353) Position after 19. B—K 6 ch

	AGUILERA *White*	CARLSSON *Black*
1.	P—K 4	P—K 4
2.	P—K B 4	P × P
3.	Kt—K B 3	P—K R 3
4.	B—B 4	P—K Kt 4
5.	P—Q 4	B—Kt 2
6.	P—B 3	Q—K 2
7.	O—O	P—Q 3
8.	P—K 5	P × P
9.	Kt × K P	B × Kt
10.	R—K 1	P—K B 3
11.	P—Q Kt 3	Kt—Q 2
12.	Q—R 5 ch	K—Q 1
13.	B—R 3	Q—Kt 2
14.	Kt—Q 2	Kt—K 2
15.	P × B	Kt × P
16.	Q R—Q 1	B—Kt 5

And White's Queen is now trapped.

17.	Kt—B 3 disc ch	K—B 1
18.	Kt × Kt	

White has no need to worry about his Queen for it is Black who is in trouble.

18.	. . . .	B × Q
19.	B—K 6 ch	Resigns

Black cannot stop mate. e.g. 19. . . . . K—Kt 1 ; 20. Kt—Q 7 ch, K—B 1 ; 21. Kt—B 8 disc ch, K—Kt 1 ; 22. R—Q 8 ch, Kt—B 1 ; 23. R × Kt mate.

This game shows that the attempt by Black to hold on to the Pawn advantage by . . . . P—K Kt 4 is not without its dangers, resulting as it does in a weakened King's position.

The basic plan is to make Black's counter play in the centre difficult for him by an early attack on the Knight which is defending Black's K 4.

White	*Black*
1. P—K 4	P—K 4
2. Kt—K B 3	Kt—Q B 3
3. B—Kt5	

Attacking the Knight which is protecting Black's K P.

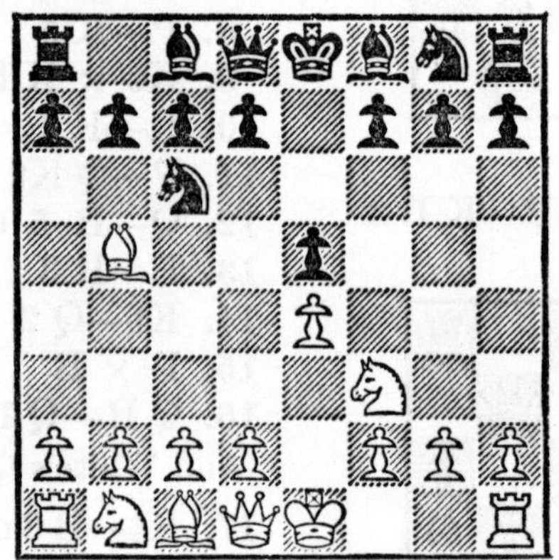

(354) Position after 3. B—Kt 5

Development by attack is a sound policy.
White's assault on the centre is both immediate and aggressive.

Variation A

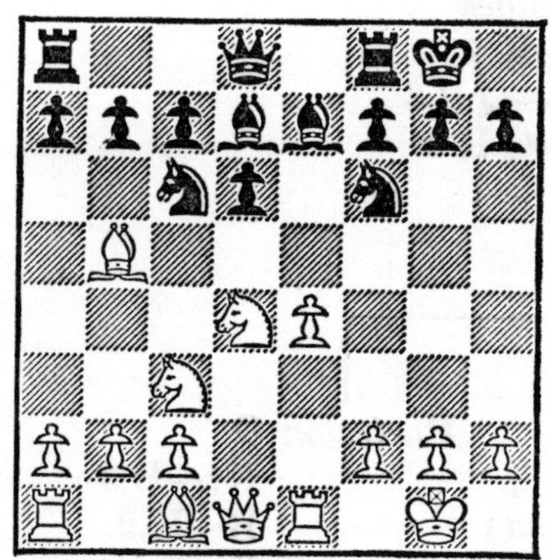

(355) Position after 8. ....O—O

	White	Black
1.	P—K 4	P—K 4
2.	Kt—K B 3	Kt—Q B 3
3.	B—Kt 5	

Variation A

3.	....	P—Q 3
4.	P—Q 4	B—Q 2
5.	Kt—B 3	Kt—B 3
6.	O—O	B—K 2
7.	R—K 1	P × P
8.	Kt × P	O—O

Variation B

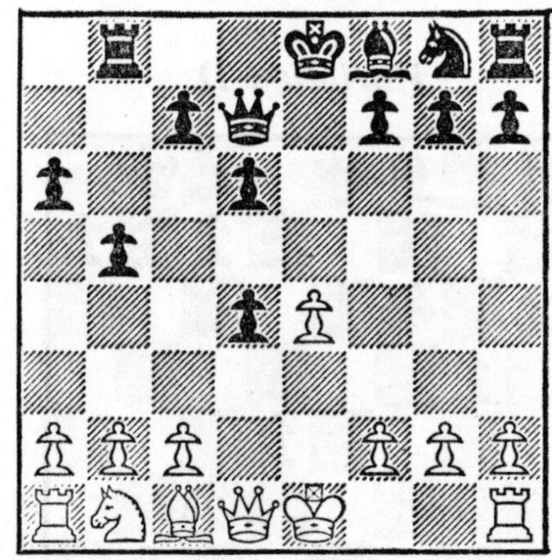

(356) Position after 10. ....Q × B

Variation B

3.	....	P—Q R 3
4.	B—R 4	P—Q 3
5.	P—Q 4	P—Q Kt 4
6.	B—Kt 3	Kt × P
7.	Kt × Kt	P × Kt
8.	B—Q 5	

Not 8. Q × P because of 8. ....P—Q B 4 attacking Queen, followed by ....P—B 5, and White's Bishop is trapped.

8.	....	R—Kt 1
9.	B—B 6 ch	B—Q 2
10.	B × B ch	Q × B

In variations with 3...... P—Q R 3 it might appear that, after 4. B × Kt, White may win the now unprotected King's Pawn with 5. Kt × P. However after 4. B × Kt, Q P×B; 5. Kt × P, Black replies 5..... Q—Q5 and both White's King's Pawn and Knight are threatened. Black then regains the Pawn with advantage in position.

	White	*Black*
1.	P—K 4	P—K 4
2.	Kt—K B 3	Kt—Q B 3
3.	B—Kt 5	P—Q R 3
4.	B—R 4	

Variation C

4.	....	Kt—B 3
5.	O—O	Kt × P
6.	P—Q 4	P—Q Kt 4
7.	B—Kt 3	P—Q 4
8.	P × P	B—K 3
9.	P—B 3	B—K 2

Variation D

4.	....	Kt—B 3
5.	O—O	B—K 2
6.	R—K 1	P—Q Kt 4
7.	B—Kt 3	P—Q 3
8.	P—B 3	O—O

Variation C *Variation D*

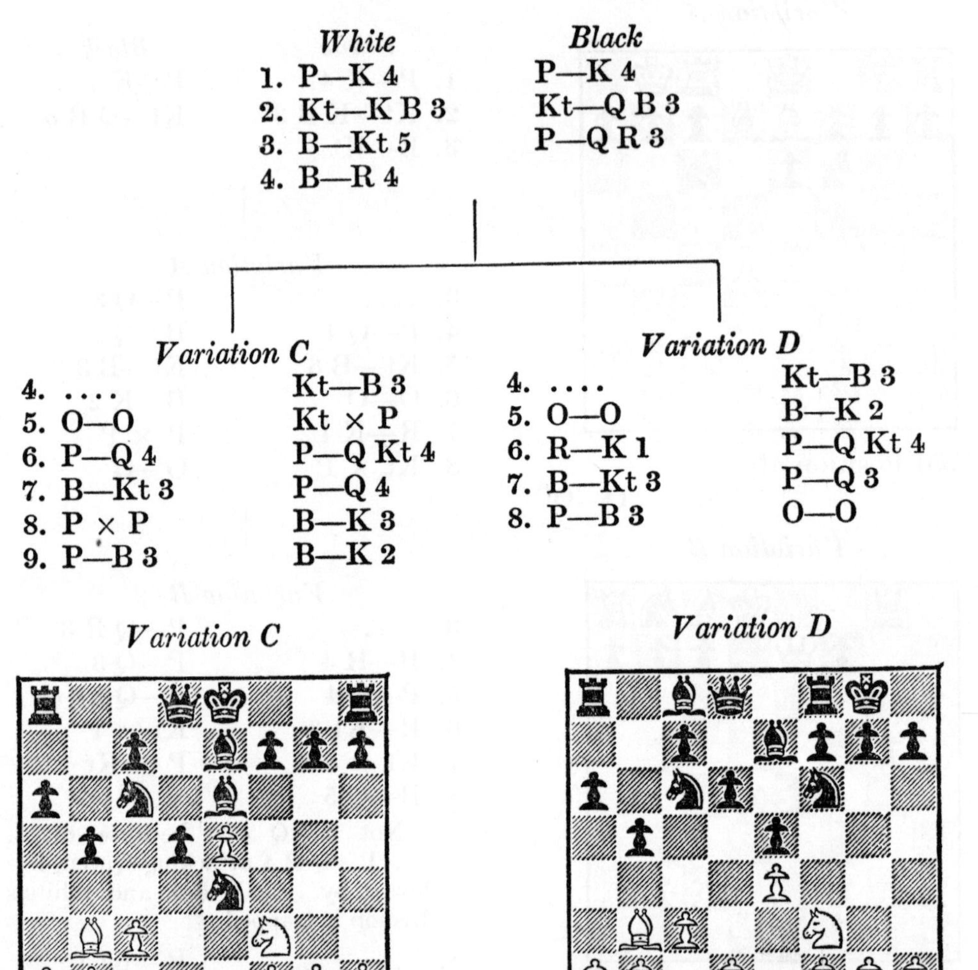

(357) Position after 9. ....B—K 2

(358) Position after 8. ....O—O

In variations B, C and D, Black has opportunities for a Queen's side counter-attack provided White's pressure in the centre can be held.

Illustrative Game, Margate, 1937

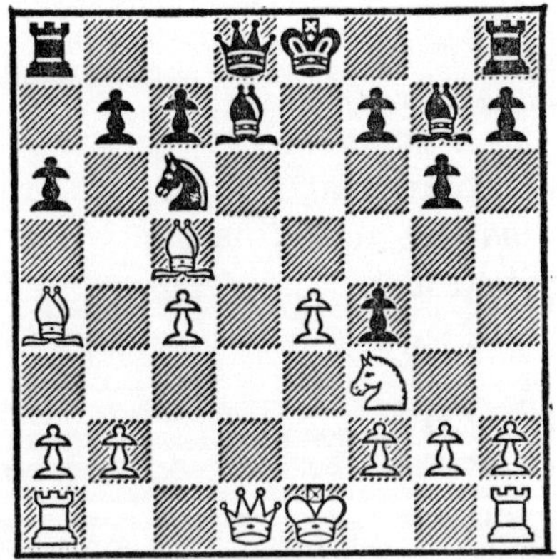

(359) Position after 12. ....P × Kt

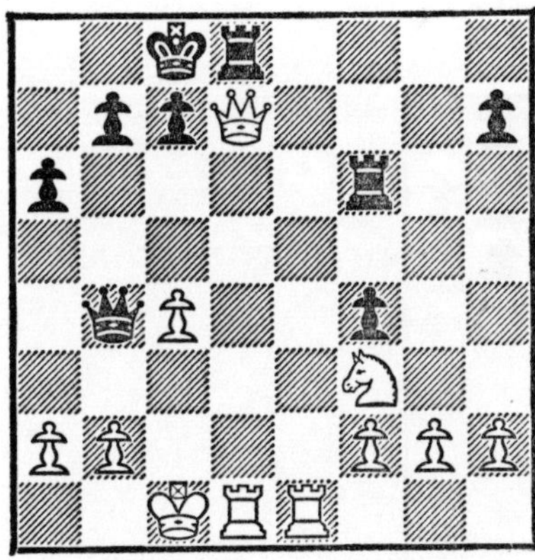

(360) Final position after 23. Q × B ch

	KERES *White*	ALEKHINE *Black*
1.	P—K 4	P—K 4
2.	Kt—K B 3	Kt—Q B 3
3.	B—Kt 5	P—Q R 3
4.	B—R 4	P—Q 3
5.	P—B 4	B—Q 2
6.	Kt—B 3	P—K Kt 3
7.	P—Q 4	B—Kt 2
8.	B—K 3	Kt—B 3
9.	P × P	P × P
10.	B—B 5	

Stopping Black from castling King's side.

10.	....	Kt—K R 4
11.	Kt—Q 5	Kt—B 5
12.	Kt × Kt	P × Kt
13.	P—K 5	P—K Kt 4
14.	Q—Q 5	B—K B 1
15.	B × B	R × B
16.	O—O—O	Q—K 2

Black wishes to castle Queen's side as well.

17.	B × Kt	B × B
18.	Q—Q 3	B—Q 2
19.	Kt × P	O—O—O

Not 19.....Q × Kt ? ? 20. Q × B mate !

20.	Kt—B 3	P—K B 3
21.	P × P	R × P
22.	K R—K 1	Q—Kt 5 ?
23.	Q × B ch !	Resigns

If 23. ....R × Q; 24. R—K 8 ch, R—Q 1; 25. R × R mate.

	White	*Black*
1.	P—K 4	P—Q B 4 challenging control of White's Q 4

The idea behind this defence is a counter-attack on the Queen's side using the Q B file as the main line of pressure. The Sicilian is well described as a " fighting defence ! "

2.	Kt—K B 3	Kt—Q B 3
3.	P—Q 4	P × P
4.	Kt × P	Kt—B 3

Black develops with attack.

5.	Kt—B 3	P—Q 3
6.	B—K 2	P—K Kt 3
7.	B—K 3	B—Kt 2
8.	O—O	O—O

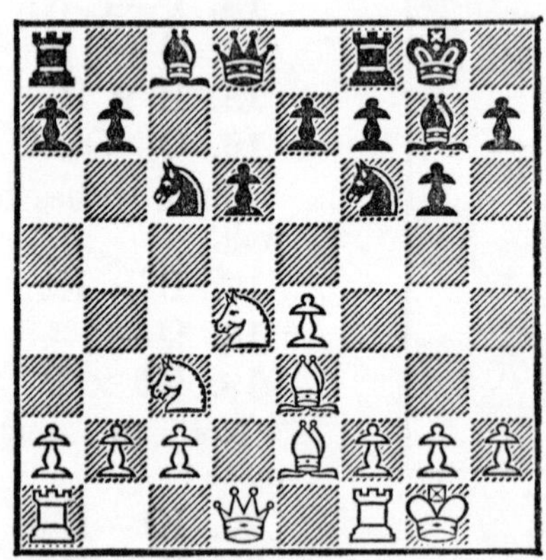

(361) Position after 8. . . . .O—O

White will try to maintain superiority in the centre in order to overcome Black's counter-attack on the Queen's side.

SICILIAN DEFENCE (*cont.*)

	White	*Black*
1.	P—K 4	P—Q B 4
2.	Kt—K B 3	Kt—Q B 3
3.	P—Q 4	P × P
4.	Kt × P	Kt—B 3
5.	Kt—B 3	P—Q 3
6.	B—K 2	P—K Kt 3
7.	B—K 3	B—Kt 2
8.	O—O	O—O

Variation A

9.	Kt—Kt 3	B—K 3
10.	P—B 4	Kt—Q R 4
11.	P—B 5	B—B 5
12.	Kt × Kt	B × B
13.	Q × B	Q × Kt

Variation B

9.	Q—Q 2	P—Q 4
10.	P × P	Kt × P
11.	Q Kt × Kt	Kt × Kt
12.	B—Q B 4	Kt—B 3

Variation A

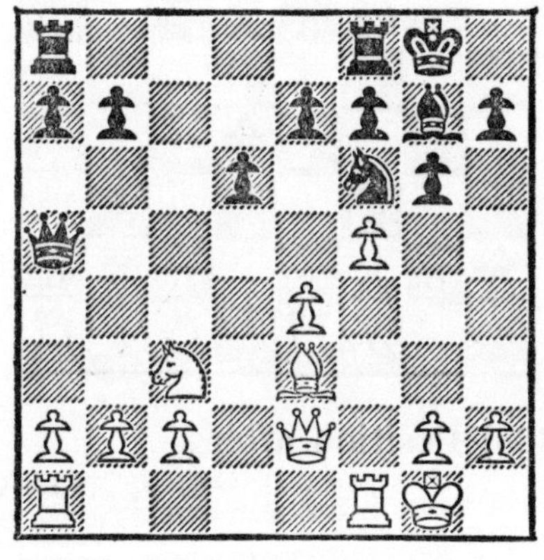

(362) Position after
13. . . . . Q × Kt

Both sides have attacking chances.

Variation B

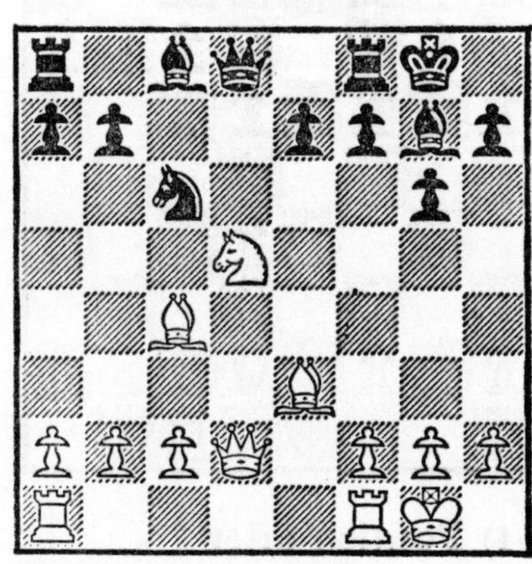

(363) Position after
12. . . . . Kt—B 3

With both White's centre Pawns gone, Black's Bishop on K Kt 2 exerts much pressure on its long diagonal, while White's minor pieces have taken up strong positions in the centre.

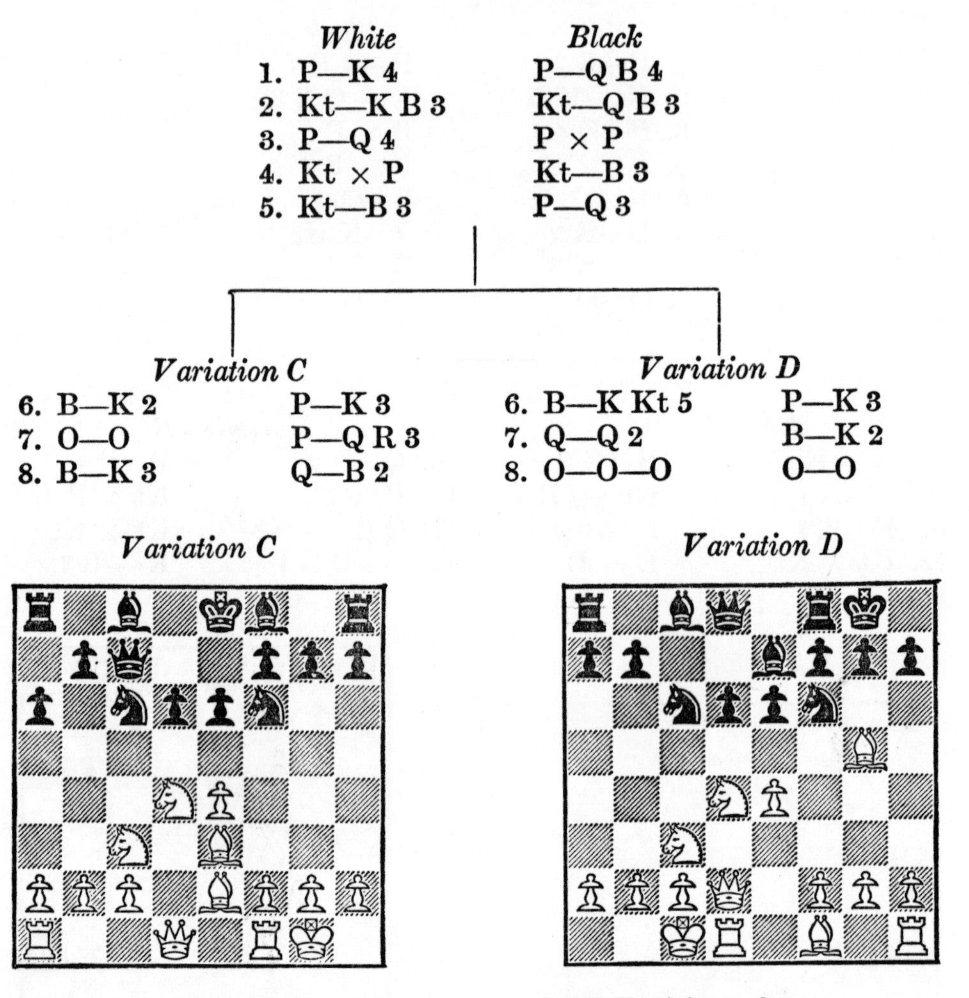

	White	*Black*
1.	P—K 4	P—Q B 4
2.	Kt—K B 3	Kt—Q B 3
3.	P—Q 4	P × P
4.	Kt × P	Kt—B 3
5.	Kt—B 3	P—Q 3

Variation C

6. B—K 2 — P—K 3
7. O—O — P—Q R 3
8. B—K 3 — Q—B 2

Variation D

6. B—K Kt 5 — P—K 3
7. Q—Q 2 — B—K 2
8. O—O—O — O—O

Variation C

(364) Position after 8. . . . . Q—B 2

Variation D

(365) Position after 8. . . . . O—O

In the above variations Black is content to submit to a cramped early development, but with the chances of ultimate freedom which the counter-attack on the Queen's side offers.

Illustrative Game, Aberystwyth, 1955

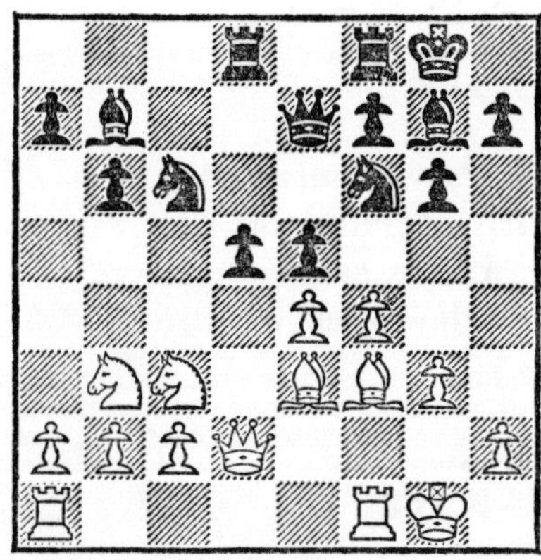

(366) Position after
13. ....P—Q 4

White's King's position has been weakened and Black opens up the centre in order to bring his pieces to bear upon the exposed King.

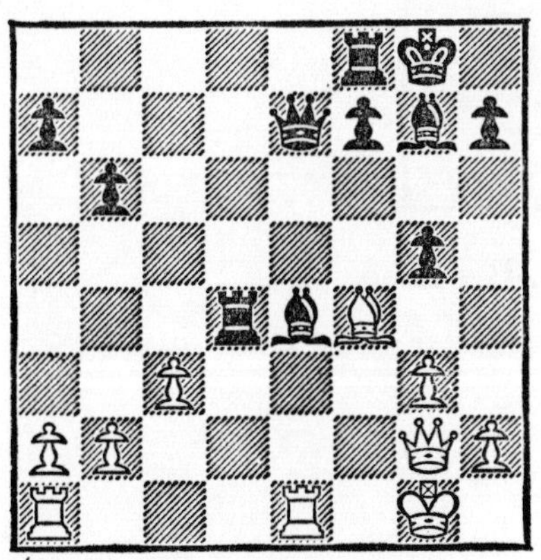

(367) Final position after
20. ....R × Kt

MILNER-BARRY *White*	WADE *Black*
1. P—K 4	P—Q B 4
2. Kt—K B 3	Kt—Q B 3
3. P—Q 4	P × P
4. Kt × P	P—K Kt 3
5. Kt—Q B 3	B—Kt 2
6. B—K 3	Kt—B 3
7. Kt—Kt 3	O—O
8. B—K 2	P—Kt 3
9. P—B 4	B—Kt 2
10. B—B 3	P—K 4
11. O—O	Q—K 2
12. P—Kt 3	Q R—Q 1
13. Q—Q 2	P—Q 4
14. Q—Kt 2	K P × P
15. B × B P	Kt—Q 5
16. Kt × Kt	P × P
17. Kt × P	Kt × Kt
18. P—B 3	P—K Kt 4
19. B × Kt	B × B
20. K R—K 1	R × Kt !
Resigns	

For if 21. P × R, B × P ch; and if White's King moves to B 1 or R 1 Black will be able to play ....B × Q with *check,* after which Black's Queen can be moved to safety.

	White	*Black*
1.	P—Q 4	P—Q 4
2.	P—Q B 4	

The gambit Pawn.

White's aim is eventually to create a Pawn centre with Pawns at Q 4 and K 4 coupled with pressure on the Queen's side using the Q B file. Here, as in most variations of the Queen's Gambit, the offer of the Gambit Pawn is declined.

2.	....	P—K 3
3.	Kt—Q B 3	Kt—K B 3
4.	B—Kt 5	

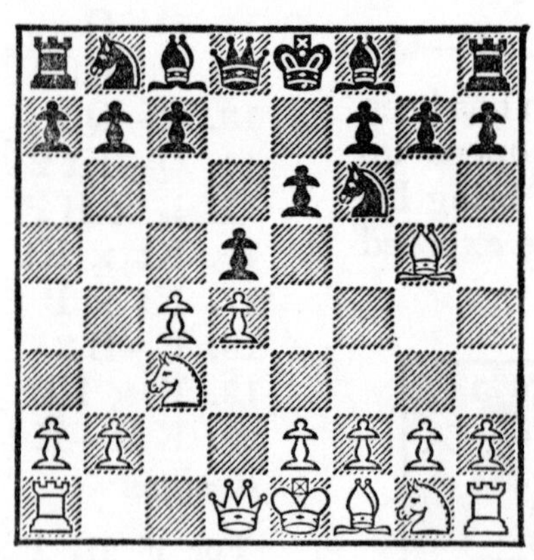

(368) Position after 4. B—Kt 5

	White	*Black*
1.	P—Q 4	P—Q 4
2.	P—Q B 4	P—K 3
3.	Kt—Q B 3	Kt—K B 3
4.	B—Kt 5	

Variation A

4.	....	B—K 2
5.	P—K 3	O—O
6.	Kt—B 3	Q Kt—Q 2
7.	R—B 1	P—B 3
8.	B—Q 3	

Variation B

4.	....	Q Kt—Q 2
5.	P—K 3	P—B 3
6.	Kt—B 3	Q—R 4
7.	B × Kt	Kt × B
8.	B—Q 3	

Variation A

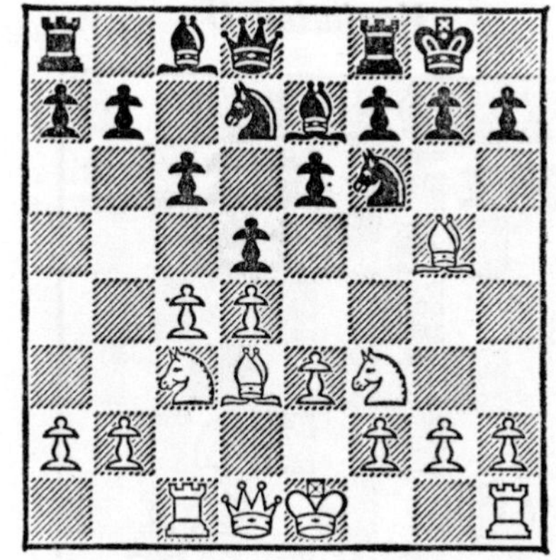

(369) Position after 8. B—Q 3

Variation B

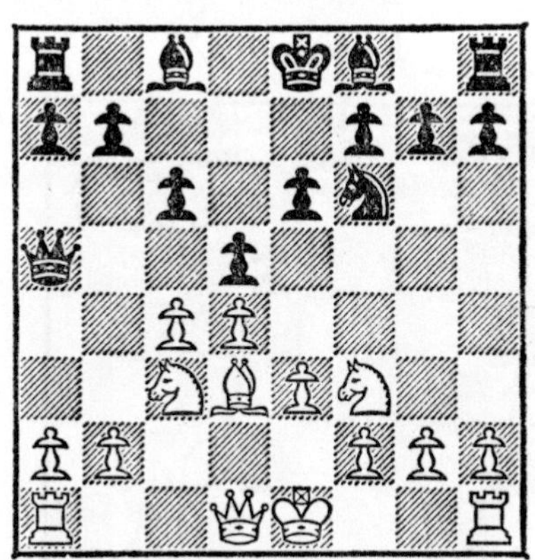

(370) Position after 8. B—Q 3

When the defence of the King's side makes a Knight at K B 3 desirable, it is often advisable to support it by playing the Queen's Knight to Q 2. If then the King's Knight is captured by White's Queen's Bishop, Black may recapture with the Queen's Knight and thus a Knight is maintained at Black's K B 3.

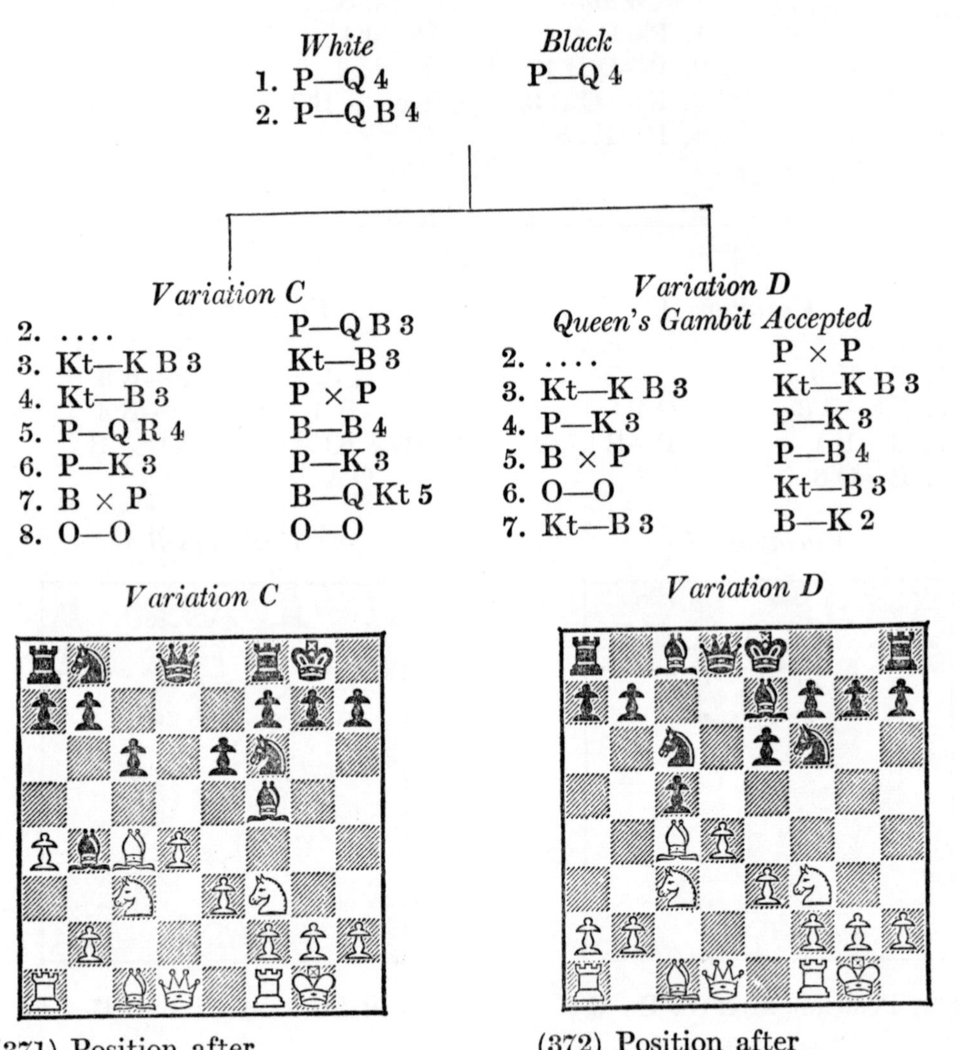

	White	*Black*
1.	P—Q 4	P—Q 4
2.	P—Q B 4	

Variation C

2.	....	P—Q B 3
3.	Kt—K B 3	Kt—B 3
4.	Kt—B 3	P × P
5.	P—Q R 4	B—B 4
6.	P—K 3	P—K 3
7.	B × P	B—Q Kt 5
8.	O—O	O—O

Variation D
Queen's Gambit Accepted

2.	....	P × P
3.	Kt—K B 3	Kt—K B 3
4.	P—K 3	P—K 3
5.	B × P	P—B 4
6.	O—O	Kt—B 3
7.	Kt—B 3	B—K 2

Variation C

(371) Position after 8. ....O—O

Variation D

(372) Position after 7. ....B—K 2

Although in the above variations White appears to have good prospects in the centre, Black may be comforted by the fact that the effective development of White's Queen's Bishop must be delayed.

QUEEN'S GAMBIT (*cont.*)

Illustrative Game played in Leningrad, 1951

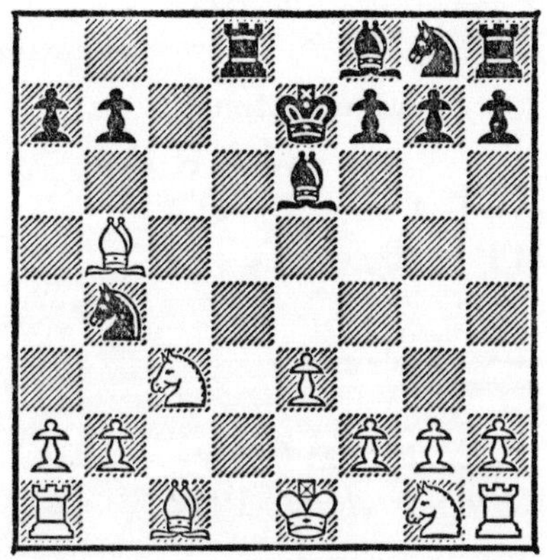

(373) Position after 10. . . . .K—K 2

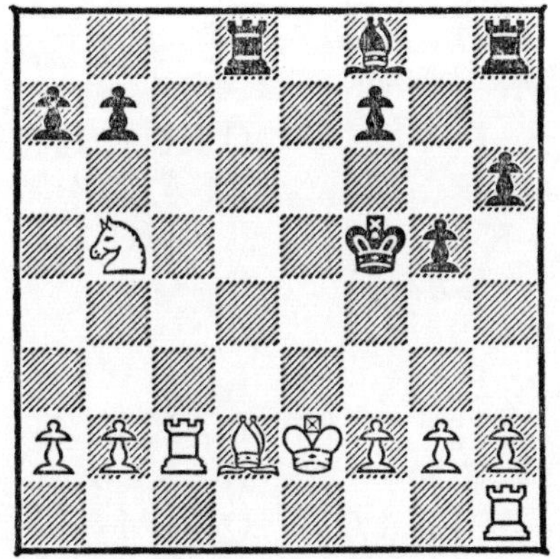

(374) Final position after 21. K—K 2

SMYSLOV *White*	ESTRIN *Black*
1. P—Q 4	P—Q 4
2. P—Q B 4	P—K 3
3. Kt—Q B 3	P—Q B 4
4. B P × P	B P × P
5. Q × P	Kt—Q B 3
6. Q—Q 1	

Of course not 6. P × Kt ? ? because of 6. . . . .Q × Q.

6.	P × P
7. Q × P	B—K 3
8. Q × Q ch	R × Q
9. P—K 3	Kt—Kt 5
10. B—Kt 5 ch	K—K 2
11. K—B 1	Kt—K B 3
12. Kt—B 3	Kt—B 7
13. R—Q Kt 1	B—B 4

threatening discovered attack against White's Queen's Rook.

14. B—Q 2	P—Kt 4
15. R—B 1	P—K R 3
16. P—K 4	Kt × P
17. R × Kt	Kt—Q 3
18. Kt—Q 4	

If now 18. . . . .B × R ; 19. Kt—Q 5 mate ! !

18.	Kt × B
19. Kt × B ch	K—B 3
20. Kt × Kt	K × Kt
21. K—K 2	

and Black resigned as he is a piece down with no chance of holding out for long.

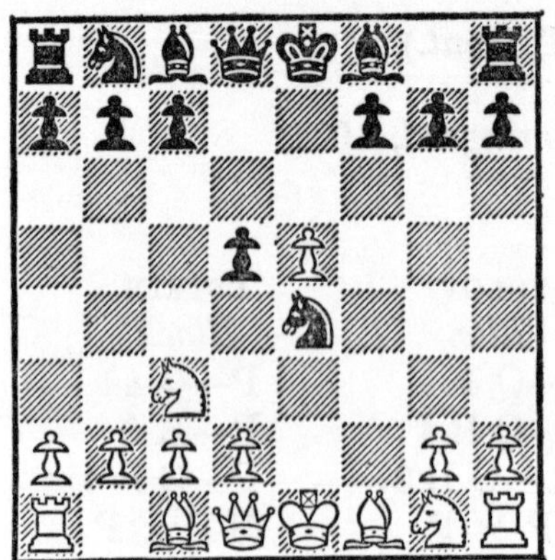

(375) Position after 4. ....Kt × P

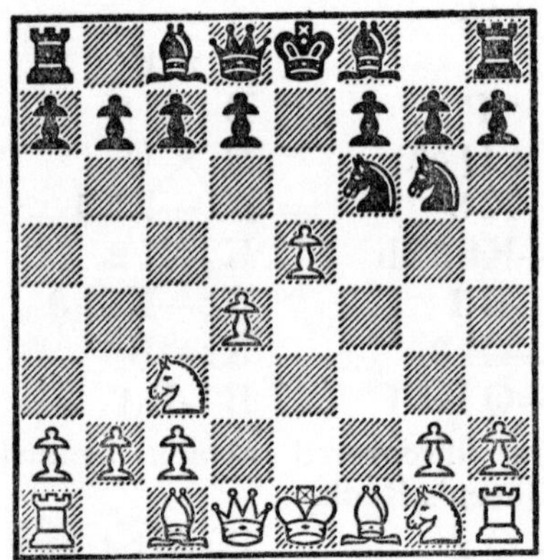

(376) Position after 6. P—K 5

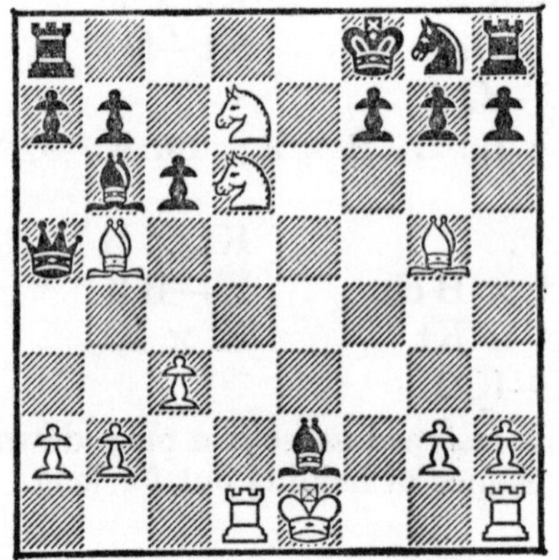

(377) Final position

VIENNA GAME

White starts a King's side attack with pressure down the King's Bishop file.

	White	*Black*
1.	P—K 4	P—K 4
2.	Kt—Q B 3	

A variation continues

2.	....	Kt—K B 3
3.	P—B 4	P—Q 4
4.	B P × P	Kt × P

Illustrative Game,
Buenos Aires, 1942

	NAJDORF *White*	A. N. OTHER *Black*
1.	P—K 4	P—K 4
2.	Kt—Q B 3	Kt—K B 3
3.	P—B 4	Kt—B 3 ?

correct is 3. ....P—Q 4

4.	P × P	Q Kt × P
5.	P—Q 4	Kt—Kt 3
6.	P—K 5	Kt—Kt 1
7.	Kt—B 3	P—Q 3
8.	B—Q 3	P × P
9.	P × P	B—Q B 4
10.	Q—K 2	B—K Kt 5
11.	Kt—K 4	B—Kt 3
12.	B—K Kt 5	Q—Q 4
13.	R—Q 1	Q—R 4 ch
14.	P—B 3	Kt × P
15.	B—Kt 5 ch	K—B 1
16.	Kt × Kt	B × Q
17.	Kt—Q 7 ch	K—K 1
18.	Kt—Kt 8 disc ch	P—B 3
19.	Kt—Q 6 ch	K—B 1
20.	Kt—Q 7 mate	

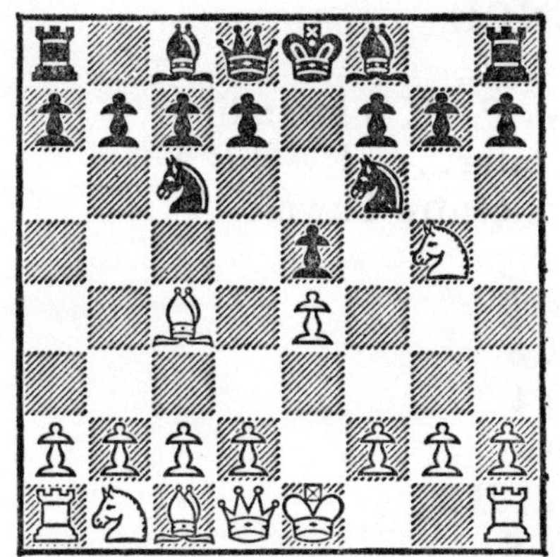

(378) Position after 4. Kt—Kt 5

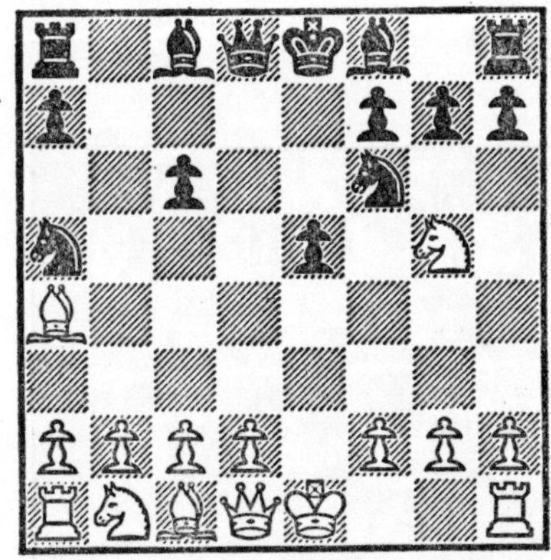

(379) Position after 8. B—R 4

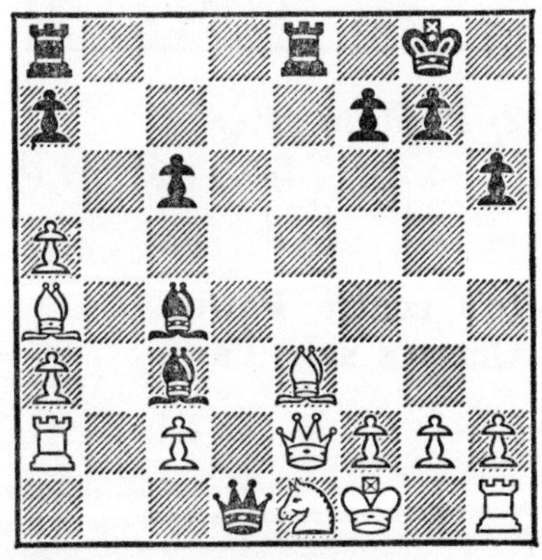

(380) Final position

TWO KNIGHTS' DEFENCE

	White	*Black*
1.	P—K 4	P—K 4
2.	Kt—K B 3	Kt—Q B 3
3.	B—B 4	Kt—B 3

these moves constitute the Two Knights' Defence.

4. Kt—Kt 5

The most common reply.

4.	....	P—Q 4
5.	P × P	Kt—Q R 4
6.	P—Q 3	P—K R 3
7.	Kt—K B 3	

Illustrative Game, Margate, 1935

	LEAN *White*	MISS GRAF *Black*
1.	P—K 4	P—K 4
2.	Kt—K B 3	Kt—Q B 3
3.	B—B 4	Kt—B 3
4.	Kt—Kt 5	P—Q 4
5.	P × P	Kt—Q R 4
6.	B—Kt 5 ch	P—B 3
7.	P × P	P × P
8.	B—R 4	P—K R 3
9.	Kt—K B 3	P—K 5
10.	Q—K 2	B—Q 3
11.	P—Q 3	O—O
12.	P × P	Kt × P
13.	B—K 3	B—K Kt 5
14.	P—Q R 3	R—K 1
15.	P—Kt 4	B—K 4
16.	R—R 2	Kt—B 6
17.	Kt × Kt	B × Kt ch
18.	K—B 1	B—K 3
19.	P × Kt	B—B 5
20.	Kt—K 1 Resigns	Q—Q 8

If 21. Q × B, Q × Kt mate!

FRENCH DEFENCE

After White 1. P—K 4, Black plays P—K 3 intending to follow up with ....P—Q 4 and later.... P—Q B 4 with a view to breaking up White's centre Pawns.

	White	*Black*
1.	P—K 4	P—K 3
2.	P—Q 4	P—Q 4
	A variation	continues
3.	Kt—Q B 3	Kt—K B 3
4.	B—K Kt 5	B—K 2
5.	P—K 5	K Kt—Q 2
6.	B × B	Q × B
7.	Q—Q 2	O—O
8.	P—B 4	P—Q B 4

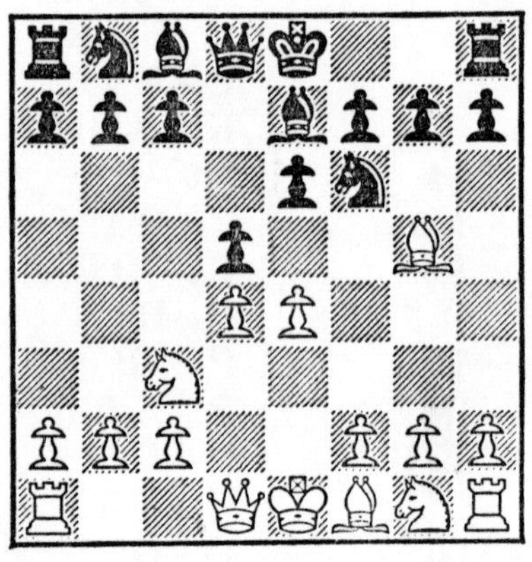

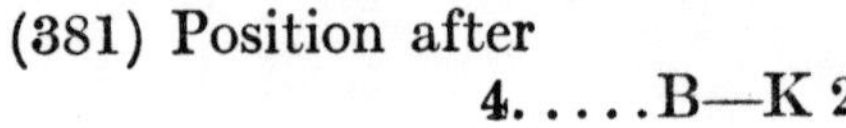

(381) Position after 4. ....B—K 2

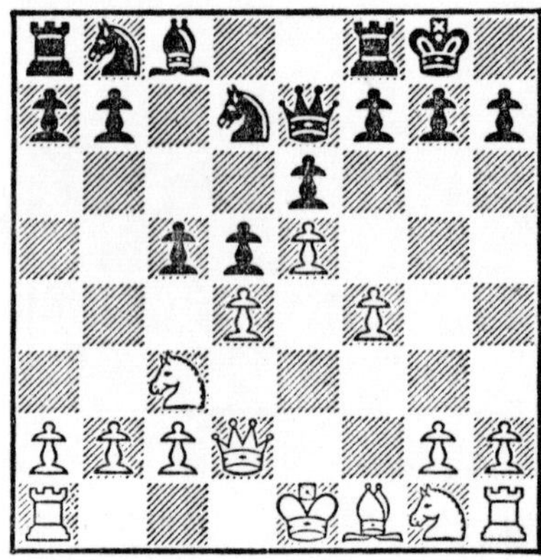

(382) Position after 8. ....P—Q B 4

If successful in breaking up White's centre Pawns, Black is well placed to launch a Queen's side Pawn attack.

QUEEN'S PAWN

In the following variation both sides follow correct principles of development and there are equal chances.

	White	*Black*
1.	P—Q 4	P—Q 4
2.	P—K 3	Kt—K B 3
3.	B—Q 3	P—B 4
4.	P—Q B 3	Q Kt—Q 2
5.	P—K B 4	P—K Kt 3
6.	Kt—B 3	B—Kt 2
7.	O—O	O—O

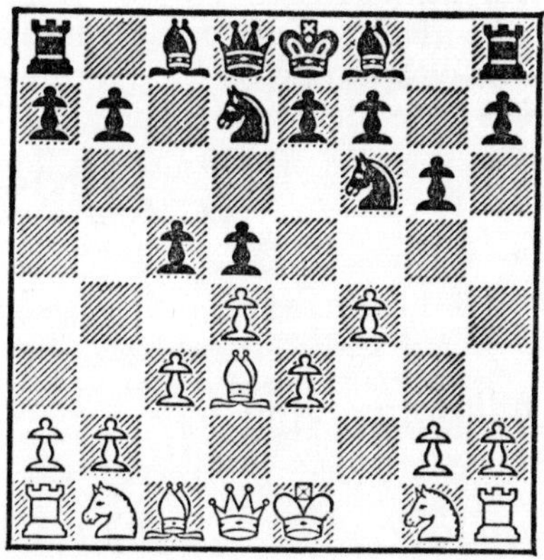

383) Position after 5. . . . . P—K Kt 3

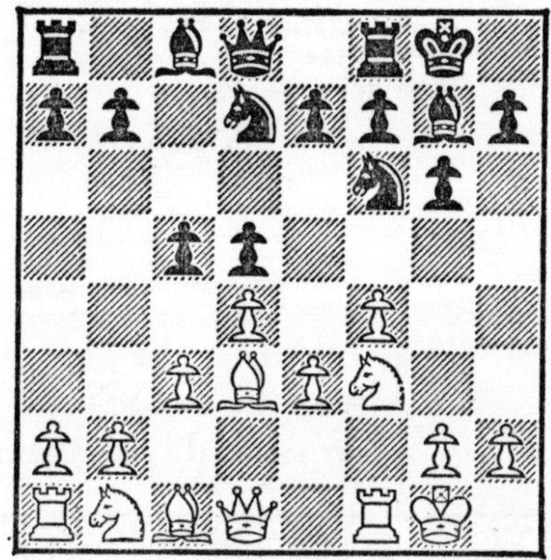

(384) Position after 7. . . . . O—O

FOUR KNIGHTS' GAME

Although not an aggressive opening it follows sound principles of rapid development on both sides.

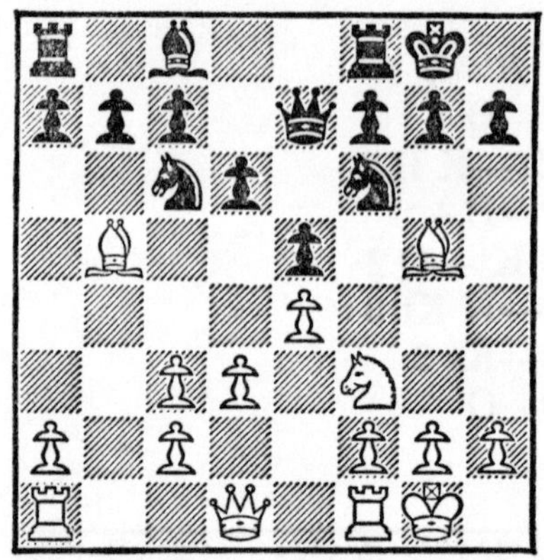

(385) Position after 8. . . . . Q—K 2

	White	*Black*
1.	P—K 4	P—K 4
2.	Kt—K B 3	Kt—Q B 3
3.	Kt—B 3	Kt—B 3
4.	B—Kt 5	B—Kt 5
5.	O—O	O—O
6.	P—Q 3	P—Q 3
7.	B—Kt 5	B × Kt

This is to stop White from playing Kt—Q 5 doubly attacking the pinned King's Knight, for if after Kt—Q 5 White follows up with B × K Kt or Kt × Kt ch Black must recapture with the Pawn and the King's side defence is dangerously weakened.

8. P × B Q—K 2

SCOTCH GAME

A violent attack on the centre following rapid and aggressive development.

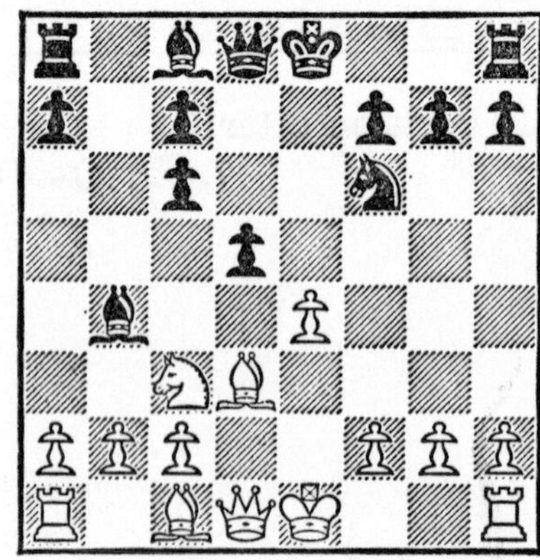

(386) Position after 7. . . . . P—Q 4

	White	*Black*
1.	P—K 4	P—K 4
2.	Kt—K B 3	Kt—Q B 3
3.	P—Q 4	P × P

Not 3. . . . . P—Q 3 ? otherwise we have 4. P × P, Kt × P ; 5. Kt × Kt, P × Kt ; 6. Q × Q ch, K × Q and Black cannot castle.

4.	Kt × P	Kt—B 3
5.	Kt—Q B 3	B—Kt 5
6.	Kt × Kt	Kt P × Kt

Not 6. . . . . Q P × Kt or White plays 7. Q × Q ch, K × Q.

7. B—Q 3 P—Q 4

KING'S INDIAN DEFENCE

In this opening, after White's 1. P—Q 4 Black replies 1. . . . Kt—K B 3 preventing 2. P—K 4.

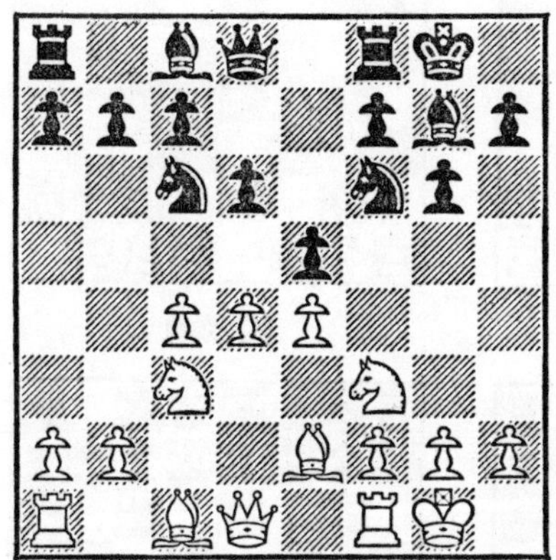

(387) Position after
7. . . . . Kt—B 3

White	Black
1. P—Q 4	Kt—K B 3
2. P—Q B 4	P—K Kt 3
3. Kt—Q B 3	B—Kt 2
4. P—K 4	P—Q 3
5. Kt—B 3	O—O
6. B—K 2	P—K 4
7. O—O	Kt—B 3

GRUNFELD DEFENCE

This opening is related to the King's Indian Defence. In the Grunfeld, Black challenges in the centre on the third move by . . . . P—Q 4.

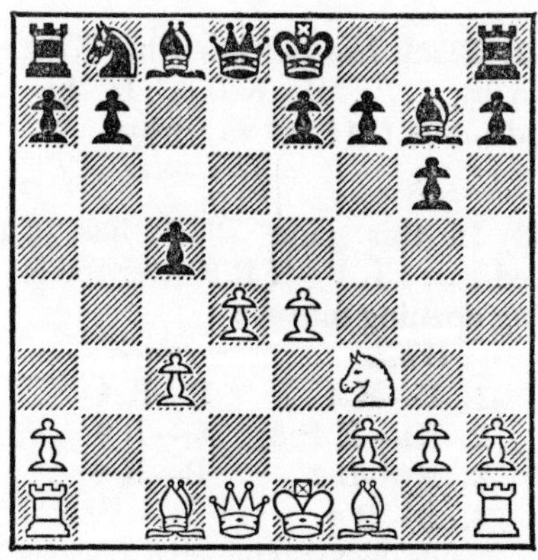

(388) Position after
7. . . . . B—Kt 2

White	Black
1. P—Q 4	Kt—K B 3
2. P—Q B 4	P—K Kt 3
3. Kt—Q B 3	P—Q 4
4. P × P	Kt × P
5. P—K 4	Kt × Kt
6. P × Kt	P—Q B 4
7. Kt—B 3	B—Kt 2

QUIZ ON "OPENING PLAY"

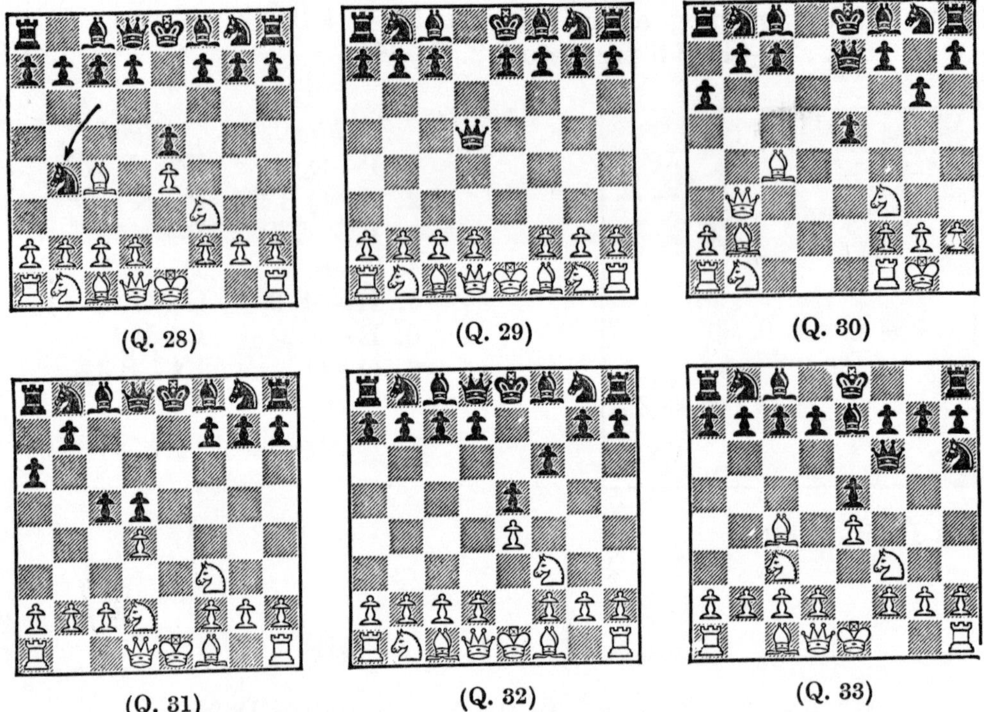

(Q. 28) (Q. 29) (Q. 30)

(Q. 31) (Q. 32) (Q. 33)

(Q.28) Black has just played .... Kt—Kt 5. This is a bad move for it breaks the principle of rapid development. Suggest a good move for White.

(Q.29) This position is reached after

	White	*Black*
1.	P—K 4	P—Q 4
2.	P × P	Q × P

Give White's best reply and give your reason.

(Q.30) White to play.
Black is three Pawns up. Who stands the better and say why?

(Q.31) White to play.
Suggest a good Pawn move.

(Q.32) Black has defended his King's Pawn by ......P—K B 3. Is this a sound move? If not say why.

(Q.33) In this game Black has just played .... K t—K R 3 after the following opening moves:

	White	*Black*
1.	P—K 4	P—K 4
2.	Kt—K B 3	Q—B 3
3.	Kt—B 3	B—K 2
4.	B—B 4	

Who stands better and give reasons?

Answers to Quiz on "Opening Play" on page, 194-5.

Exchanges and Sacrifices

1. EXCHANGES

DURING the course of a game many pieces will be captured. In some cases a player will be faced with little or no choice but to exchange pieces if he is to maintain or improve his position. But frequently positions occur where a player has to decide whether to create situations where exchanges can take place so that he can gain advantage.

Here are some reasons for exchanging pieces

(*a*) To gain in tempo or pressure.

(*b*) To remove an active enemy piece.

(*c*) To increase the ratio of forces.

(*d*) To destroy a defender.

(*e*) To create an open file.

(*f*) To break a Pawn centre.

(*a*) GAINING TEMPO

In the following position Black and White are disputing control of the open Queen's file.

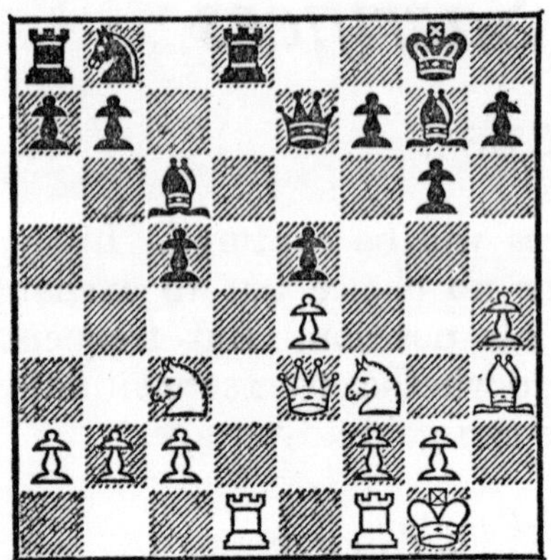

(389) Position before
1. R × R ch

It is White's turn to move and by means of exchanging off a Rook he is able to establish his other Rook in a much more active role.

1. R × R ch Q × R
2. R—Q 1

and now Black's Queen's best move is to vacate the open file leaving White with command of it.

Let us assume Black plays 2. . . . Q—K 2 in order to protect the Q B Pawn which is attacked by White's Queen.

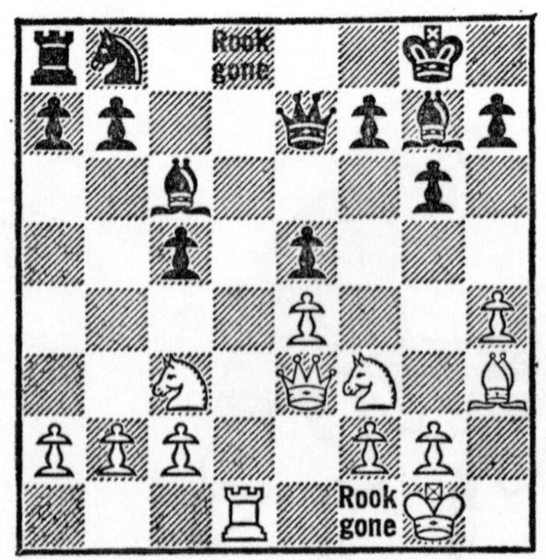

(390) After 2. . . . Q—K 2

We would then have the position as shown in diagram 390, which is similar to the first position but with the Black Rook on Q 1 and White Rook on K B 1 removed. Clearly White has exchanged a passive Rook for an active one—a positional gain.

Let us now consider a simple example where the use of an exchange provides such a gain in time that a win immediately results.

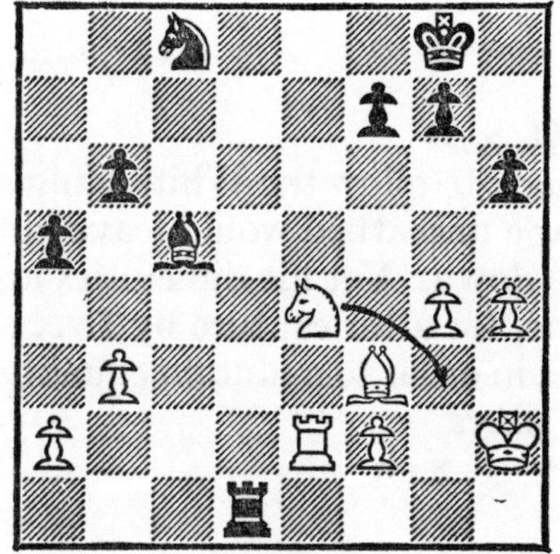

(391) White plays 1. Kt—Kt 3

White to play.
This position shows equal material, yet White would be able to win material if the King's file were clear for the action of his Rook, i.e. R—K 8 ch followed by R × Kt. But his own Knight is in the way on K 4. If he were to move it away, say to Kt 3, Black has time to deal with the threat and would play ....Kt—Q 3.

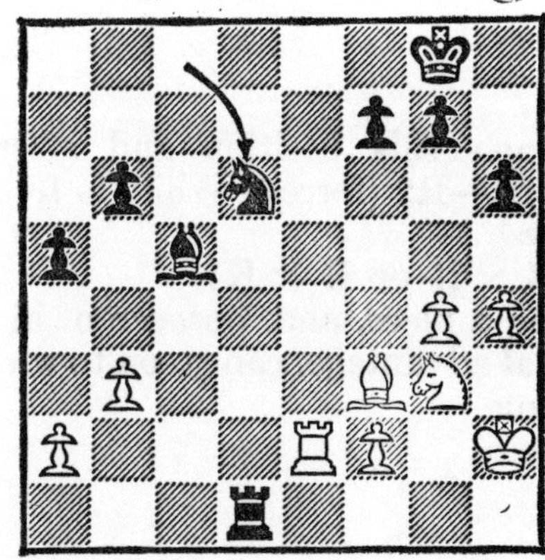

(392) Black plays
1. ....Kt—Q 3

We would then have this position and clearly White's threat no longer exists.

White is able to deny Black time to deal with the threat, however!

We return to the original position

In this example more violent methods are successful.

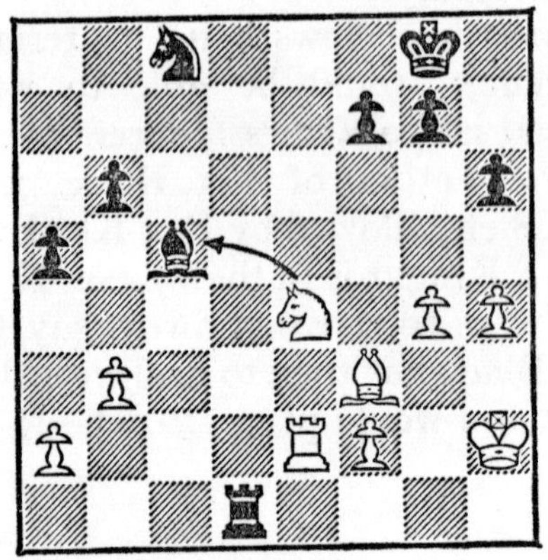

(393) 1. Kt × B !

1. Kt × B
For Black to allow the White Knight to escape unscathed would leave him a piece down. Yet his difficulties are extreme, for after capture by 1. .... P × Kt in order to maintain equality, White plays
2. R—K 8 ch

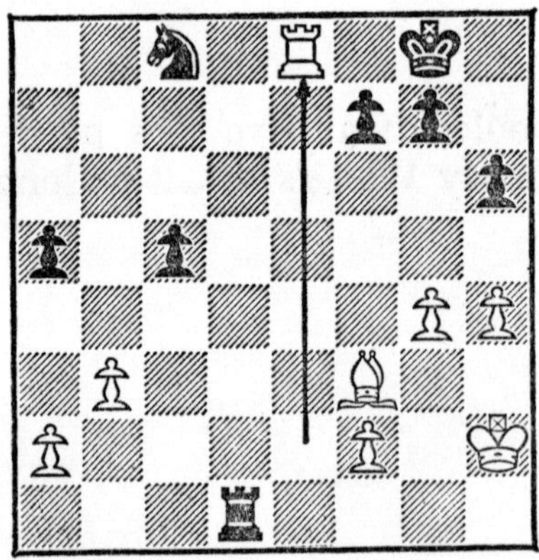

(394) Position after
2. R—K 8 ch

We reach this position and after 2. . . .K—R2 (forced) White is free to play
3. B × R or R × Kt
winning a piece, and, because of his material advantage, can go on to win the game.

The lesson we learn from this simple manœuvre is that in recapturing Black *lost time*, or to put it another way, White *gained a tempo*.

(*b*) REMOVING AN ACTIVE ENEMY PIECE

In the position shown in diagram **395** it is White to play. We see that White has a number of serious threats to face. Most immediate is Black's .... Q—Kt 8 mate. If White plays **1.** Kt—K 2 covering the mating square, he loses drastically, for this move gives Black fatal use of White's Q 1. **1.**....R—Q 8 ch and White is left with the dismal prospect of interposing Queen and Knight only delaying the inevitable mate on Black's K Kt 8.

The spearhead of this violent attack by Black is the Black Queen. Fortunately, White has one resource which blunts Black's offensive and gives White valuable breathing space in which to repair his defences.

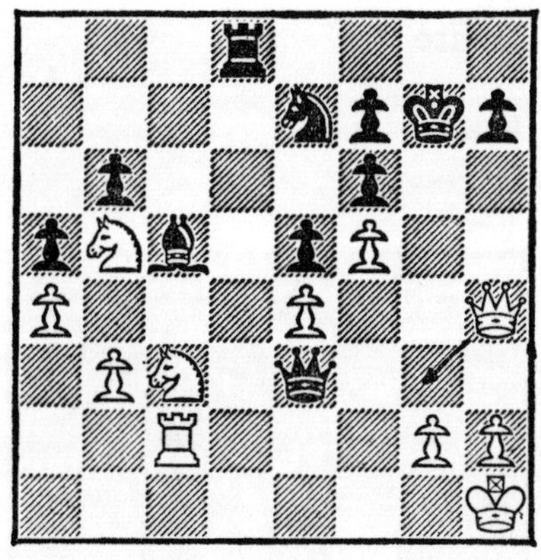

(395) Position before
1. Q—Kt 3 ch

1. Q—Kt 3 ch !

This move gives White the opportunity of exchanging Queens. Black has three reasonable choices :

(*a*) to move the King (to B 1, R 1 or R 3)

(*b*) interpose Queen on Kt 4

(*c*) exchange Queens.

Whichever choice Black adopts, White has averted the immediate dangers and is given chances to fight back.

Here are the resulting three positions that occur after each of Black's possible choices.

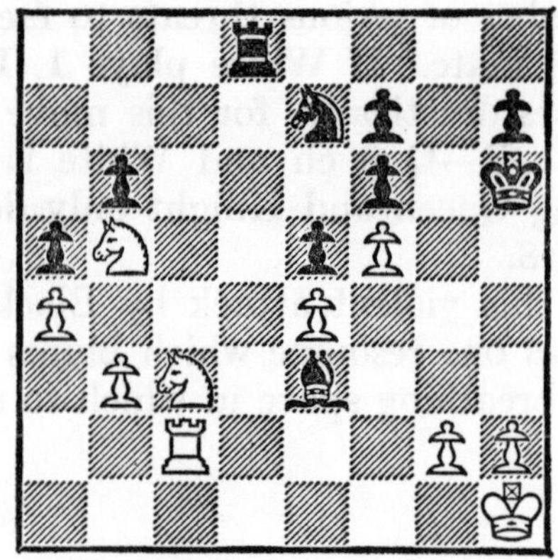

(396) Position with White to play after
1. Q—Kt 3 ch K—R 3
2. Q × Q ch B × Q

(397) Position with White to play after
1. Q—Kt 3 ch Q—Kt 4
2. Q × Q ch P × Q

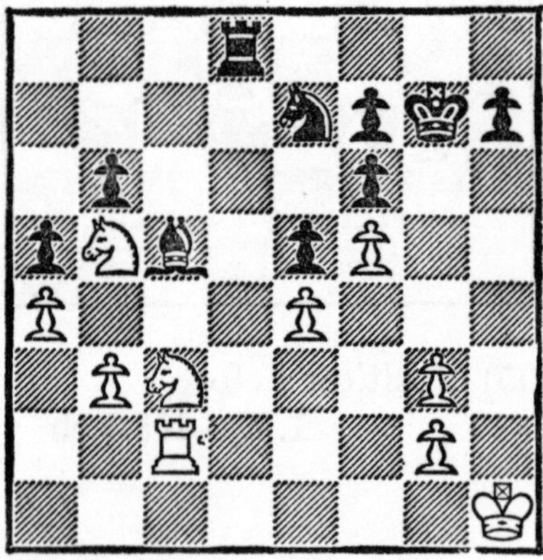

(398) Position with Black to play after
1. Q—Kt 3 ch Q × Q
2. P × Q

A trio of saved situations thanks to exchanging off Black's active Queen.

Here is another example

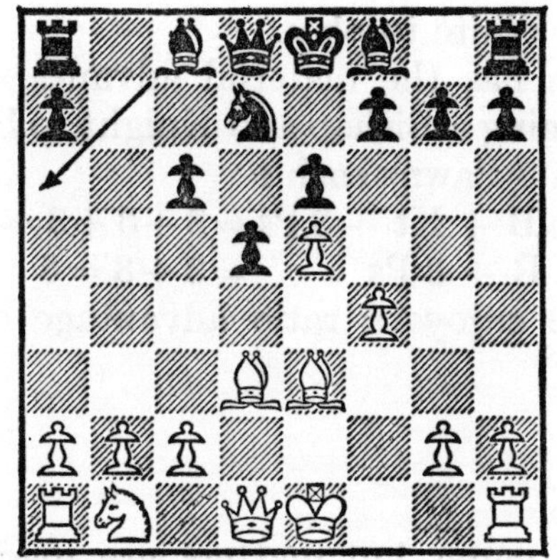

Black to play.
Black's Queen's Bishop is going to find it difficult to become active with his central Pawns all on White squares restricting its movement. By contrast White's King's Bishop is well established in a central position. Black therefore plays

1. . . . . B—R 3

(399) Position before
1. . . . . B—R 3

White cannot safely move the Bishop on Q 3 off the diagonal, and the move 2. P—B 4 just gives up a Pawn. If White decides on any other move then Black simply plays 2. . . . . B × B and the exchange is achieved.

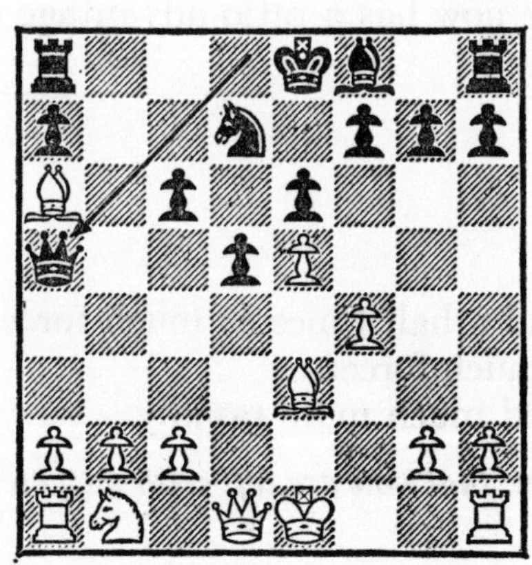

If White plays
2. B × B
Black replies with
2. . . . . Q—R 4 ch
The Black Queen attacks King and Bishop simultaneously and the Bishop goes. Black exchanges a Bishop with poor prospects, for an active one.

(400) After 2. . . . . Q—R 4 ch

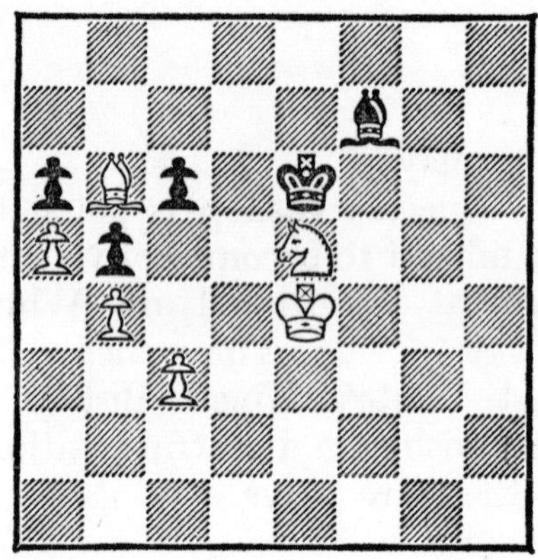

(401) White to play.
White has the material advantage. Assuming a Bishop and Knight to be worth 3 Pawns each:
White B + Kt + 3 Ps = 3 + 3 + 3 = 9
Black B + 3 Ps = 3 + 3 = 6
White enjoys a ratio advantage of 9 : 6

Certainly White should win this end game, but matters are made simple by an exchange of material.

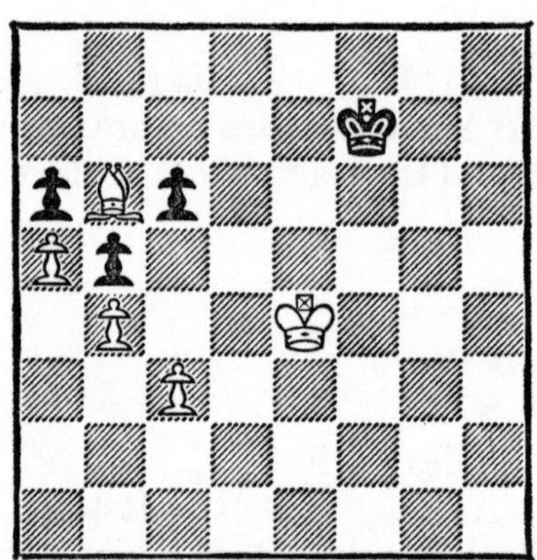

(402) 1. Kt × B K × Kt
Now the material is as follows:
White B + 3 Ps = 6
Black 3 Ps = 3
White now has a ratio advantage of 6 : 3

Before the exchange White had one and a half times as much force.
After exchanging, White has twice as much force.
The end game should now be concluded much more rapidly.

In such exchanges you must always ensure that you are left with sufficient material with which to checkmate!

In this particular example White will eventually be able to queen a Pawn with little difficulty.

(*d*) DESTROYING A DEFENDER

In this position Black and White have equal material. Both sides have the problem of trying to queen a Pawn. Black's King, though enjoying a more attacking position, is faced with the difficulty of overcoming the defence of White's Pawns by the Bishop on Q B 3.

(403) Position before
1. ....Kt × B

Black to play.
The solution lies in destroying the defender !

1. .... Kt × B
2. K × Kt and now

White's King has replaced the Bishop as the Pawns' defender.

(404) Position after
3. ....K × P

2. .... P—Kt 4 !

preventing a Pawn move by White and now White's King is forced to desert the Queen's Pawn.

3. K—Kt 3 K × P
and wins.

Note—3. K—Kt 2, B 2 or Q 2 clearly bring about similar results.

In this position White can rapidly achieve increased scope for his doubled Rooks by the exchange 1. P × P, opening up the Queen's file.

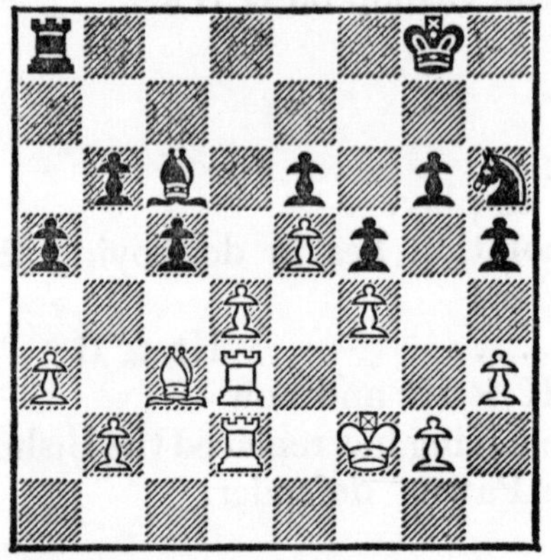

White to play.

1. P × P   P × P

White acquires the open file for his two Rooks.

(405) White plays 1. P × P

Here we see the resulting position with White's threat of invading Black's defences.

(406) Position after 1. . . . .P × P

(*f*) BREAKING A PAWN CENTRE

On page 124 we discussed how Pawns established in the centre act as a barrier keeping opponents' pieces away. Often a player will attempt to break up such a centre for his own use and occupy it with his pieces.

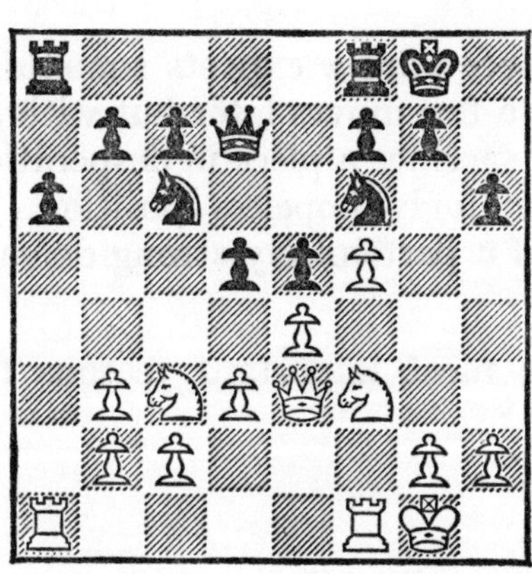

Nottingham, 1946

MILNER-BARRY *v* A. R. B. THOMAS

(407) White to play.

This is a position reached after 13 moves in a game in which White played the Vienna Opening. Black has not played vigorously enough in the centre and White breaks up the central position. This enables him to bring a Rook rapidly into active play and move a Knight on to a more dangerous square preparatory to a direct assault on Black's King.

The game continued

1. Kt × Q P	Kt × Kt
2. P × Kt	Q × Q P
3. P—B 6	K R—K 1
4. R—R 4	R—K 3
5. Kt—Q 2	

preparing to move the Knight up to the centre.

5.	K—R 2
6. R—K Kt 4	

The Rook moves across the free central rank and becomes the spearhead of the attack.

6.	R—K Kt 1
7. Kt—K 4 !	

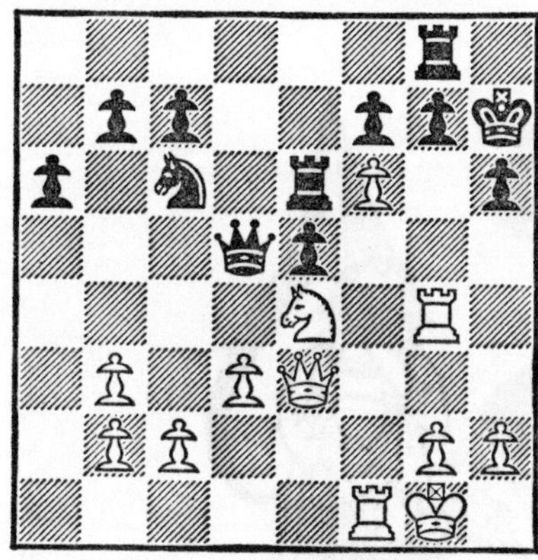

(408) Position after
7. Kt—K 4

If you now contrast this position with that in diagram 407 immediately before the central break-up, you can readily see how White has greatly improved his chances. All four of his pieces—both Rooks, Queen and Knight, are co-operating together in a direct assault on Black's King. All are active. Nine moves later Black resigned in a hopeless position.

2. SACRIFICES

The usual meaning of the word *sacrifice* is to give up something for the sake of something else—just as a smoker may give up cigarettes for the sake of his health, or parents may give up a holiday so that the money can be spent on their children.

In chess the player who sacrifices a piece *always* expects something in return ! Sometimes he recovers the loss a few moves later but with an improved position ; at other times he may sacrifice a piece in desperation in order to extricate himself from a seemingly hopeless position. A sacrifice may involve the breaking down of a particularly strong defence built up by an opponent.

We are going to consider two of the most important reasons for offering a sacrifice :

(*a*) those which lead to checkmate ;

(*b*) those which gain more material.

Here is a simple example from an actual game, where a sacrifice leads to an immediate mate on the back rank.

(409) White plays 1. Q × R ch

White to play.
1. Q × R ch
and Black is forced to capture the White Queen.

In giving up Queen for Rook, White gains something decisive in return —immediate control of Black's back rank, forcing mate.

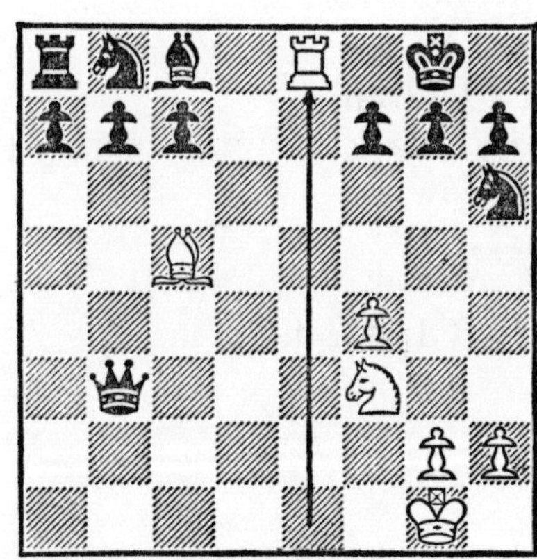

(410) Position after
3. R—K 8 mate

1.	K × Q
2. B—B 5 ch	K—Kt 1 (fcd.)
3. R—K 8 mate	

and Black's great superiority in material is to him like money to a starving man in a desert!

We now see another example based on the idea of breaking through the Pawn barrier in front of a castled King.

Magdeburg, 1927

SPIELMANN *v* L'HERMET

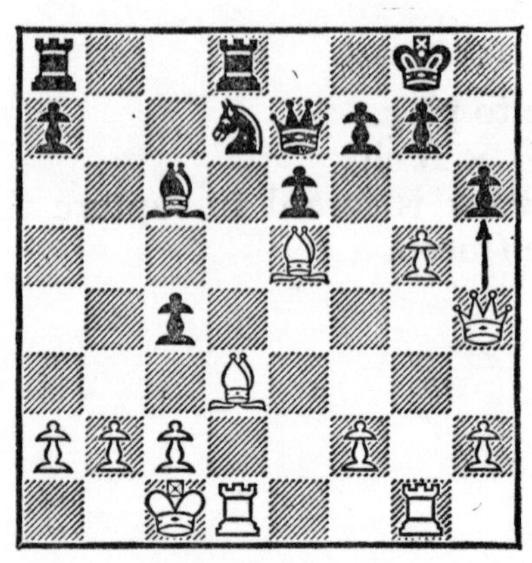

(411) White plays 1. Q × R P

White to play.

1. Q × R P

This move threatens mate either by 2. Q × Kt P or 2. Q—R 7 ch followed by 3. Q—R 8 mate. Black can hardly play 1. . . . . Kt—B 3 covering the dual threat, for 2. P × Kt wins immediately. Black can do little else but play 1. . . . . P × Q.

The White Queen is given up, but what an investment ! !

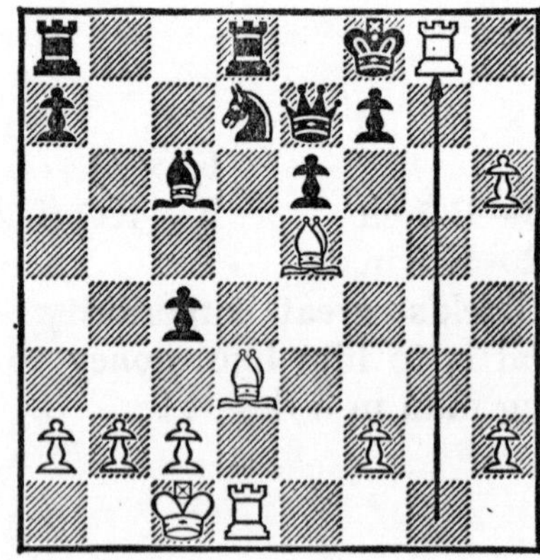

(412) Final position after 3. R—Kt 8 ch

2. P × P disc ch !	K—B 1
3. R—Kt 8 ch	

and here Black resigned for there would follow

3.	K × R
4. P—R 7 ch	K—B 1
5. P—R 8 = Q mate	

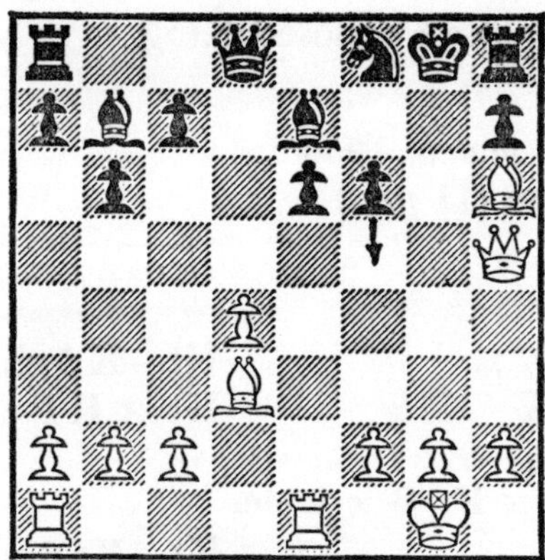

(413) Position before
1. . . . . P—K B 4

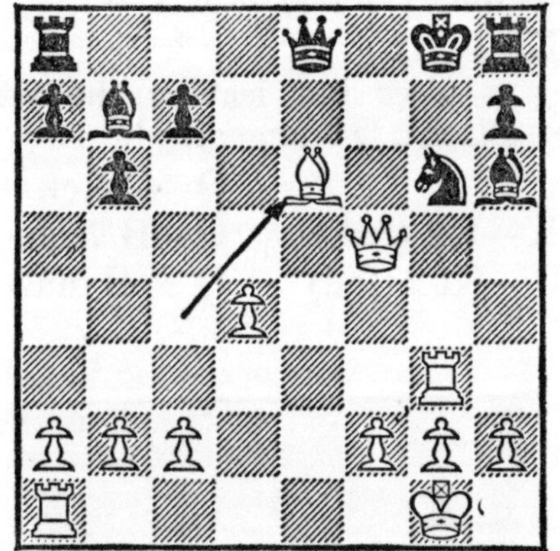

(414) Position immediately after
6. B × P ch

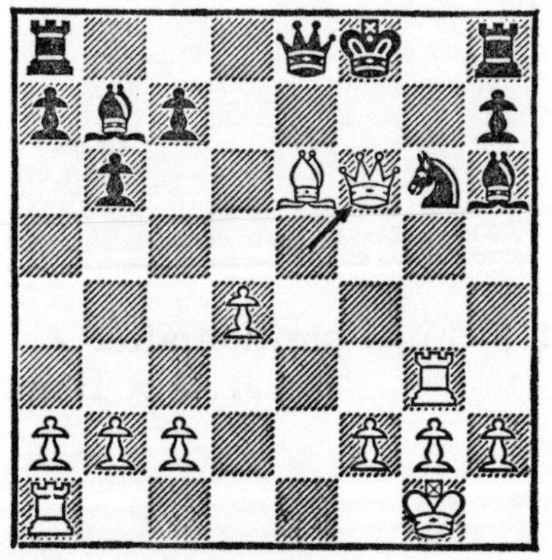

(415) Final position

Another example

Riga, 1934

TRAUTMANIS *v* HAENFUSS

Black to play.

White is a piece down, but the Black King is exposed and both Black's Rooks are out of play. Both White's Bishops are very active, the White Queen in a dangerously aggressive position and a White Rook about to enter into the attack

1. . . . . P—K B 4

to avoid the dangers of White's Q—Kt 4 ch.

2. R—K 3 Q—K 1

3. R—Kt 3 ch Kt—Kt 3

4. B—Q B 4

attacking the now undefended King's Pawn.

4. . . . . B—K B 1

and the K P is now defended by the Black Queen.

5. Q × P !

Black's K P is pinned.

5. . . . . B × B

losing vital time.

6. B × P ch K—Kt 2

Black's game is lost because of the mating combination. . . .

7. Q—K 5 ch

The Black Knight is pinned by White's Rook on Kt 3.

7. . . . . K—B 1

8. Q—B 6 ch Resigns

Black resigned because of 8. . . . . Q—B 2 (forced); 9. Q × Q mate.

Another example of an attack against an exposed King

London Primary Schools' match, 1958
P. HOWARD *v* R. TAYLOR (11 *yrs.*)

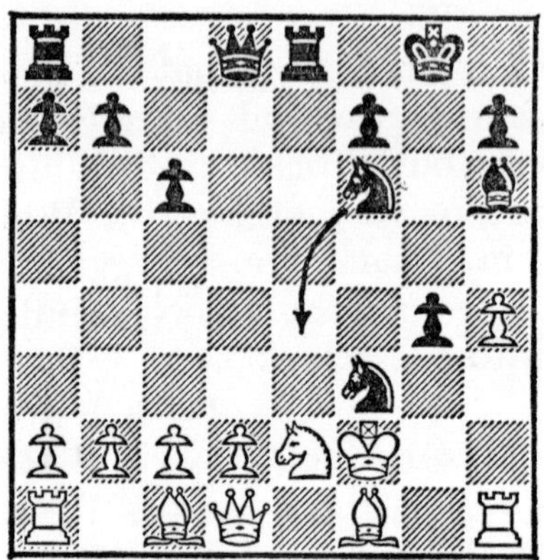

(416) Position before
1. . . . . Kt—K 5 ch

1.	Kt—K 5 ch
2. K—Kt 2	Kt × R P ch
3. K—Kt 1	

If 3. R × Kt, Q × R etc.

3.	Kt—Kt 6

attacking Rook. If Rook moves to R 2, then 4. . . . . B—K 6 ch winning Queen for White is forced to play 5. P × B

4. Kt × Kt

winning a piece but leaving the vital square—Black's Q 5 unguarded.

4.	Q—Q 5 ch
5. K—R2 (fcd.)	Q—B 7 ch
6. B—Kt 2 (fcd)	Q × B mate

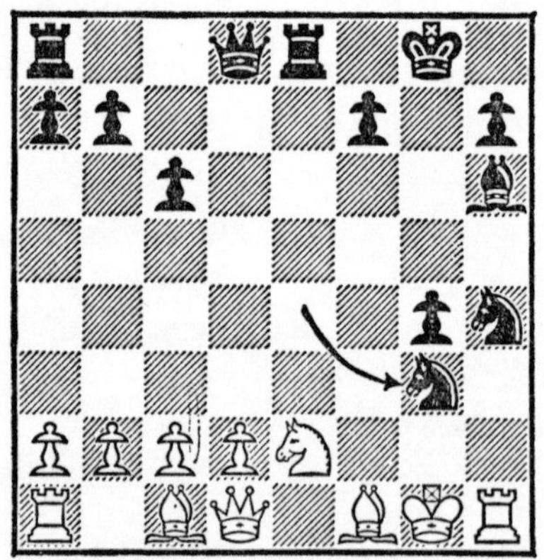

(417) After 3. . . . . Kt—Kt 6
offering Knight

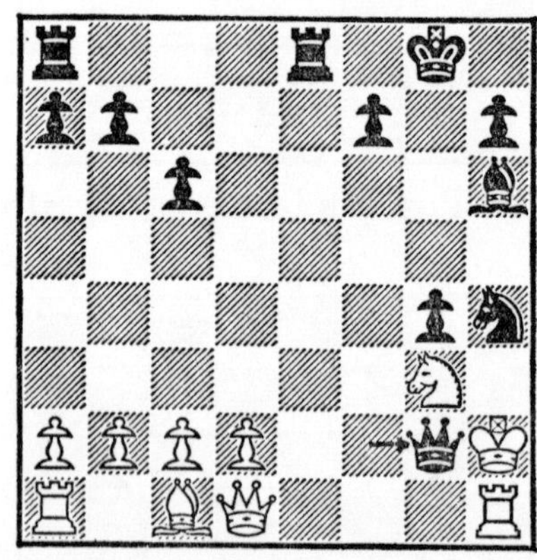

(418) Final position after
6. . . . . Q × B mate

We now examine a typical position where a sacrifice is effective against a castled King position. In this position we have the opportunity of B × P ch. Greco's sacrifice which commences with this move is effective if there is control of the Rook's file by the attacking Queen, and there is Knight support at Kt 5.

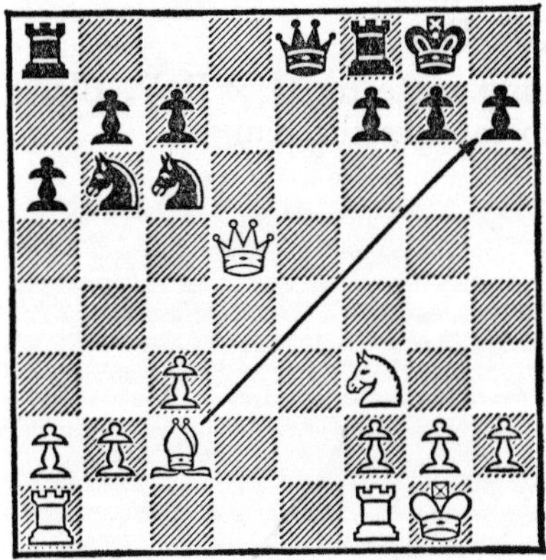

(419) Position before 1. B × P ch

White to play.

1. B × P ch

The offered sacrifice of the Bishop. If Black declines and plays 1. . . . . K—R 1 we have 2. Q—K R 5 threatening discovered check with mate to follow.

1.	K × B
2. Q—K R 5 ch	K—Kt 1

No doubt Black regrets not having one of his Knights over on the King's side—anyway it is too late now!

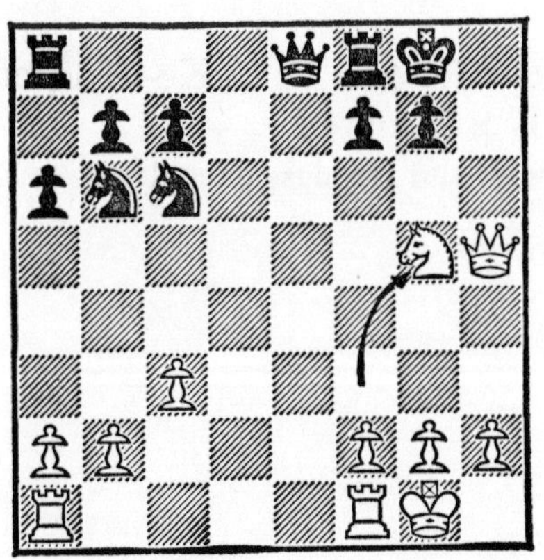

(420) Position after 3. Kt—Kt 5

3. Kt—Kt 5

Black can only prevent an immediate mate by replying 3. . . . . Q—K 5 which loses the Queen at once. Any other move by Black allows White to win by

4. Q—R 7 mate!

Breaking open a castled King's position on the Knight's file.

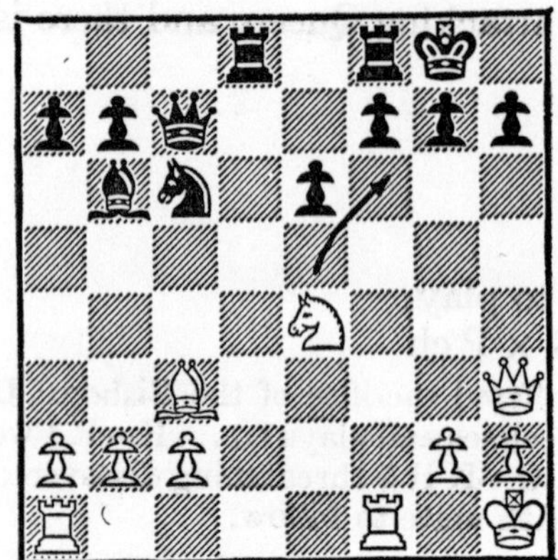

(421) Position before 1. Kt—B 6 ch

White to play.

1. Kt—B 6 ch!

threatening mate by Q × R P. Black is forced to capture the Knight.

1. .... P × Kt

Ample return for the loss of the Knight—a gaping hole in front of the Black King.

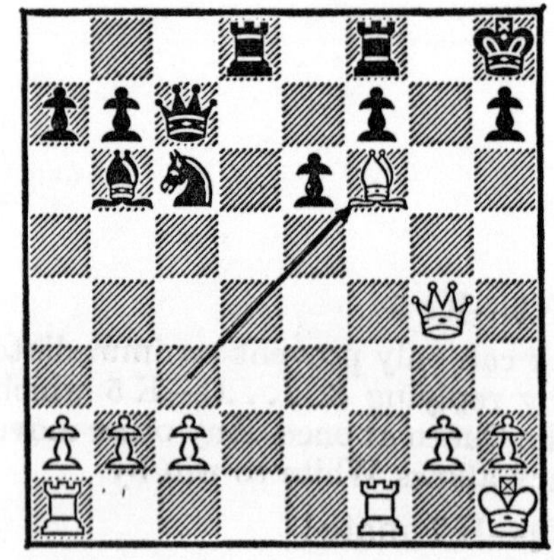

(422) Final position after 3. B × P mate

2. Q—Kt 4 ch K—R 1 (fcd.)

3. B × P mate!

A swift and painless execution.

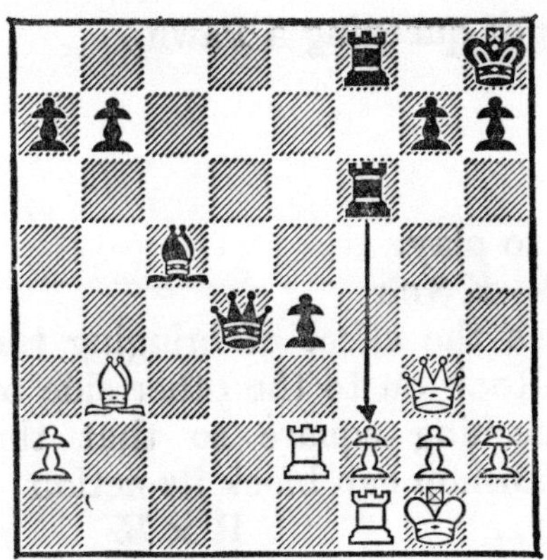

(423) Position before
1. . . . . R × P

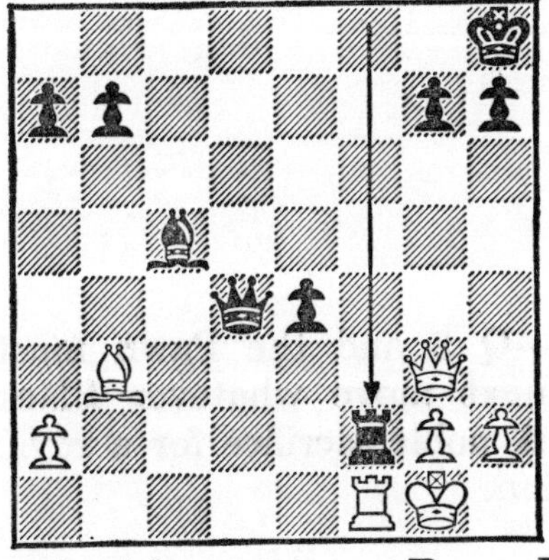

(424) After 2. . . . . R × R. Interesting to note that 3. Q—Kt 8 ch is met by 3. . . . . R—B 1 disc ch winning Queen !

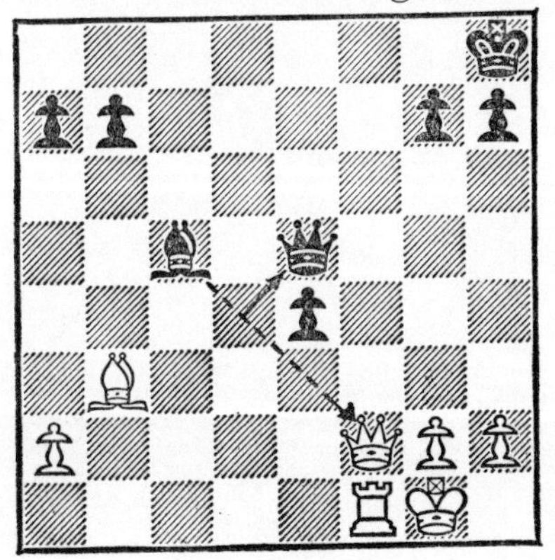

(425) After 3. . . . . Q—K 4

(*b*) SACRIFICING TO GAIN MORE MATERIAL

Magdeburg, 1927

BOGOLJUBOW *v* SPIELMANN

Black to play.
The battle rages about White's square K B 2. Black, with doubled Rooks on this target plus Queen and Bishop, launches a decisive combination giving up a Rook, only to regain more material almost immediately.

1. . . . . R × P

threatening 2. R × R mate. White has no less than four choices, all of which lose :

(*a*) 2. R (K 2)—K 1, R × R mate ! Although White's Rook covers square K B 1, Black's move is a double checkmate by Rook and Queen.

(*b*) 2. R(B 1) × R, Q—R 8 ch ;
3. B—Q 1, Q × B ch ;
4. R—K 1, Q × R mate.

(*c*) 2. Q × R, R × Q winning Queen for Rook with more threats to follow.

(*d*) 2. R (K 2) × R. This is what White actually played.

2. R (K 2) × R R × R
3. Q × R

No choice, for again if 3. R × R, Q—R 8 ch ; 4. B—Q 1, Q × B mate.

3. . . . . Q—K 4

White's Queen is neatly pinned against the King by the Black Bishop. Black went on to win the end game, for Queen plus the extra Pawns were too much for Rook and Bishop.

A sacrifice can often be the means of queening a Pawn.

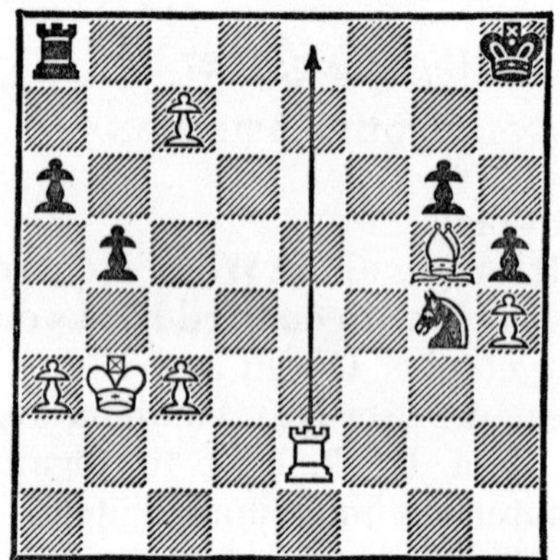

White to play.

1. R—K 8 ch

This has the effect of bringing the Black Rook on to the other side of the queening square so that the White Bishop can block its action

1. .... R × R

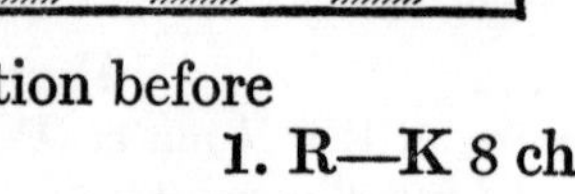

(426) Position before
1. R—K 8 ch

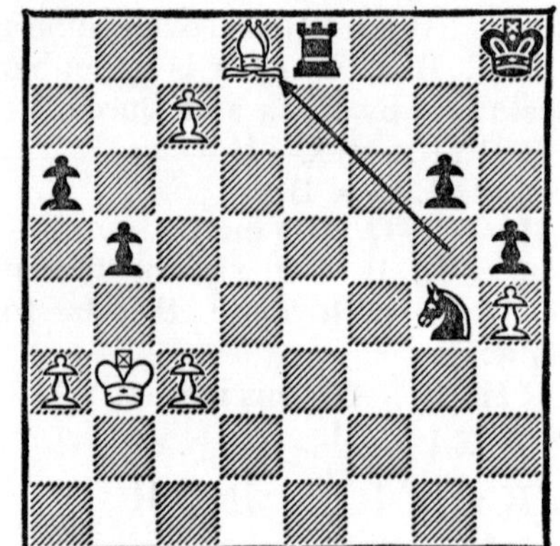

2. B—Q 8 and the Pawn must queen next move whatever Black plays. A noble sacrifice for a royal succession.

(427) After 2. B—Q 8

QUIZ ON "EXCHANGES AND SACRIFICES"

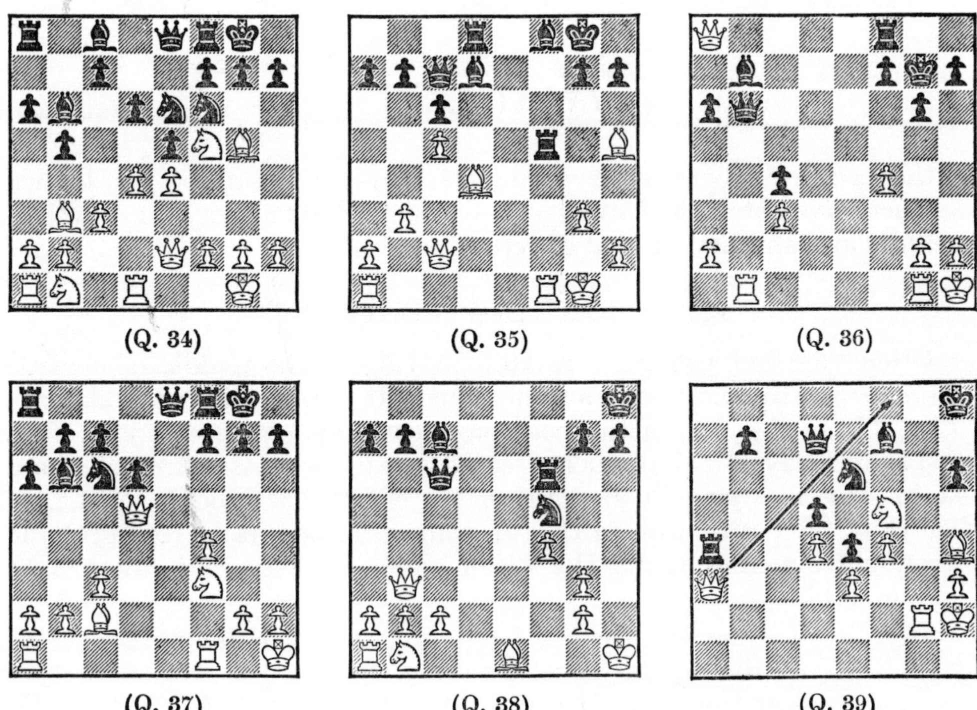

(Q. 34) (Q. 35) (Q. 36)

(Q. 37) (Q. 38) (Q. 39)

(Q.34) White to play.
White has a Knight on B 5 threatening Black's K Kt 2 and a Queen which can also move on to the King's Knight's file in order to attack the same square. Suggest exchanges which can bring this plan to a successful conclusion.

(Q.35) White to play.
Exchanges enable White to penetrate Black's defences. Suggest a plan to bring this about.

(Q.36) Black to play.
Note that Black is already the exchange down. What is Black's best move in the circumstances ?

(Q.37) White to play.
An offer of a piece which wins by mate or loss of Black Queen, whether Black accepts the sacrifice or not ! Can you find the move ?

(Q.38) Black to play.
Black with a mating threat, sacrifices a piece in order to gain more material. Can you work out this plan ?

(Q.39) White to play.
A Queen sacrifice forces mate in five moves.
We give you the first move:

1. Q—B 8 ch

Answers to Quiz on "Exchanges and Sacrifices" on page 195-6.

Notation

In this book we have been recording the moves in chess notation known as Descriptive notation. Now we want to show you two ways of recording *positions* and another method of recording *games*.

1. RECORDING POSITIONS

Often you find you have to stop playing in the middle of a game and will wish to continue it another time. It is useful in cases like this to be able to copy down the position when play was interrupted. The most simple way of making such a record is to use what is called a diagram blank. This is a printed diagram of the empty chessboard. You may then copy the position on to this diagram using letters to represent the pieces, putting rings round the Black pieces to distinguish them from those of White.

Here is an example. On the left is a position with ordinary chess symbols and on the right with letters :

(428) Position on the chessboard.
Black to play.

JACK SMITH to move

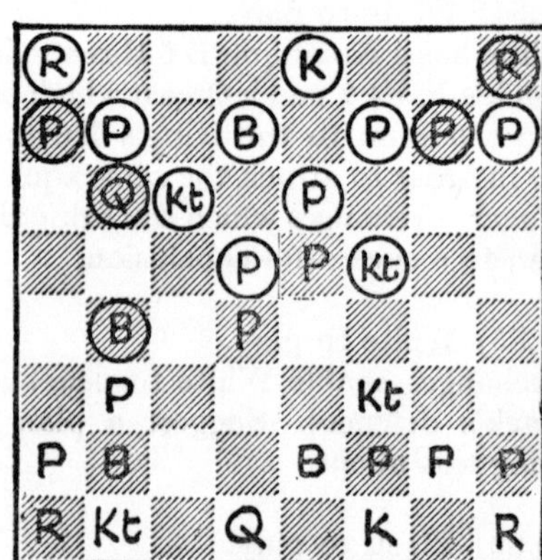

JOHN BROWN

(429)

You will notice that the names of the players have been written in and whose turn it is to move. This is essential to avoid confusion, particularly if you have a number of unfinished games to complete.

Such unfinished games are known as *adjourned* games. To adjourn means to put off until a later date.

If you do not happen to have a diagram blank there is another simple method of writing a position down. This is known as **Forsyth** notation, so named after its inventor. The same letter symbols are used, and numbers are used to indicate the squares which have no pieces upon them. Each rank of the chessboard is recorded in turn, as from White's point of view, starting from *Black's QR* 1, and you record from left to right. Let us see how this works with Black's first rank (which is White's 8th rank, of course) in the position we recorded in diagrams 428 and 429. It looks like this :

(430) Starting from the left (Black's Q R 1) we have

Black Rook—three empty squares—Black King—two empty squares —Black Rook. We again distinguish the Black pieces by putting rings round them.

In *Forsyth* notation we write

(R) 3 (K) 2 (R)

Here is the complete position, alongside which we have written the Forsyth notation rank by rank.

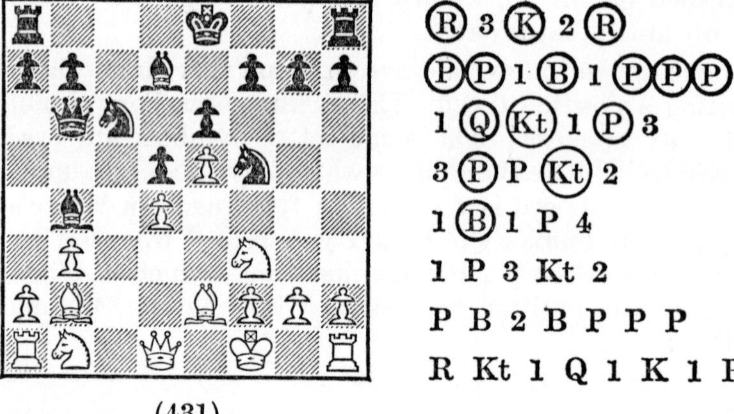

(431)

Usually the position is written down with commas between each rank, in order to save space like this :

(R) 3 (K) 2 (R), (P)(P) 1 (B) 1 (P)(P)(P), 1 (Q)(Kt) 1 (P) 3,
3 (P) P (Kt) 2, 1 (B) 1 P 4, 1 P 3 Kt 2,
P B 2 B P P P, R Kt 1 Q 1 K 1 R.

John Brown *v* Jack Smith (to move).

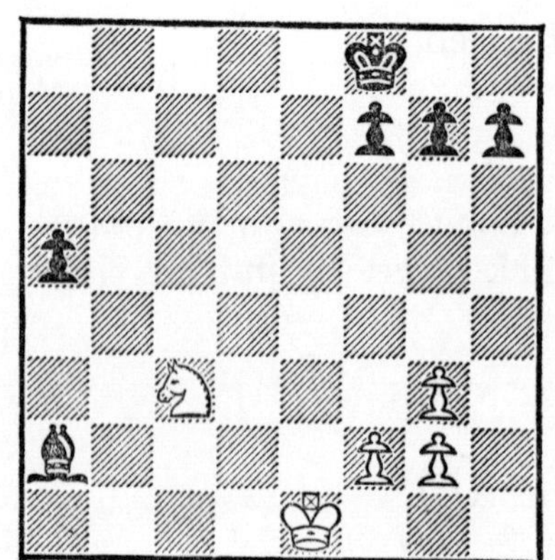

(432) Another example, showing some ranks without any pieces upon them.

Forsyth notation

5(K)2, 5(P)(P)(P), 8, (P)7, 8, 2 Kt 3 P 1, (B)4 P P 1, 4 K 3

2. RECORDING GAMES

Almost all chess books printed in the English language use the Descriptive notation, but almost all chess books published in other countries use a much better kind of notation known as the Algebraic system. One reason why it is better is because each square has only *one* label whilst in Descriptive notation it has two—one for White and one for Black, e.g.

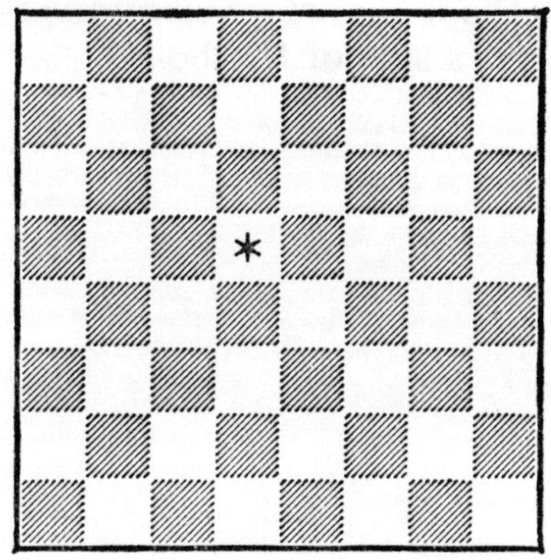

(433) If we want to identify this square marked * it is not sufficient to say it is the square Q 5. We must either say it is *White's Q* 5 or *Black's Q* 4.

Then another difficulty with Descriptive notation is that the chessboard has to be divided into two—a King's side and a Queen's side.

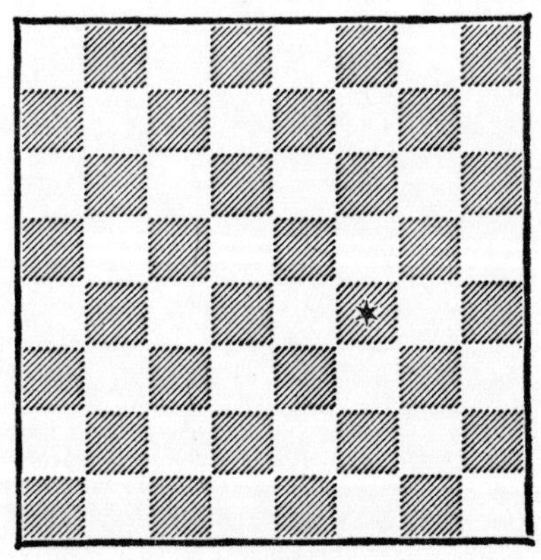

(434) Thus the square marked * in this diagram is not just White's B 4, for White has another B 4, so it must be described as White's King's Bishop 4 (K B 4).

Both these difficulties are overcome by Algebraic notation, and when players are writing down their moves there is less chance of mistakes being made.

Let us see how it works

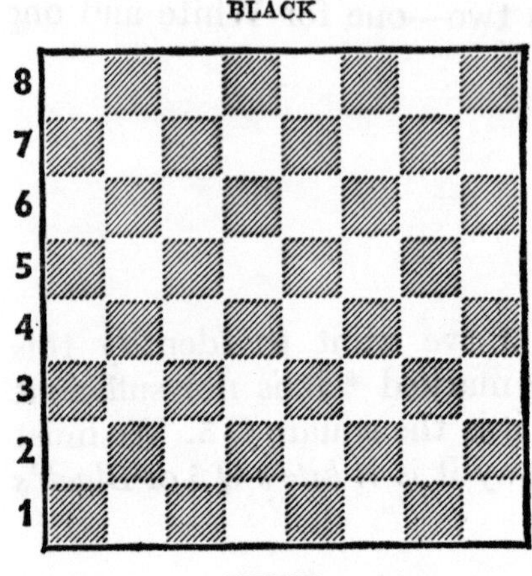

(435) All the ranks are given numbers from *White's* side of the board.

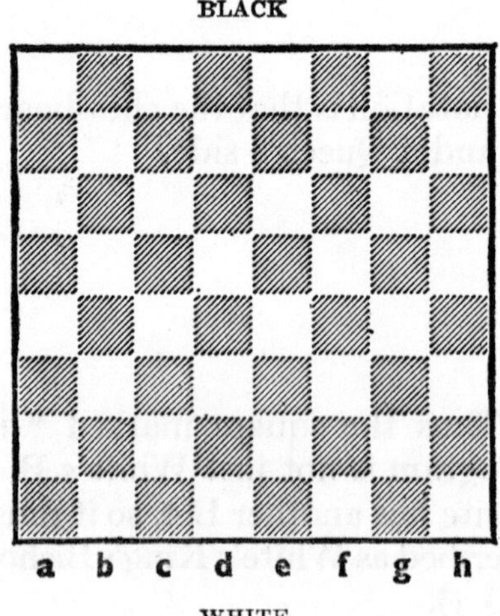

(436) All the files are given letters starting from *White's left-hand* side of the board (White's Q R 1).

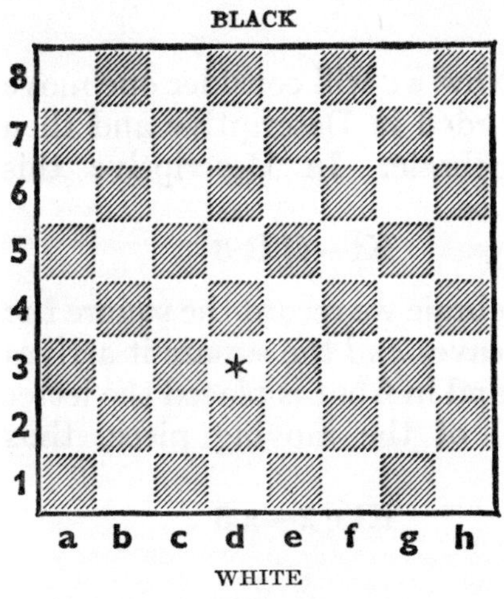

(437) Each square can now be identified in a similar way to giving a map reference in longitude and latitude. For each square you just write down the file letter followed by the number of the rank it is on, thus the one marked * is on file d and rank 3, and so is known as square d 3.

BLACK

a8	b8	c8	d8	e8	f8	g8	h8
a7	b7	c7	d7	e7	f7	g7	h7
a6	b6	c6	d6	e6	f6	g6	h6
a5	b5	c5	d5	e5	f5	g5	h5
a4	b4	c4	d4	e4	f4	g4	h4
a3	b3	c3	d3	e3	f3	g3	h3
a2	b2	c2	d2	e2	f2	g2	h2
a1	b1	c1	d1	e1	f1	g1	h1

WHITE

(438) Here are all the squares labelled. You will note that White's left-hand square is a 1 and Black's left-hand square is h 8.

WHITE

h1	g1	f1	e1	d1	c1	b1	a1
h2	g2	f2	e2	d2	c2	b2	a2
h3	g3	f3	e3	d3	c3	b3	a3
h4	g4	f4	e4	d4	c4	b4	a4
h5	g5	f5	e5	d5	c5	b5	a5
h6	g6	f6	e6	d6	c6	b6	a6
h7	g7	f7	e7	d7	c7	b7	a7
h8	g8	f8	e8	d8	c8	b8	a8

BLACK

(439) This is how the labels appear if you are Black. The numbers remain the *same*—a 1 still being White's left-hand corner square.

(440) Now we will consider one move as recorded in Descriptive and then in Algebraic. In Descriptive this would be

Kt—Q R 3

In Algebraic we record the square the piece leaves *and* the square it arrives upon, and in front is placed the letter symbol of the moving piece, thus

Kt c 2—a 3

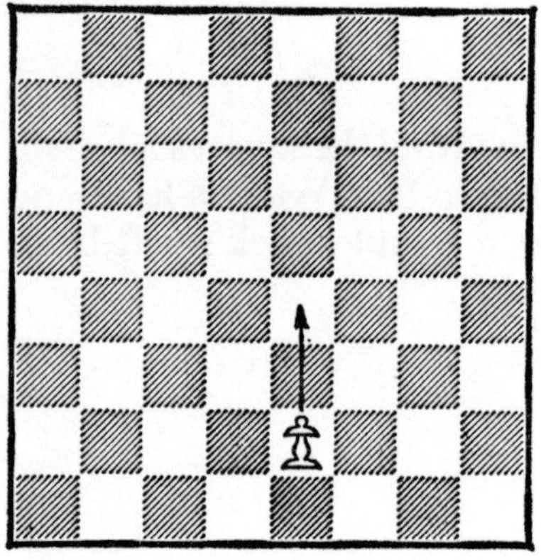

(441) The only exception is the Pawn move. In this case only the squares are indicated and no piece letter appears in front.

Thus P—K 4 is written

e 2—e 4

The symbols for castling O—O or O—O—O and for capture × are the same as in Descriptive, but in Algebraic check is usually shown by the sign + and checkmate by #.

Here is a complete game recorded in both Descriptive and Algebraic notation for comparison. Play it over and see how it works.

	DESCRIPTIVE		ALGEBRAIC	
	White	*Black*	*White*	*Black*
1.	P—Q4	P—Q4	d2—d4	d7—d5
2.	P—QB4	P—QB3	c2—c4	c7—c6
3.	Kt—QB3	Kt—KB3	Ktb1—c3	Ktg8—f6
4.	Kt—B3	P—K3	Ktg1—f3	e7—e6
5.	B—Kt5	Q Kt—Q2	Bc1—g5	Kt b8—d7
6.	P—K3	B—Kt5	e2—e3	Bf8—b4
7.	B—Q3	Q—R4	Bf1—d3	Qd8—a5
8.	O—O	B × Kt	O—O	Bb4 × c3
9.	P × B	Q × BP	b2 × c3	Qa5 × c3
10.	Q—K2	O—O	Qd1—e2	O—O
11.	QR—B1	Q—R4	Ra1—c1	Qc3—a5
12.	Kt—K5	P × P	Ktf3—e5	d5 × c4
13.	R × P	Q—B2	Rc1 × c4	Qa5—c7
14.	P—B4	Kt—Q4	f2—f4	Ktf6—d5
15.	Q—R5	P—K Kt3	Qe2—h5	g7—g6
16.	Q—R6	P—KB4	Qh5—h6	f7—f5
17.	Kt × Kt P	Kt × KP	Kte5 × g6	Ktd5 × e3
18.	Kt—K7 ch	K—R1	Ktg6—e7 +	Kg8—h8
19.	Q × R ch	Kt × Q	Qh6 × f8 +	Ktd7 × f8
20.	B—B6 mate		Bg5—f6 #	

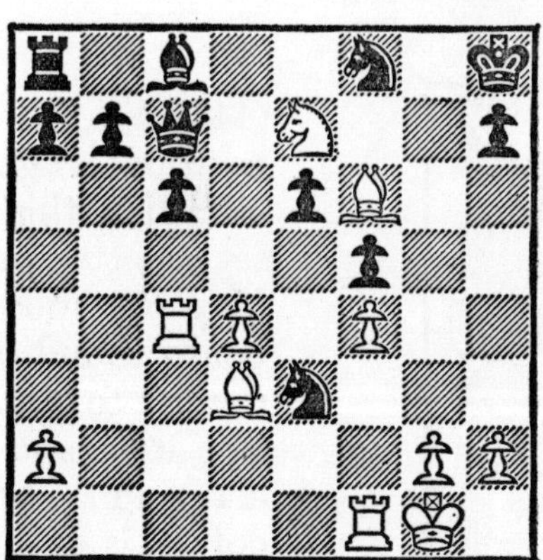

(442) The final position.

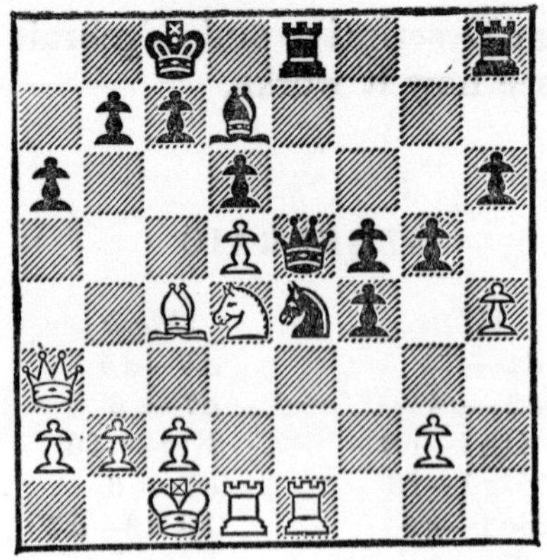

(443) Now set up this position reached after Black's 18th move in a game between Juliusson and Gudnason in Iceland 1933. Both players almost certainly recorded their moves in Algebraic notation.
See if you can follow the concluding moves of this game on your chess-board. It is White to play.

	White	*Black*
19.	Bc4×a6	b7×a6
20.	Qa3×a6+	Kc8—d8
21.	Qa6—b7	Qe5—g7
22.	a2—a4	Kte4—c5
23.	Ktd4—c6+	Bd7×c6
24.	Qb7—b8+	Kd8—d7
25.	d5×c6+	Kd7×c6
26.	Qb8—b5#	

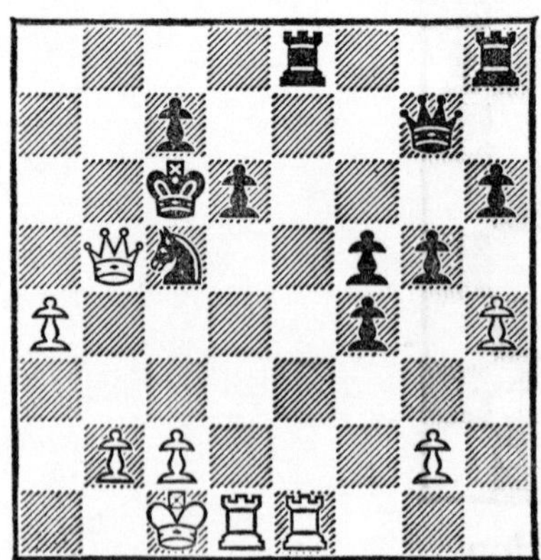

(444) You should have reached this position. A good test of your skill at following this notation would be to set up the first position again and play the moves over, but turn the board round so that you have Black nearest to you. Remember your near-side left-hand corner is now *h* 8 not *a* 1 and your nearside right-hand corner is *a* 8.

Once you have become fairly proficient with this system of notation it is possible to use it in a shortened form. In this form of Algebraic notation the square of departure is omitted except in the case of Pawn captures and where similar pieces can move to the same square. We show below once again the game which was recorded on page 189 but this time in the abbreviated form :

	White	*Black*
1.	d4	d5
2.	c4	c6
3.	Ktc3	Ktf6
4.	Ktf3	e6
5.	Bg5	Ktb8 d7
6.	e3	Bb4
7.	Bd3	Qa5
8.	O—O	B × c3
9.	b2 × c3	Q × c3
10.	Qe2	O—O
11.	Ra1 c1	Qa5
12.	Kte5	d5 × c4
13.	R × c4	Qc7
14.	f4	Ktd5
15.	Qh5	g6
16.	Qh6	f5
17.	Kt × g6	Kt × e3
18.	Kte7 +	Kh8
19.	Qf8 +	Kt × f8
20.	Bf6 ⧺	

A difficulty when using the shortened form is that when two similar pieces can move to the same square, confusion may arise. This is overcome by stating the departure square as in the normal Algebraic form. For example see Black's 5th and White's 11th moves. You would be more likely to make an accurate record of a game by using the full Algebraic method.

QUIZ ON "FORSYTH NOTATION" *Answers on page* 196-7.

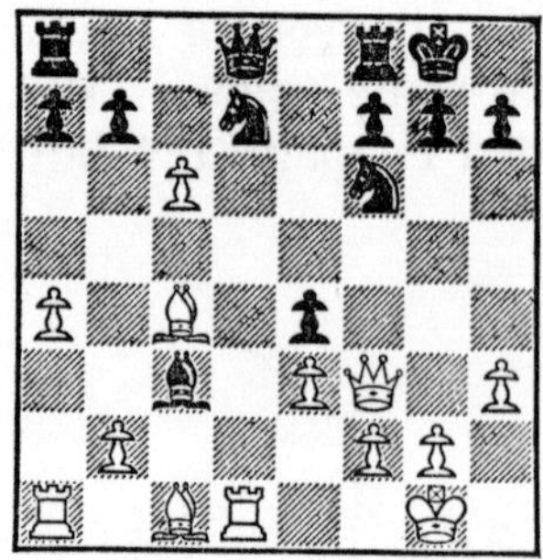

(Q.40) Record this position in Forsyth notation.

(Q.41)

Set up on your chessboard the following position which is recorded in Forsyth notation:
6 ⓇⓀ, 2 Ⓠ 2 Ⓟ 1 Ⓟ,Ⓟ 2 Ⓑ 1 Ⓟ 2, 1 ⒷⓅ 2 P 2, 8, 4 Ⓡ B P 1, P P Q 1 Kt R 1 P, R 6 K.

(Q.42)

Set up the following position on your chessboard:
1 ⓇⒷ 2 ⓇⓀ 1, Ⓟ 2 (Kt) 1 ⓅⓅⓅ,
1 Ⓠ 1 P 4, 1 ⓅⓅ R 4, 4 Kt 3, P 3 P 3,
B P Q 2 P P P, 5 R K 1.

QUIZ ON "ALGEBRAIC NOTATION" *Answers on page* 197.

(Q.43) Play over the following game and see if you reach the correct final position as shown on the answer page:

	White	*Black*
1.	e2—e4	e7—e5
2.	Ktg1—f3	Ktb8—c6
3.	Bf1—b5	Ktg8—f6
4.	O—O	d7—d6
5.	d2—d4	Ktf6 × e4
6.	d4—d5	a7—a6
7.	Bb5—d3	Kte4—f6
8.	d5 × c6	e5—e4
9.	Rf1—e1	d6—d5
10.	Bd3—e2	e4×f3
11.	c6 × b7	Bc8×b7
12.	Be2—b5 #	

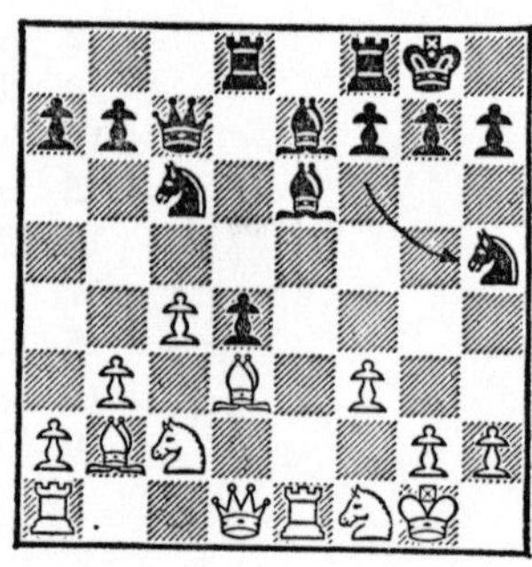

(Q.44) Describe in Algebraic notation Black's move as arrowed.

(Q.45) The White Knight's Pawn captures Black's Knight as shown by the arrow. Record this move in Algebraic notation.

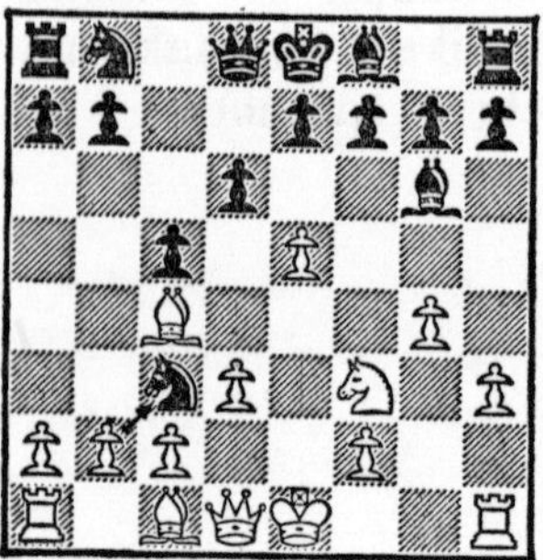

ANSWERS TO QUIZ QUESTIONS

(Q.1) 1. . . . . R—R 8 ch
2. B—B 1 (forced) R × B ch
3. K × R Kt—Q 7 ch
Winning Queen with a Knight fork.

(Q.2) Yes. Black plays.
1. . . . . B—Kt 4
White's Rook is pinned and doubly attacked and so must be lost.

(Q.3) 1. B—K 6 disc ch K—K 1
2. Q—Q 7 mate

(Q.4) 1. R × Kt Q × R
2. Q—K 8 ch
Forking King and Rook.
2. . . . . K—Kt 2
3. Q × R

(Q.5) 1. Kt—Q 6 double checkmate.

(Q.6) 1. P—Kt 8 = Q ch
for after 1. . . . . Q × Q
2. R—R 8 ch
and Black's King and Queen are skewered.
2. . . . . K moves
3. R × Q

(Q.7) 1. Q × R Q × Q
2. R—Q 8 ch Q × R
King and Queen were forked.
3. P × Q = Q ch

(Q.8) (*a*) White to play.
1. K—K 1 moving *into* the facing position.
If now 1. . . . . P—Q 7 ch
2. K—Q 1—a drawn game either by stalemate or capture of the Pawn.

(*b*) Black to play.
1. . . . . P—Q 7
2. K—B 2 K—K 7
and the Pawn Queens next move.

(Q.9) 1. . . . . R—K Kt 8 ch
2. K moves P—B 8=Q
and Queen and Rook support each other.

(Q.10) 1. R—R 1—*behind* the Pawn otherwise if White plays 1. P—R 6 Black would reply 1. . . . . R—Q R 4 and the Pawn is lost. If Black's Rook is then stationed at Q R 1 to prevent White's Pawn from queening, the White King should be moved over to its support—see diagram 167.

(Q.11) As the two White Pawns are self-supporting, they do not need the protection of the King, which may move across and capture Black's Rook's Pawn. It may then return to shepherd one of the Pawns to the queening square.

(Q.12) After White's King moves to Q 2, Q 3 or Q 4 we are in a position to use our counting rule for it is now the Pawn's turn to move. We find the Pawn has four moves to reach the queening square, the same number as the White King. The Pawn will be captured on queening.

(Q.13) 1. Q—K 6 ch K—R 1 (fcd.)
2. R × R mate

(Q.14) 1. . . . . Q × P ch
2. R × Q R—Kt 8 ch
if 2. K—R 1, Q × R mate
3. R—B 1 (forced) B—Q 5 ch
4. K—R 1 (forced)
The White Rook is pinned
4. . . . . R × R mate

(Q.15) 1. Kt—Kt 6 d. ch K—B 2 (fcd.)
2. Kt × R mate

(Q.16) 1. . . . . Q × P ch
2. R × Q (forced) R—Kt 8 mate

(Q.17) 1. .... Q—B 8 ch
2. Q—Q 1 B × P ch
3. Kt—B 3 or Q 2 B × Kt mate

(Q.18) 1. Q—R 5 threatening Q × R P mate. Black may postpone the evil day with 1. .... P—K R 3 but after 2. Q × R P, mate follows next move. If 1. .... K R moves to give the King a flight square, White replies 2. Q × R P ch, K—B 1; 3. Q × P mate. If Black replies to 1. Q—R 5 with 1. .... P × Q; 2. B × P mate!

(Q.19) 1. .... Q × R!
If 2. Kt × Q Black mates in three on the back row as follows:
2. .... R × B ch
3. Q—K 1 R × Q ch
4. R—B 1 R × R mate

(Q.20) 1. .... R × P ch!
2. K × R Q—Kt 5 ch
not 2. K—R 1 because of 2. .... Q—R 6 mate.
3. K—R 1 Q—R 6 ch
4. K—Kt 1 R—Kt 2 ch
5. K—B 2 R—Kt 7 ch
6. K—B 1 Q—R 8 mate

(Q.21) 1. .... R—Kt 7!
and now White must give up the Queen or be mated. e.g.
2. Q—Q 1 or B 3 Kt × P mate

(Q.22) 1. Kt × Kt P × Kt
2. R × P
The Rook now dominates the open file whilst the White Bishop is destined to enjoy much freer mobility than before.

(Q.23) Black's position is much superior to White's. Although White has more material than Black, all Black's pieces are active against an open King's position, whilst most of White's pieces are out of play and might as well be back in their box! Black may now play
1. .... Q—Q 4 ch.
2. K—B 1 B—K 6 ch
3. K—Kt 1, Q—Kt 4 ch; 4. K—R 2, Q—Kt 7 mate. Or after 2. K—B 1 Black may play 2. .... Q—Q 7 ch
3. K—Kt 1 Q—Q 8 ch
4. K—R 2 Q × P mate
All White's moves are forced.

(Q.24) White is much stronger in this position. White's King's Rook acts strongly at K R 3 and the Queen's Rook is well placed to support the Queen by moving to Kt 2. As these major pieces are supported by the Knight outpost at K 5 White's King's side attack is strong indeed. Black's major pieces, unlike those of White, enjoy little freedom of movement. White's next move? 1. Kt—Kt 5! threatening 2. R × P.

(Q.25) Black has a backward Pawn at Q 3 and if it is pushed forward it will be lost. It is attacked twice and defended twice. White plays 1. Kt—B 5 attacking the Pawn a third time and it must fall.

(Q.26) 1. .... Q—R 4 followed by 2. .... B—K 4 and White's Pawn on Q B 3 is lost for it has only the Queen to defend it.

(Q.27) There is a "hole" at Black's K Kt 3; in addition to which all the white squares round the position of the Black King are weak.
1. B—R 7 ch K—R 1
if 1. .... K—B 2; Q—Kt 6 mate
2. Kt—Kt 6 ch K × B forced
3. Kt × Q ch
with an easy win.

(Q.28) Rather than play Kt × P which leads to complicated possibilities, White should proceed with his development. He can do this either by 1. P—B 3 driving the Knight away and preparing the way for 2. P—Q 4 or by 1. O—O. Black had no good reason for moving this Knight twice before completing his development.

(Q.29) White should play
3. Kt—QB 3. This is a good move since it combines development with attack.

(Q.30) Although Black is three Pawns up, White is much better off since his pieces are so well placed. White, who has control of the centre, now plays 1. Kt × P threatening not only a discovered attack upon Black's King's Rook, but 2. B × P ch or 2. R—K 1 as well. With careful play White will not only win back his Pawns but in short time, the game as well. Black's appalling lack of development is certainly not worth three Pawns.

(Q.31) 1. P—B 4!
White has made a better start to his development than Black. In cases like this the player with the better position should strive to *keep* his lead. If now Black plays 1. .... Q P × P; 2. B × P gives White another well-placed piece and his position becomes stronger still.

(Q.32) *Never* play 2. .... P—K B 3 to defend the King's Pawn after the following moves:

1. P—K 4	P—K 4
2. Kt—K B 3	Here Black

should play 2. .... Kt—Q B 3.
2. ....P—K B 3 weakens Black's King's position. 2. .... Kt—Q B 3 is a much more sensible move since it protects the King's Pawn and develops a piece at the same time. Moreover, the Pawn at K B 3 deprives Black's King's Knight of the square to which it is normally developed.

(Q.33) White stands much better than Black in this position. Already White controls the centre whilst Black's Queen is occupying a square to which the King's Knight should have been played. The Black Knight is of very little use at K R 3 and White will soon harass Black's Queen by further sound developing moves.

(Q.34) 1. B (Kt 5) × Kt P × B
Black has to regain the lost piece, or accept playing on a Knight down.
This exchange has had the effect of opening the Knight's file in front of the Black King.
2. B × Kt removing the defence of Black's K Kt 2 square.

If Black replies 2. ....P × B there follows 3. Q—Kt 4 ch Q—Kt 3 (the only move to stop mate).
4. Kt—K 7 ch forking King and Queen. The Queen is lost.

If Black replies 2. ....Q or B × B there follows 3. Q—Kt 4 ch K—R 1 (forced) and there follows 4. Q—Kt 7 mate.

An important point to notice is that if White commences these exchanges with the capture of Black's Knight on K 3 first, instead of that on B 3, then the planned attack does not materialise. After

1. B (Kt 3) × Kt	Q × B!
2. B × Kt	Q × B

Black's square KKt 2 is no longer vulnerable.

Thus it can be seen that the *order* in which these exchanges take place is vital for White's success.

(Q.35)

1. R × R	B × R
2. Q × B	R × B

3. R—K B 1 threatening Q × B mate.

If Black replies 3. .... R—Q 1 there follows 4. B—B 7 ch K—R 1 forced.

5. B—K 8 ! ! with more mating threats.

If Black replies 3. . . . . Q—K 2 there follows 4. B—B 7 ch K—R 1 (moving away from the defence of the square K B 1). 5. B—Q 5

Now the mating threat is on again, and White's Bishop prevents the Black Rook from moving on to the back rank to cover the defence of the Bishop on K B 1. Should Black try 5. . . . . Q—B 3 then White can reply 6. Q—B 8 discovering an attack on the Queen with other unpleasant threats.

Should Black try 5. . . . . Q—K 6 check then White simply plays 6. K—R 1 and with no effective checks to follow, Black is in a worse plight.

(Q.36) If Black decides to capture White's Queen at once, then White will promptly play R × Q. Black's best move is to win as much material as possible with his Queen, before the exchange of Queens takes place.

1. . . . . Q × R ch.

White replies with 2. K × Q or R × Q. Black will capture White's Queen and will have won a Rook into the bargain.

(Q.37) 1. B × P ch !

If Black replies 1. . . . . K × B there follows

2. Q—R 5 ch K—Kt 1 (fcd.)

3. Kt—Kt 5 and whatever Black plays White must win.

Any move by Black other than 3. . . . . Q—K 5 results in 4. Q—R 7 mate.

If 3. . . . . Q—K 5 in a vain attempt to cover Black's square K R 2, then the Queen is lost by 4. Kt × Q.

If Black replies 1. . . . . K—R 1 declining to take the offered Bishop, then White plays.

2. Q—R 5 and Black is unable to avoid mate. For example:

2. . . . . P—Kt 3 ; 3. Q—R 6 and whatever Black plays White replies by moving the Bishop away, discovering check, and mating next move.

(Q.38) 1. . . . . Kt—K 6 threatening Q × P mate.

White's only reply to save the situation is 2. Q × Kt. Black now forces the White King on to the same diagonal as its Queen.

2. . . . . R—R 3 ch ! ! 3. K—Kt 1 (the only move).

3. . . . . B—Kt 3 and the White Queen is neatly pinned against the King.

(Q.39) 1. Q—B 8 ch already given you.

Black must reply Kt × Q or be mated for if 1. . . . . B—Kt 1 ; 2. Q × B mate. Or if 1. . . . . K—R 2 (only other move).

2. Q × P mate.

Thus the following takes place:

1.	Kt × Q
2. B—B 6 ch	K—R 2 fcd.
3. R—Kt 7 ch	K—R 1 fcd.
4. R × B disc ch	K—Kt 1 fcd.
5. Kt × P mate ! !	

(Q.40) (R)2(Q)1(R)(K)1,(P)(P)1(Kt)1(P)(P)(P), 2 P 2 (Kt)2, 8, P 1 B 1 (P)3, 2(B)1 P Q 1 P, 1 P 3 P P 1, R 1 B R 2 K 1.

(Q.41)

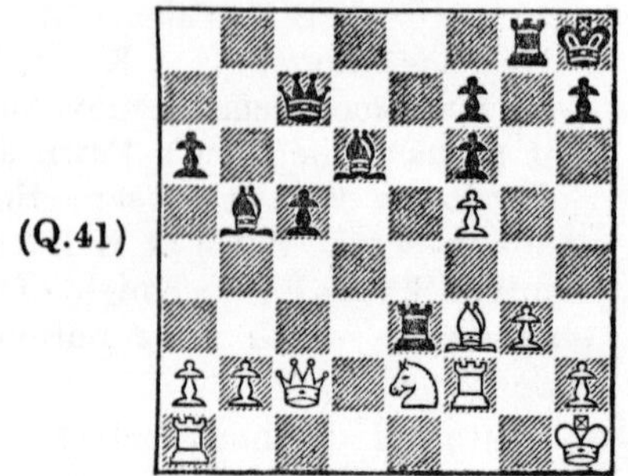

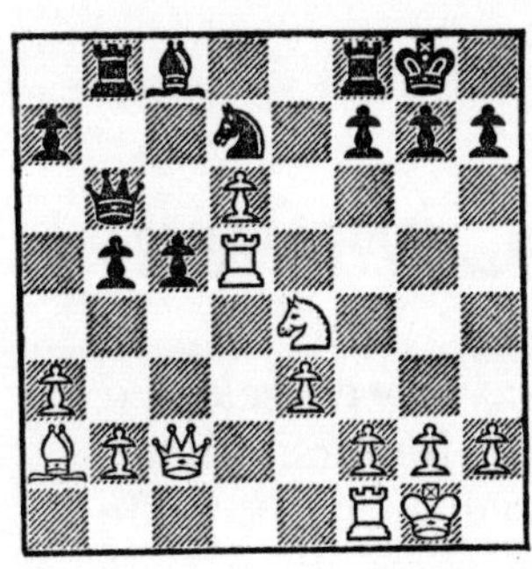

(Q.42)

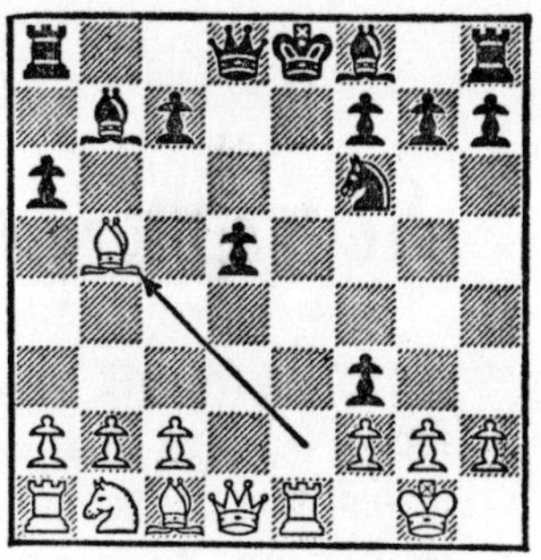

(Q.43) Position after
12. Be 2—b 5 ≠

(Q.44) Kt f 6—h 5

(Q.45) b 2×c 3

Some Games with Comment

THESE are not master games, but have been selected from a very large number played by juniors. In all cases the reasons for our choice have been that the games are fairly short, contain lively chess ideas that illustrate much that we have been trying to say in this book and, most important of all, are examples of imaginative junior chess.

Played in London Primary Schools Individual Championship, London, 1959.

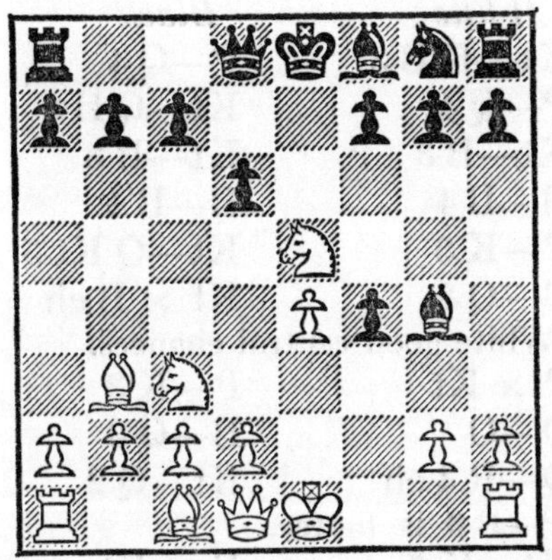

(445) Position after 7. Kt × Kt

Vienna Gambit

B. TOMBLESON[1] *White*	A. N. OTHER *Black*
1. P—K 4	P—K 4
2. Kt—Q B 3	Kt—Q B 3
3. P—B 4	P—Q 3
4. Kt—B 3	P × P
5. B—B 4	Kt—K 4
6. B—Kt 3	B—Kt 5
7. Kt × Kt !	

offering the White Queen Black accepts the bait.

7.	B × Q ?
8. B × P ch	K—K 2 (fcd.)
9. Kt—Q 5 mate	

A neat example of Legal's mate, still winning games since first demonstrated in 1750 by Kermur de Legal, a well-known French player of that time.

If you set up the position once again as shown in diagram 445 you can consider some of Black's alternatives :

(*a*) 7.	Q—R 5 ch
8. P—Kt 3	B × Q
9. P × Q	P × Kt

10. Kt × B with material gain for White.

(*b*) 7.	Q—R 5 ch
8. P—Kt 3	P × P ?
9. B × P ch	

Not 9. Q × B because of 9. ....P—Kt 7 ch ! ! 10. Q × Q, P × R = Q ch

9.	K—Q 1

The Black King is forced on to a Black diagonal.

10. Q × B with winning material advantage for now 10. ....P—Kt 7 ch is not good enough because 11. Q × Q ch, B—K 2 ; 12. Q × B ch, Kt × Q ; 13. R—K Kt 1, P × Kt and White remains material up.

[1] B. Tombleson, age 11 (co-holder of London Primary Schools Individual title 1959).

Played in a School match, London, 1959

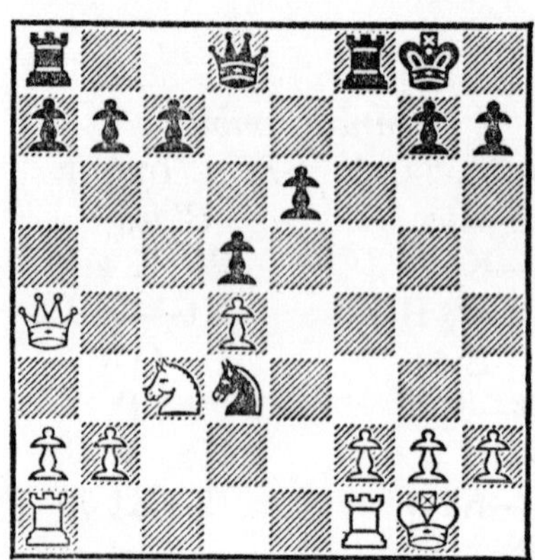

(446) Position after 14. ....P × P

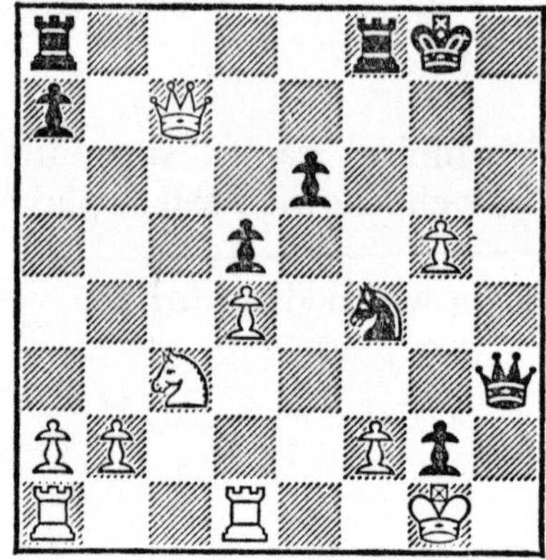

(447) Position after 23. ....Q—R 6

[1] Lynda Biggs, age 11 (London Primary Schools Joint Champion 1959 and co-holder of the Southern Counties 1959 under 15 Girls Championship title).

Queen's Pawn

M. INNES *White*	LYNDA BIGGS[1] *Black*
1. Kt—K B 3	P—Q 4
2. P—Q 4	Kt—Q B 3
3. Kt—B 3	Kt—B 3
4. B—B 4	B—B 4
5. P—K 3	Kt—Q Kt 5
6. B—Q 3	Kt × B ch

giving White good central chances.

7. P × Kt	P—K 3
8. O—O	B—Q 3
9. Q—R 4 ch	Kt—Q 2

9.....P—B 3 is better.

10. Kt—K 5	B × Kt
11. B × B	O—O
12. P—K 4	Kt × B
13. P × B	

P × Kt would have been better since Black's Bishop would have limited scope.

13.	Kt × P
14 P × P ?	P × P

White has now opened up Black's game.

15. Q—Kt 5	Kt—B 5
16. Q × Kt P	Q—Kt 4
17. P—K Kt 3	P—K R 4
18. P—K R 4	Q—Kt 5
19. Q × B P	

still continuing a Pawn snatching campaign in the face of a well-managed King's side attack by Black.

19.	P—Kt 4
20. P × P	P—R 5
21. K R— Q 1?	P × P
22. K—B 1	P—Kt 7 ch
23. K—Kt 1	Q—R 6
24. Resigns	

Black threatens 24.....Q—R 8 mate. If 24. P—B 3, Q—Kt 6 threatens mate by ....Kt—R 6 which can only be avoided by giving up White Queen for Knight.

Played in Southern Counties under 15 Boys Championship, Bognor 1959.

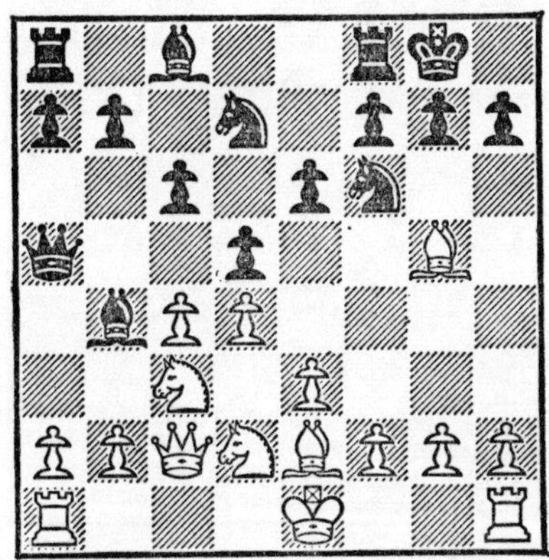

(448) Position after 9. B—K 2

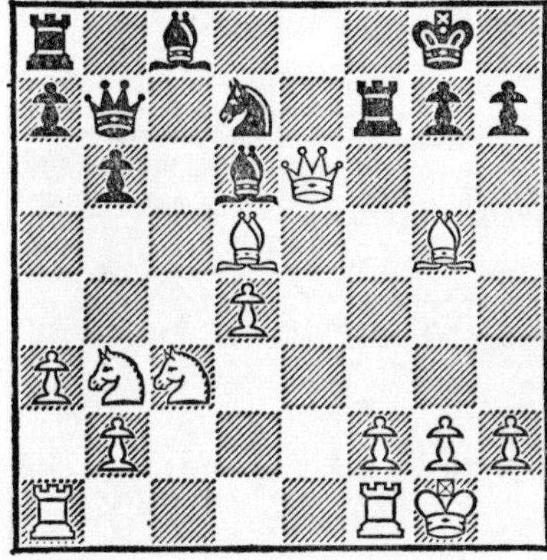

(449) Position after 19. B × Kt

Queen's Gambit Declined
Cambridge Springs Defence

G. H. MASON	A. FIRMIN
White	*Black*
1. P—Q 4	P—Q 4
2. P—Q B 4	P—K 3
3. Kt—Q B 3	Kt—K B 3
4. B—Kt 5	Q Kt—Q 2
5. Kt—B 3	P—B 3
6. P—K 3	Q—R 4
7. Kt—Q 2	B—Kt 5
8. Q—B 2	O—O
9. B—K 2	P—B 4 ?

9. . . . . P × P is better.

10. O—O

Here 10. P—Q R 3 would have forced the exchange, and given White use of the Q Kt file.

10.	B P × P
11. K P × P	P—Q Kt 3 ?

Black's Queen now becomes hemmed in.

12. Kt—Kt 3	Q—R 3
13. P × P	

uncovering an attack on the Black Queen.

13.	Q—Kt 2
14. P × P	P × P
15. P—Q R 3	B—Q 3
16. B—B 3	Kt—Q 4
17. Q—K 4 !	

threatening 18. Q × P ch winning Bishop, and also 18. Kt × Kt, P × Kt; 19. Q × P ch, Q × Q; 20. B × Q ch winning Rook.

17.	R—B 4
18. Q × P ch	R—B 2
19. B × Kt !	

threatening mate and the Black Queen.

19.	Resigns

Played in a Junior International match at the Hague, Holland, 1954

King's Indian Defence

W. J. P. VINK	M. MACDONALD-ROSS[1]
White	*Black*
1. P—Q 4	Kt—K B 3
2. P—Q B 4	P—K Kt 3
3. P—K Kt 3	B—Kt 2
4. B—Kt 2	O—O
5. Kt—Q B 3	P—Q 3
6. P—K 4	P—K 4
7. K Kt—K 2	Kt—B 3
8. P—Q 5	Kt—K 2
9. O—O	Kt—Q 2

Black aims to keep the centre closed, and start a King's side attack.

10. B—K 3	P—K B 4
11. P—B 3	P—K R 3
12. P—Q Kt 4	P—B 5
13. P × P	P × P
14. B—Q 4	Kt—K 4
15. P—B 5	P—K Kt 4
16. R—B 1	Kt(K2)—Kt 3
17. K—R 1	P—Kt 5
18. Kt—K Kt 1	Kt—R 5

Black's King's side attack has now expanded well into White's territory.

19. B × Kt	Kt × B
20. B × B	Kt—K 6
21. Q—Q 4	P—Kt 6

threatening 22. ....P—Kt 7 mate.
If 22. R P × P, B P × P!

22. Kt (Kt 1)—K 2	P—Kt 7 ch
23. K—Kt 1	P × R = Q ch
24. R × Q	Q—Kt 4 ch
25 Kt—Kt 3	

Not 25. K—R 1, Q—Kt 7 mate; or if 25. K—B 2, Q—Kt 7 ch; 26. K—K 1, Kt—B 7 ch winning Queen.

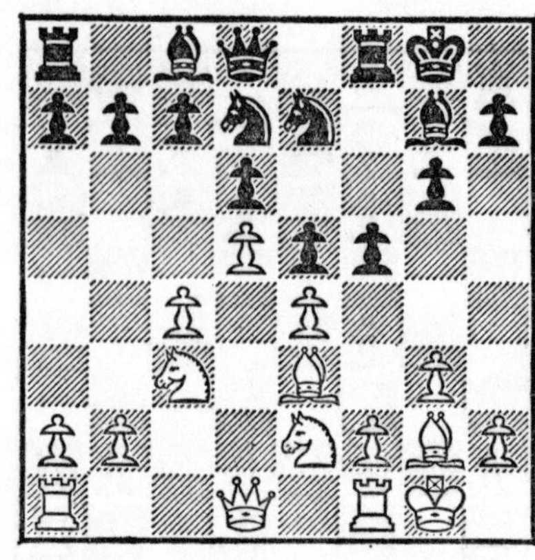

(450) Position after 10. .... P—K B 4

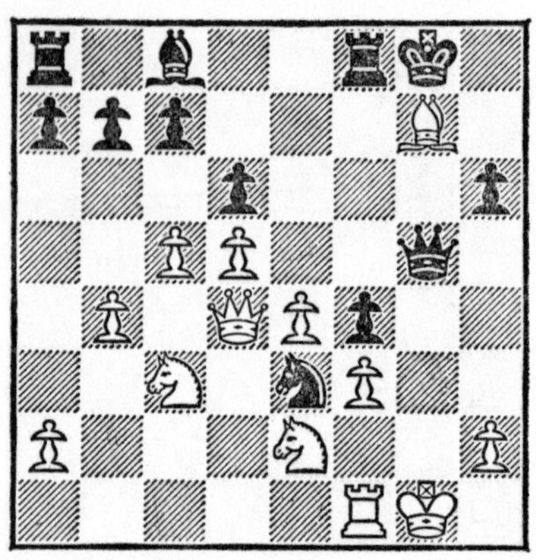

(451) Position after 24. ....Q—Kt 4 ch

25.	P × Kt
26. B × R	P × P ch
27. K—B 2	Kt × R
28. Resigns	

for Black's Pawn must queen.

[1] M. Macdonald-Ross, age 15.

Played in the British Boys Championship, Hastings, 1932

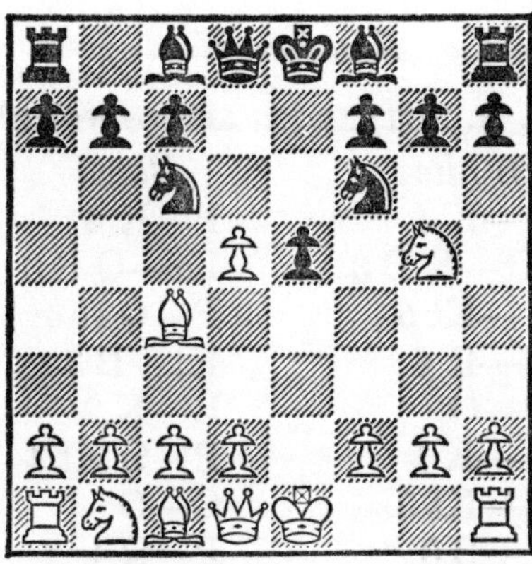

(452) Position after 5. P × P

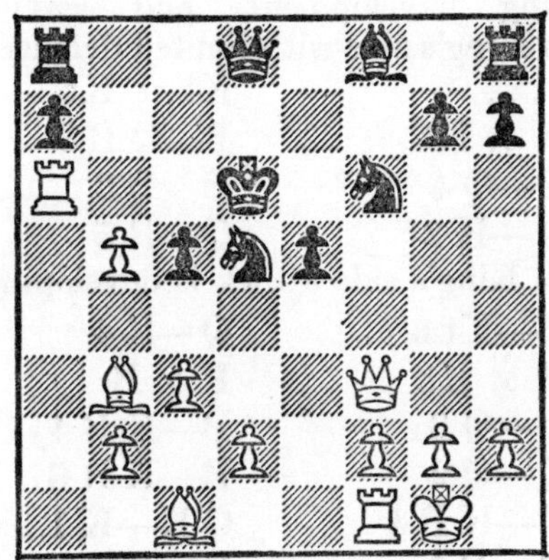

(453) Position after 17. R—R 6 ch

Two Knights' Defence

S. BLACK[1] *White*	P. B. COOK *Black*
1. P—K 4	P—K 4
2. Kt—K B 3	Kt—Q B 3
3. B—B 4	Kt—B 3
4. Kt—Kt 5	P—Q 4
5. P × P	Kt × P ?

Black's troubles begin from this move. His best reply was 5. . . . . Kt—Q R 4 after which usually follows: 6. B—Kt 5 ch, P—B 3; 7. P × P, P × P; 8. B—K 2, P—K R 3.

6. Kt × B P !	K × Kt
7. Q—B 3 ch	K—Q 3

to save the Knight from capture

8. Kt—B 3	Kt—Kt 5
9. O—O	P—B 3
10. Q—K 4	P—Q Kt 4
11. B—Kt 3	P—B 4
12. Kt × P	B—R 3
13. P—Q R 4	B × Kt
14. P × B	K—Q 3

to free the pinned Knight

15. P—Q B 3	Kt—K B 3
16. Q—B 3	Kt(Kt 5)—Q 4
17. R—R 6 ch	

Making good use of the Rook's file, which Black permitted to be opened by 13. . . . . B × Kt, 14. P × B.

17.	K—K 2
18. R—K 1	P—K 5
19. R × K P ch !	Kt × R
20. Q × Kt ch	K—Q 2
21. Q × Kt ch	K—K 1

21. . . . . K—B 2 would have lasted a little longer.

22. Q—B 7 mate

[1] S. Black, age 16.

Played in a Glorney Cup match, a Junior International Team Tournament, Dublin, 1951.

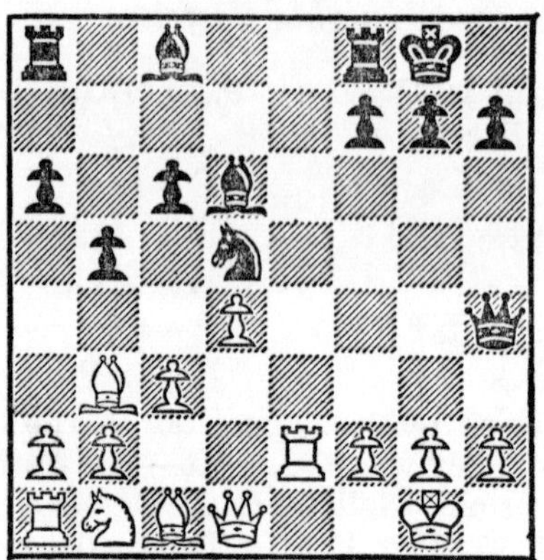

(454) Position after 13. ....Q—R 5

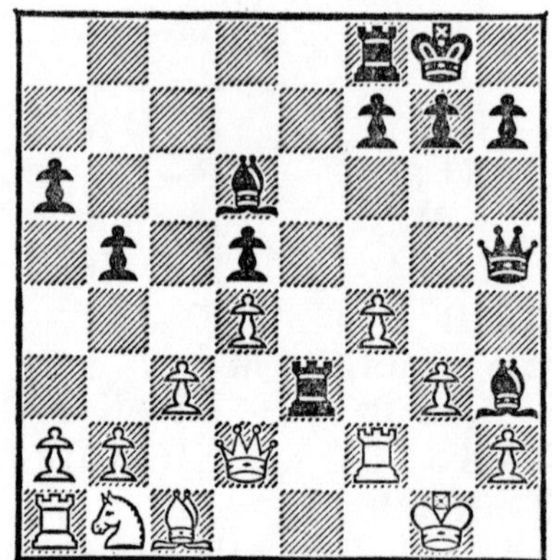

(455) Position after 19. ....R—K 6

Ruy Lopez

R. W. M. BUTLER	N. LITTLEWOOD[1]
White	*Black*
1. P—K 4	P—K 4
2. Kt—K B 3	Kt—Q B 3
3. B—Kt 5	P—Q R 3
4. B—R 4	Kt—B 3
5. O—O	B—K 2
6. R—K 1	P—Q Kt 4
7. B—Kt 3	O—O
8. P—B 3	P—Q 4
9. P × P	Kt × P
10. Kt × P ?	

neglecting development, and leaving White's King's side with limited defences.

10.	Kt × Kt
11. R × Kt	P—Q B 3
12. P—Q 4	B—Q 3
13. R—K 2	Q—R 5

Black King's side attack is developing.

14. P—Kt 3	Q—R 4
15. B × Kt	P × B
16. Q—Q 3	B—K B 4
17. Q—Q 2	B—K R 6
18. P—K B 4	Q R—K 1
19. R—B 2	R—K 6 !
20. Kt—R 3	K R—K 1

If 20. Q × R, Q—Q 8 ch and mate in two!

21. Kt—B 2	R—K 7 !
22. Resigns	

If 22. R × R, R × R; 23. Q—Q 3, B—K B 4 ! 24. Q—Q 1, Q × P ch ! etc., and Black mates in two. Or 22. R × R, R × R; 23. Q—Q 1, R—Kt 7 ch ! again mate in two for Black.

[1] N. Littlewood, age 17.

Played in the British Boys Championship, Hastings, 1946

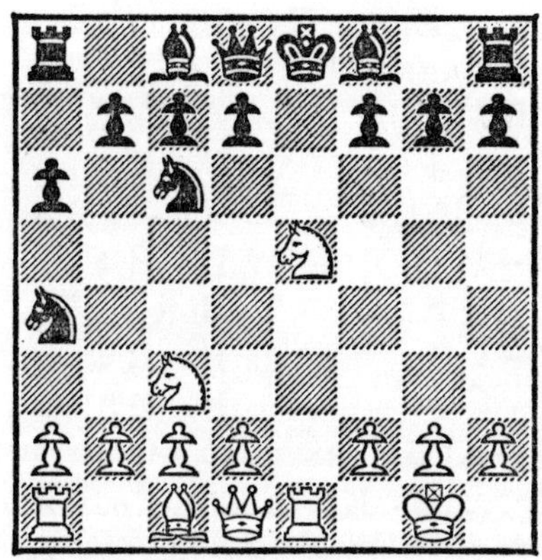

(456) Position after 8. Kt × P

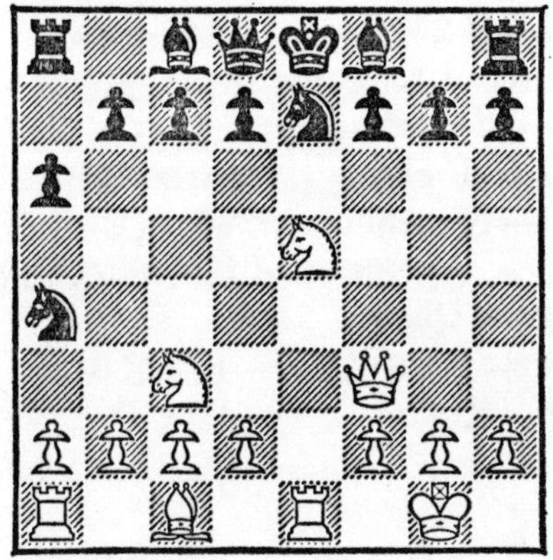

(457) Position after 9. Q—B 3

Ruy Lopez

J. A. FULLER[1] *White*	G. T. CROWN *Black*
1. P—K 4	P—K 4
2. Kt—K B 3	Kt—Q B 3
3. B—Kt 5	P—Q R 3
4. B—R 4	Kt—B 3
5. O—O	Kt × P
6. R—K 1	Kt—B 4
7. Kt—B 3	Kt × B
8. Kt × P	Kt—K 2 ?

Correct play is 8. . . . .Kt × K Kt.

9. Q—B 3 !	Resigns

for White threatens Q × P mate. Black's only replies are 9. . . . .P—K B 3 or K B 4 when follows either 10. Q—R 5 ch, Kt—Kt 3; 11. Kt × Kt disc ch etc. Or if 10. Q—R 5 ch, P—Kt 3; 11. Kt × P, and if 11. . . . .P × Kt; 12. Q × P mate !

[1] J. A. Fuller, age 17 (British Boy Champion, 1946).

Played in British qualifying competition for World Junior Championship, Birmingham, 1951.

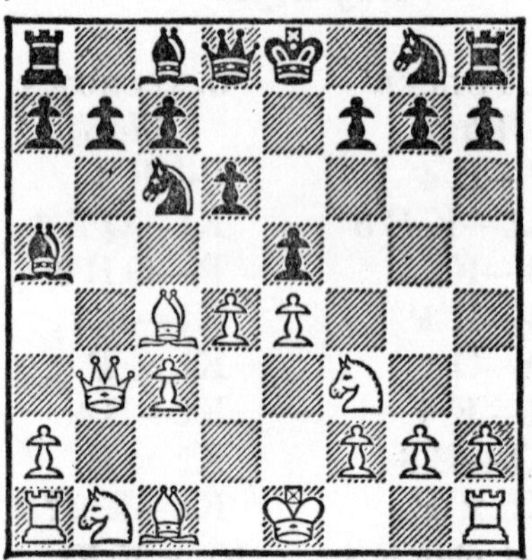

(458) Position after 7. Q—Kt 3

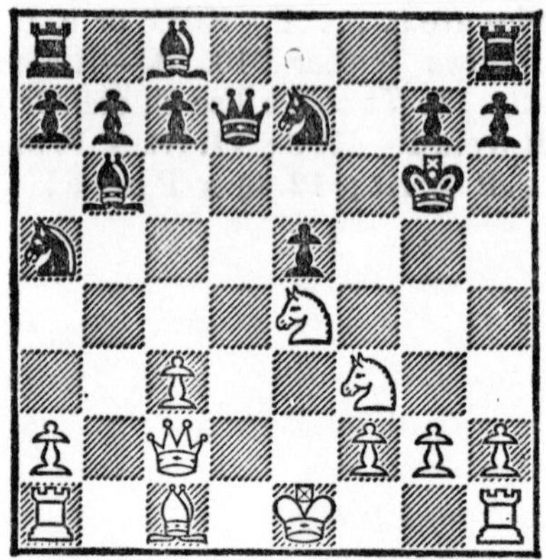

(459) Position after 16. Kt—K B 3

Evans Gambit

M. N. BARKER[1] *White*	W. MARSHALL *Black*
1. P—K 4	P—K 4
2. Kt—K B 3	Kt—Q B 3
3. B—B 4	B—B 4
4. P—Q Kt 4	B × Kt P
5. P—B 3	B—R 4
6. P—Q 4	P—Q 3
7. Q—Kt 3	Q—Q 2

Not 7. .... Q—K 2 because of 8. P—Q 5 and after the Black Knight moves—9. Q—Kt 5 ch winning Bishop.

8. P × P	B—Kt 3
9. Q Kt—Q 2	Kt—R 4
10. Q—B 2	Kt—K 2

10. ....Kt × B would have prevented White's next move.

11. B × P ch!	K × B
12. P—K 6 ch	K × P

If 12. ....Q × P then 13. Kt—Kt 5 ch winning the Queen.

13. Kt—Kt 5 ch	K—B 3
14. P—K 5 ch	P × P

14. ....K × Kt exposes Black to a fatal attack.

15. Q Kt—K 4 ch	K—Kt 3
16. Kt—K B 3	

threatening to win Black's Queen in either of two ways.

16.	Q Kt—B 3

Black prevents 17. Kt × P ch by this move, and accordingly goes down to the second threat.

17. Kt—B 5 disc ch	Q—B 4
18. Kt—R4 ch	Resigns

[1] M. N. Barker, age 17 (British Boy Champion, 1949, '50 and '51).

Dictionary of Chess Terms

Active. A piece is said to be active when it is well positioned.

Algebraic Notation. A system of notation for recording games.

Back Row. The first rank on either side of the board.

Checkmate. When a King cannot escape from check.

Combination. When two or more pieces work together compelling an opponent to move in a particular way.

Defend. To protect, guard or support a piece against an attack.

Deflection. Forcing a piece away from its required role.

Development. Bringing pieces on to squares where they are more active.

Discovered Check. A position in which one piece has been moved to uncover check by another piece.

Double Attack. Two pieces attacked at the same time.

Double Check. A position in which a King is in check from two pieces at once.

Doubled Pawns. Pawns of the same colour standing on the same file.

En passant. A special kind of Pawn capturing move.

En prise. A piece is said to be "*en prise*" when it is being attacked.

Exchange. A series of moves in which each side captures pieces.

Flight Square. A square to which an attacked piece may go.

Forced Move. No other move possible.

Fork. A particular type of double attack.

Forsyth Notation. Name given to a kind of notation for recording positions.

Gambit. An opening where a piece (usually a Pawn) is given up, with the idea of gaining an advantage in development.

Illegal Move. A move that is not allowed. One that breaks the rules of the game.

Interpose. To move a piece in between an attacked piece and its attacker.

J'adoube. "I adjust." Spoken by players when they wish to make it clear that they are not making a move but merely standing a piece correctly on its square.

Minor Piece. A Bishop or Knight.

Mobile. Able to move freely.

Open File. A file on which there are no Pawns.

Opening. The first few moves of the game.

Overworked Piece. A piece which is performing two or more defensive roles at the same time.

Passed Pawn. A Pawn which has no opponent's Pawn in front of it on its own file, and which in moving to the 8th rank does not have to pass an opponent's Pawn on either of the adjoining two files.

Passive. Not performing any useful function : non-active.

Pin. A piece is pinned when it cannot move without exposing another piece to attack.

Simultaneous Display. An event in which one player plays a number of opponents at the same time, where the principal player makes a move on each board in turn.

Sacrifice. Giving up a piece in order to gain some kind of advantage.

Skewer. An attack upon two pieces on the same line where the piece nearest the attacker is compelled to move, leaving the other piece to be taken.

Stalemate. A drawn position, where a player is not in check but is unable to move any piece anywhere.

Tempo. Time taken to move pieces into required positions. A manœuvre that need only take one move that is performed in two moves is said to lose a tempo. To force your opponent to make such time-wasting moves gains tempo for you.

! Used in notation to indicate either a good move or the best move available.

? Used in notation to indicate a bad move.